# CHINESE
# FILM THEORY

# CHINESE FILM THEORY

## *A Guide to the New Era*

Edited by
George S. Semsel, Xia Hong,
and Hou Jianping

Translated by
Hou Jianping, Li Xiaohong, and Fan Yuan

Foreword by Luo Yijun

New York
Westport, Connecticut
London

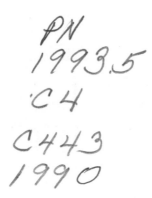

**Library of Congress Cataloging-in-Publication Data**

Chinese film theory : a guide to the new era / edited by George S.
    Semsel, Xia Hong, and Hou Jianping; foreword by Luo Yijun
        p.    cm.
    Includes bibliographical references.
    ISBN 0-275-93103-X (alk. paper)
    1. Motion pictures—China. 2. Motion pictures—Philosophy.
I. Semsel, George Stephen. II. Xia Hong. III. Hou Jianping.
PN1993.5.C4C443    1990
791.43'0951—dc20    89-23079

Library of Congress Catalog Card Number: 89-23079
ISBN: 0-275-93103-X

First published in 1990

Praeger Publishers, One Madison Avenue, New York, NY 10010
A division of Greenwood Press, Inc.

Printed in the United States of America

The paper used in this book complies with the
Permanent Paper Standard issued by the National
Information Standards Organization (Z39.48–1984).

10  9  8  7  6  5  4  3  2  1

For Ye Ye

and the students of the

People's Republic of China

# CONTENTS

# ACKNOWLEDGMENTS

We have received much help and support in this project. We would like, first of all, to thank the authors translated here for their kind permission to translate and edit their articles. This work would not have been possible without their wholehearted endorsement and cooperation. Our gratitude to Alison Bricken, our editor at Praeger, for her concern throughout this project. Luo Yijun, secretary of the Secretariat of the China Film Association, deserves special thanks for his warm concern for this project and for writing the foreword. Our special appreciation to Rong Weijing, Managing Editor of *Film Art,* for his most generous help and information. Our thanks also to Li Xiaohong, Fan Yuan, and Sun Jianrong for their dedicated work with translation. We also extend our appreciation to Dr. David O. Thomas, director of the Ohio University School of Film, for his concern and assistance.

# FOREWORD

China has one-fifth of the world's population; however, its cultural life is limited. Film, a product of modern Western science and technology, came to China while still in its infancy, took root, blossomed, and gave forth fruit in this ancient country. For a long time filmgoing was the major entertainment in China and the film audience numbered as many as 20 billion people annually. Even now, the Chinese film audience far surpasses that of any other country.

From its very beginnings, film revealed more of an international character than other art forms. However, in the past, film exchanges between China and the West went primarily in one direction. During different periods of time, Western films, especially those of France, Italy, Russia, and the United States, poured into China's film market. Similarly, the writings of Western film theoreticians such as Rudolf Arnheim, Sergei Eisenstein, Vsevolod I. Pudovkin, Bela Balasz, André Bazin, Seigfried Kracauer, Jean Mitry, and Christian Metz were introduced into China, while conversely, Chinese film and film theory until recently remained completely foreign to the West. At the onset of the 1980s, this one-way exchange began to change. Chinese film, heavily influenced by Eastern culture, has gradually awakened interest in the West, and a few Western scholars have written on the subject. Chinese film theory, however, has remained virgin territory. *Chinese Film Theory: A Guide to the New Era,* edited by George Semsel, Xia Hong, and Hou Jianping, is the first of its kind.

China, for thousands of years a unified and continuous civilization, maintains an independent cultural system quite different from that of any other. In 1840, after the cannons of the Opium War burst through the closed doors of the country, China began to recognize the challenge of modern industry in the West, and realized that its own civilization lagged far behind. The economic base of the peasantry made it stagnant. Chinese civilization has gone through many twists and turns on its way to modernization. The significant changes taking place in politics, economics, and culture for more than a hundred years now, in scale and in depth have no parallel in Chinese history. However, the modernization of China is not exclusively a Westernization. The cultural tradition of the people and the historical accumulation of their cultural psychology have been handed down tenaciously. All Western concepts, be they political, economic, philosophical, sociological, literary, or aesthetic, to take root in China, inevitably must undergo changes and transformations wrought by the people, albeit to varying degrees, whether this nationalization is carried out consciously or not. Western film and film theory have gone through this process. The development of Chinese film and film theory embodies the Chinese cultural spirit; at the same time it is constrained by the social realities of the country.

Emphasis upon the function of film as a means of social education has always been a major characteristic of Chinese film theory. In its earliest days the representative trends of thought were that film should depict life, educate society, and enlighten the people. Later the emphasis shifted from moral to political education. The concept of film as a tool of political education that dominated the film circles of mainland China for more than half a century can be traced to a cultural tradition that centers on human relations. Chinese philosophy stresses ethics and neglects epistemology or ontology. Chinese aesthetics places emphasis on the unity of beauty and kindness — relating the appreciation of the beautiful with moral and ethical conduct. For centuries, the ideas that "literature expresses ideology" and "art contains morality and ethics" dominated the ancient theories of literature and art. The establishment of film as a tool for political education probably resulted from the culture that formed when changes in Chinese society took the political standard as its essence.

In terms of ontology, film, from its beginning until the late 1970s, was generally regarded as recorded drama, moving images reflected on the screens of China. The term "filmed drama," frequently used in the early days of film, accurately summarized this concept. In early Western film theory, similar concepts also appeared, but they lost their position soon after. Such a concept lasted seventy to eighty years in China because of its cultural tradition and social reality. Chinese philosophy centers upon the exploration of the functions and relations of phenomena, while it neglects analyses of substance and structure. It stresses unity and neglects detail. The style of Chinese thinking places emphasis on a command of general and whole ideas as opposed to the scientific spirit that stresses concrete, deep, multilayered and multifaceted analyses.

That ancient popular Chinese novels and dramas excel in the complexities of their plots and in their presentations of emotions certainly helped condition the Chinese to prefer dramatic situations. This prefilmic psychology of appreciation constrains the situation and the concept of Chinese film. The tastes of the masses do not conflict with the concept of film as recorded drama and the purpose of film as political tool. Theoretical studies of Chinese filmscripts focus more on shots than on anything else, for scripts as a whole embody the political and ideological tendencies of film. While it is true that Chinese film theory also studies film structure, the composition of visual images, and camera movement, this is done primarily to make comparisons with the devices of other arts, especially those of drama. Montage heavily influenced Chinese film, but was accepted more as a technique than an ontological factor.

Chinese culture is effective in the spirit of practice, but not at abstract thinking. It encourages artists to inherit from their ancestors, rather than to be creative and to surpass them. The culture, based on political standards, is closer to utilitarianism, eager for quick successes and instant benefits. Consequently, Chinese film theory has distinguished practice-oriented characteristics. The close relationship between Chinese film theory and filmmaking makes it difficult to distinguish film theory from film criticism. The truth is, many film artists are both theoreticians and film critics. Chinese film theory, more often than not, is the summary and distillation of filmmaking practices and, in turn, directly affects how films are made. As a result, it has not developed a strict and methodological way of theoretical thinking, with its dependence mostly on instinctive empirical judgments.

From the early 1930s to the late 1970s the power that dominated the development of Chinese film and film theory was politics. When China faced the armed invasion of imperialist countries and its people were on the dangerous verges of extinction, all cultural activities, including film, centered on the political struggle for survival. This was a natural and reasonable consequence of history. Later, as the resultant revolutionary literature and art progressed into the countryside, it came to be summarized as "literature and art serving politics and the workers, peasants, and soldiers." This principle bestowed on Chinese film and film theory new agendas such as kindling ideas of the relation between art and life and between art and the people. But this position, so closely related to the rural base areas of the war period, revealed its limitations and violation of the innate principles of literature and art when peace was achieved throughout the country, especially when mainland China formed its own national apparatus. An example is the suppression of subjectivity in theory and practice, and the abstention from freedom of academic discussion and exploration.

During the 1950s and early 1960s only a few especially influential debates in Chinese film theory appeared; however, the sphere of these debates was limited to such subjects as how film could better serve politics and the common people. At the same time, some penetrating assessments were severely criticized on political grounds. By the mid-1960s the situation reached a ridiculous extreme. While the economies of adjacent regions and countries were making significant progress, China engaged in a comprehensive ten-year-long ideological civil war. The Cultural Revolution was a feudal Fascist dictatorship that simply killed the culture. China entered a dark age similar to the Western Middle Ages. Film theory was buried, and what remained were the political verdicts of the autocracy.

In modern Chinese history, major cultural movements have always intertwined with political movements. In 1979 China entered a new historical era. The efforts to create order out of the political chaos provided a healthy environment for the development and prosperity of Chinese culture. A long-suppressed movement for spiritual liberation swept the entire country with the force of a thunderbolt, touching every realm of the culture. The year 1979 was also a turning point for Chinese film and film theory. The open-door policy unlocked the long-closed gates of the nation. Western culture, including Western film and film theory, came to China in a continuous stream and brought vitality to the movement to liberalize thought in film.

Two main trends made their appearance in the New Era. One is an awakening of the self-consciousness of human beings, a restoration of the enlightenment, esteem, and values of humanity that had been alienated by blind worship and barbarity. The other is the awakening of the self-consciousness of film — film freed from the direct control and restraints of politics so as to recognize and establish itself. Through a reconsideration of politics and culture, film theory adjusted the relationship between film and politics and reestablished the social function of film on a full scale. It extensively studied some of the common issues of literary and aesthetic theory such as nature and humanity, masses and individual, free will, realism, modernism, and the laws of art. Even more significant is that rather than comparing specific cinematic devices with those of other arts, film theory examined the laws and potentials of film itself and heightened the level of research into film ontology. In the history of Chinese film theory, there had never been such an extensive, profound, and continuous academic debate.

The first target attacked was the concept of the medium as recorded drama that long dominated Chinese film. Proposals to throw away the walking stick of drama and divorce drama and film initiated the debate. Theorists questioned the dramatized structure of Chinese film, the theatrical concepts of space and time in film, and the concept of stage performance in film. This debate was followed by a challenge to the ideas that the script is the ideological and artistic basis of film and film is literature rendered through specific cinematic techniques. Film theory sought to replace the traditional concept of Chinese film with a new concept that fit the trend of contemporary film. Along with these debates, the emphasis of Chinese film theory gradually shifted from the theoretical study of the script to film ontology — the nature of film representation, the portrayal of images, the aesthetic functions of shots, and the sound effects of film. These studies enriched to a large extent the vulnerable spots in Chinese film theory or filled in blanks that had long been empty.

To oppose the artificiality in film wrought by leftist thinking, Bazin's realism, once introduced into China, played an important role in affecting the development of Chinese film theory in the 1980s. New methodologies such as semiotics and psychoanalysis began to be introduced, enlarging the vision of Chinese film theory and enriching its patterns as well. Old issues such as the nationalization of film and the critical inheritance of the Chinese cultural tradition came again into full swing. As an imported art from the West, film contains both the ancient Western aesthetics of imitation and the traditional Chinese aesthetics of ignoring ideology and emotion. The reintroduction of this issue in the 1980s resulted from the confrontation and subsequent merger of Western and Chinese cultures brought on by the open-door policy and was intended to lead Chinese film to discover its own unique path of development.

Chinese film theory and filmmaking in the New Era stimulate and affect each other. The movement of Chinese film in the New Era can be generally observed through the development of film theory. Currently China is changing from an agrarian economy to a commercial economy. This trend has pushed Chinese film toward commercialization and, consequently, entertainment and genre films have emerged as a current hot topic in the study of Chinese film theory.

This book may not contain all of the highest achievements of Chinese film theory in the New Era. The limited space of this book has prevented the editors from including some of the important longer articles. Nevertheless, this collection clearly and objectively traces the development of Chinese film theory in the New Era and reflects its basic characteristics. Most of the chapters in this book have been highly influential in China, and several have created a furor. The overall collection and the arrangement of the individual chapters are specifically helpful in leading the Western reader to an understanding of contemporary Chinese film theory.

George S. Semsel, one of the few Western scholars who have given much interested attention to Chinese film, has edited an introductory book and written a number of articles about Chinese film. Hou Jianping, a young Chinese film scholar, has been working on the introduction of Western film into China and Chinese film into the West. I came to know them in different ways. Xia Hong is a colleague and my friend. Before he left to study film in the United States, he was managing editor of *Film Art* and worked several years with me at the China Film Association. Xia knows the current situation of Chinese film theory very well and has formulated strong opinions about it. These three people are among the few rare and suitable people qualified to undertake the translation and editing of such a project as this collection. It is courageous and admirable of them to undertake this difficult yet significant task. To date, even in China, no such systematic collection has been published. I believe that the publication of *Chinese Film Theory: A Guide to the New Era* will be a milestone in the history of the exchange of film between the United States and China.

Luo Yijun

# INTRODUCTION

China, one of the most productive filmmaking countries in the world, has maintained an average production rate for the last decade of more than 130 films annually. However, film theory in the People's Republic of China, we have to admit, remains far behind not only theoretical studies in the West, but equally far behind the level and quality of filmmaking within China itself. Although a few filmmakers such as Chen Kaige, Zhang Yimou, and Wu Tianming have become internationally known, not a single theoretician has received international recognition. Consequently when in recent years foreigners began to understand Chinese culture and to study Chinese films like *Yellow Earth* (1984) and *Red Sorghum* (1985), little was known about Chinese film theory. Yet even before the Fifth Generation* began its active explorations of filmmaking, equivalent explorations had already been initiated by scholars and writers committed to the art.

This collection is limited to the New Era, which began in 1979 after the end of the Third Plenary Session of the Eleventh Party Central Committee reestablished the policy to "let a hundred flowers blossom, let

---

*The Fifth Generation refers to a group of young filmmakers who are mostly graduates of Beijing Film Institute in 1982. The major representatives are Chen Kaige, Zhang Yimou, Tian Zhuangzhuang, Zhang Junzhao, and Wu Ziniu. Their major works are *Yellow Earth, One and Eight, On the Hunting Ground*, and *Red Sorghum.*

a hundred schools of thought contend" (Mao Zedong) and ended on June 3, 1989, when that same government crushed the student demonstration in Tiananmen Square. This time frame does not mean that there was no systematic film theory in China before 1979, nor that a complete and systematic film theory has appeared since that time. Our interest is to reflect an unprecedented era in Chinese film history, an era in which not only the most heated debates and study about film were launched, but also a period in which theoretical research flourished as it never had before. The chapters edited and translated here (with the kind permission of their authors) are among the most representative, influential, and debatable. We did not restrict our selection to only those writings considered to be the very best, but included a broad range of materials by practitioners as well as scholars. What we have provided here is a systematic understanding of the developmental processes of Chinese film theory through the major issues of debate. We hope the book will help the Western scholar to know how the Chinese study and understand film art.

Generally speaking, Chinese film of the early period was heavily influenced by Hollywood, and later, by Russian revolutionary films. After the 1950s Chinese film, for a long time, was the combined product of the Hollywood model and Russian social-realist film theory. Too much emphasis was put on the function of propaganda and film as an educational tool. In comparison to Westerners, Chinese film scholars seldom made a serious exploration of film ontology, especially of such issues as the medium's specifics and principles.

During the thirty years (1949–1979) following Liberation, there was nothing outstanding taking place in the field of Chinese film theory, though historically, filmmaking in this period was further developed than that of the 1930s and 1940s. There were some limited debates of theoretical issues, but strictly speaking, they cannot be regarded as trends of schools of film. At best, they should be seen as critical commentaries on filmmaking (such as the attack on *Wu Xun*) or limited theoretical phenomena (such as the attack on the article, "The Drum of Film"). Such debates initiated nationwide political and ideological movements, but never established themselves as serious film theory. Nonetheless, during those thirty years there were a few events worthy of mention:

Zhong Dianfei's article, "The Drum of Film," published in 1957, announced that we should respect the economic principles of film, though before the "drum" could make itself heard, the author was being criticized.

Ju Baiyin's "Monologue on Cinematic Innovation," published in 1962, announced the need to respect the aesthetics of film as well as its constant innovation, though his call didn't generate any reverberations at the time, and the article turned out to be the author's last monograph. (He was tortured to death during the Cultural Revolution because of this article.)

The "three prominences" of the Gang of Four (give prominence to the positive among all the characters; give prominence to the heroes among the positive; give prominence to the major heroes among the heroes) eventually became the only principles to follow in literature and art during the ridiculous period in which 800 million people watched only eight model dramas.

A few books such as Xia Yan's *The Problems of Screenwriting* and Zhang Junxiang's *About the Special Expressive Means of Film* were published that are regarded as classic works that first established Chinese film theory.

The overthrow of the Gang of Four in 1976 marked the end of the Cultural Revolution. Film, after suffering disastrous ruin for a decade, entered into a period of rehabilitation during the nation's economic and political reform. At that time, the major issue of theoretical study was not theory itself, but how to make the adjustment, both theoretically and ideologically, in a period of transformation: on the one hand, film theory tried to criticize and break through political restrictions and the limitations of the three prominences; on the other hand, it tried to restore and identify with the concept of art before the Cultural Revolution. It is obvious that films produced before 1979 made a great effort to break away from the models, but consciously or unconsciously, they were entrapped in them. Meanwhile, the optimistic attitudes and the restlessness that appeared in film theory circles were only concerned with whether or not the current filmmaking was catching up with the artistic standards of the seventeen-year period (1949–1966) before the Cultural Revolution.

During this period in film circles, as in those of any other art, there were some arduous debates over such issues as the relationship between film and politics, the relationship between art and reality, and discussions about realism, sentimentality, and humanity depicted in film, and other problems of the time. These debates, however, were more concerned with general problems rather than something unique and concrete to film, and the methodologies remained those of tradition, restoration, and stimulation. Yet by reestablishing distinctions between what was right and what was wrong, which had been seriously perverted during the Cultural Revolution, the understanding of these issues became more profound. At the same time, these debates also helped lay a foundation for the prosperity of filmmaking and film theory. Though it is true that those in film circles made a major effort to achieve this, there were no exciting or real changes, practically or theoretically, taking place during this period.

The year 1979 was a significant year for Chinese film. The December 1978 meeting of the Third Plenary Session of the Eleventh Communist Party Conference clarified many problems left from the Cultural Revolution as well as subsequent ones. It marked the coming of a new period in which thoughts were being liberated and the open-door policy was being carried out. A most active and prosperous situation for filmmaking and theory was formed and developed under such circumstances.

Two major events took place in film circles in 1979 that could be regarded as signs of transformation. The first was the appearance of two films, *Troubled Laughter* and *Xiao Huar*. The second was the publication of "Throwing Away the Walking Stick of Drama," by Bai Jingsheng and "The Modernization of Film Language," by Zhang Nuanxin and Li Tuo. Films, for the first time in history, experimented with the means and potentials of cinematic representation; and the essays, likewise for the first time, put forth the crucial argument that "film should be film." All played equally important roles in making the badly needed adjustments and stimulating the development of filmmaking and film research. Furthermore, they initiated a series of debates on issues like the theatricality of film, the literary quality of film, the new concept in film, the nationalization of film, and tradition and innovation of film, which turned this period into a crucial time for the development of the medium — the New Era.

# I

# The Debate on the Theatricality of Film

If "The Modernization of Film Language" by Zhang Nuanxin and Li Tuo was the major explosive, then Bai Jingsheng's "Throwing Away the Walking Stick of Drama" was the fuse. At the beginning of his article, Bai reported that for a long time, people generally understood film from the point of view of drama. "It is true that film absorbed a great deal from drama on its way to becoming an art form," he argued. "It was with the help of drama that film took its first step. However, now that film has become an independent art form, does it have to rely on the walking stick of drama forever?" His answer was very clear: "It is time that we throw away the walking stick of drama."[1] The significance of his proposal cannot be underestimated, for it was the first time in Chinese film history someone brought the issue into the open.

The first enthusiastic response came from film director Zhang Nuanxin and her husband, film critic Li Tuo. "The Modernization of Film Language" broke the silence of Chinese film theory and brought about a greater activity than had ever existed before. The article addresses two major issues: first, based on research into the development of film since the invention of the Lumiere brothers, they argue that cinematic language constantly changes, with the new continuously superceding the old. Furthermore, the rate of change is faster and more violent than that of any other linguistic form. They point out that the films of Italian Neorealism and the French New Wave broke with the conventions of drama and boldly experimented with modes of structure unique to film, bringing innovation to its narrative strategies so that by the 1970s, films were basically free from the principles governing dramatic conflict and had become more cinematic.

Second, from the perspective of representational forms, which no one had touched upon before, they analyze why Chinese film has lagged behind the West, pointing out that filmmaking in China is still "based on patterns of drama." It seems if film lost the support of the "walking stick of drama" it could hardly take another step. Therefore, film in China, instead of honestly, naturally, and vividly reflecting real life, remains little more than "canned drama." The authors conclude that the artificiality of content, a cliché-ridden film language, and the overuse of dramatization are the major reasons for the falsity. They strongly urge that the language of film be brought up to date, especially now, during the time of the four modernizations. A new circumstance should be created in which the artistic qualities of film, the techniques of representation, film aesthetics, and film language can be openly and forcefully discussed.[2]

Their opinion shocked film circles of the time and generated an arduous response and debate. The problem of the theatricality of film soon caught the attention of many people and started a long nationwide discussion. The interest of those in theoretical circles turned to the ontology of film, which had never been studied before. Soon after, the well-known theoretician Zhong Dianfei proposed the "divorce of film from drama." He believed that it was not only the natural consequence of the development of the art to get this "divorce" but also that it was the only way to stimulate the improvement of film art. His argument brought the debate to its maximum intensity.[3]

This debate lasted about three years and many artists like Shao Mujun, Yuan Wenshu, Huang Shixian, Zhang Junxiang, Zheng Xuelai, Lin Shan, Tan Peisheng, Chen Yutong, and He Ren became involved. Aside from the fact that all were interested in the issue, their opinions varied. Some were for it, some against it. In "Modernization and the Modernism," Shao Mujun was among the first to make a quick response, claiming that film language evolved gradually through a process of accumulation rather than elimination, and arguing that the move away from drama was incompatible with Marxist principles. "It's a wrong road and dangerous to vent anger on drama and to draw unconsciously to the nondramatization of the modernists in order to oppose formalism and conceptualism," he warned.[4] His concern was quite representative. Yuan Wenshu, deputy chairman of the China Film Association, also claimed in

1980 that "the spirit of the French avant-garde of the 1920s might possibly make its appearance in China in the 1980s."[5] His overly sensitive warning, which many found ridiculous, didn't find much support in film circles.[6] Other ideas appeared as well, such as that film, as a synthetic art, shouldn't "throw away the walking stick of drama," nor should it "divorce" from theatre; on the contrary, it should be "polygamous."[7]

The reasons for this debate are not complicated. With the advent of the liberation of thought and the establishment of the open-door policy, people working in film circles had their first glimpse of recent developments in world cinema and realized just how far China's film lagged behind. Their respect for their country and sense of responsibility made some people restless. They were anxious to find a way to change the backwardness; so anxious, in fact, they often engaged in practical approaches without giving them the thought they warranted. What was true of theoretical studies was equally true of filmmaking itself. Yang Yianjin, director of *Troubled Laughter,* enthusiastically and without hesitation tried any technique he could see or use, although almost all of them — flashbacks, zooms, location sound, and the like — were already clichés elsewhere. At the time in China such techniques were seen as positive and innovative. In theory circles, as will become increasingly clear, discussion of every issue was aimed at the practice of filmmaking.

The lengthy debate on the theatricality of film shattered the tranquility surrounding research into ontology and the characteristics of film, and came to the attention of all film circles in China. This debate was to some extent limited to the level of a few elemental proposals, and discussions remained superficial. No concrete conclusions were reached. Nonetheless, the debate itself, though not theoretically scientific and complete, functioned as a catalyst that stimulated the rise of a new trend in Chinese film. From that moment, Chinese film entered into a new era in which an arduous and constant study of film would be carried on, and innovation and prosperity would be achieved in the medium.

## NOTES

1.  Bai Jingsheng, "Throwing Away the Walking Stick of Drama," *Film Art Reference,* no. 1, 1979.
2.  Zhang Nuanxin and Li Tuo, "The Modernization of Film Language," *Film Art,* no. 3, 1979.
3.  Zhong Dianfei, "A Letter to Ding Qiao," *Film News Report,* October 1980.
4.  Shao Mujun, "Modernization and the Modernism," *Film Art,* no. 5, 1979.

5. Yuan Wenshu, "About Film Study," *Reference of World Cinema,* June 1980.

6. Huang Shixian, "Film Should Seek the Beauty of Its Form," *Film Art Reference,* no. 21, 1980.

7. Zhang Junxiang, "Essay Done in Film Terms," *Film Culture,* February 1980.

# 1 THROWING AWAY THE WALKING STICK OF DRAMA

Bai Jingsheng
translated by Hou Jianping

For a long time now, people have spoken of film from the perspective and concept of drama, and screenwriters, more often than not, apply dramatic structure to their scripts. It is true that film absorbed a great deal from drama on its way to becoming an art form. It was with the help of drama that film took its first step. However, now that film has become an independent art form, does it have to rely on the walking stick of drama forever?

People often say that film is a synthetic art. However, they often neglect the rich content this synthetic art contains, and the fact that this synthesis is not based on drama, nor is it a mechanical mixture of all art forms either. Film has become a unique art after absorbing a variety of art forms including drama, literature, painting, music, and photography. Film has gone far beyond the limitations of drama, as well as the limitations of any other art.

## UNDERSTANDING DRAMATIC CONFLICT

The basis of drama is conflict. There would be no drama at all without characters and the conflicts among them. This unvarying principle has been with drama since its inception. On the stage, settings and properties can be omitted, but not the characters and their conflicts. Without characters, drama would lose its prerequisite, and without conflicts, there would be no contradictions through which to stimulate development of the situation.

But not all art forms base their existence on conflict. Painting, for example, depicts a variety of subjects such as landscapes, still lifes, flowers, and birds. Obviously, such paintings do not present conflict, though a few thematic paintings such as Da Vinci's *The Last Supper* do. But in the end, most paintings do not touch upon the representation of character conflicts.

In music, too, except for opera, which is closely related to drama, conflicts are not addressed. Although certainly we can argue that conflicts exist in the melody, these are not within the sphere of character conflicts.

In literature, descriptive prose that focuses on landscapes, or poetry and lyrics that express human emotions, do not directly represent character conflicts. Only narrative literature contains them, but its means of representation is different from that of drama. In drama, conflicts are centralized and condensed, starting with a beginning from which they undergo complications and developments that lead, in the end, to their resolution. The entire process centers on the conflicts of characters and formulates a structure unique to drama. In drama, aside from character there is almost nothing else, or nothing is permitted to exist. The novel, on the other hand, does not require such compression. A novel can contain narration, description, lyrical passages, and commentaries. Though all relate to theme, they are not direct representations of character conflicts.

On this point, film is closer to the novel. The feature film, one kind of film that contains dramatic situations, also represents the conflicts of characters, but does not have to follow their development as strictly as does drama. It can certainly present conflicts indirectly, reveal emotion, and depict landscapes without any characters on the screen. In drama, the environment (setting) and the objects (properties) cannot exist independently, without the appearance of characters. But in film, natural landscapes and objects can appear in a series of scenes without characters. Though these natural landscapes and objects are also used to express emotions indirectly, they obviously do not directly represent conflicts. When, for example, in *Spring Comes to the Withered Tree* — in the scene in which "time passes and people die," and the male and female protagonists meet — a brooklet, a bridge, and a flock of ducks appear on the screen. Though they serve workably as foils to emotions, such vivid images certainly cannot appear on the stage. Such representations are unique to film. Sometimes natural settings can be used independently to express a symbolic meaning. In *The Lin Family Store,* a basin of dirty water is poured into the river to symbolize characteristics of the period and the environment.

In film, parallel editing creates symbols and associations and often uses the images of settings instead of characters in conflict. Eisenstein in *The Battleship Potemkin* cuts rapidly from the cannon to three stone lions, each in a different position. The montage creates the impression that a lone lion is shocked and leaps forward. Characters in conflict are not represented.

In such ways film differs from drama, which reveals its content by relying entirely on the direct depiction of the conflicts of characters. Film contains not only elements of drama, but also those of painting, prose, poetry, and music, and thus does not have to center on the presentation of conflicts to reveal its content.

## THE FORM OF TIME AND SPACE

The most significant difference between film and drama lies in the form of time and space. The scenes and acts of dramatic structure determine a limited sphere for time and space. The space of a scene can only be a fixed space, and time, equally fixed. The first act of *Thunderstorm* is set entirely in Zhou's living room during one morning in the summer. The passage of time in the drama is basically the same as that of reality. The limitations of the stage determine that content can only be revealed by separate scenes and acts. If too many scenes and acts are fragmented, the presentation of characters and their dramatic conflicts would lack unity.

Film does not have this time and space limitation. It can constantly change its space, from Nanjing to Beijing, from Earth to the moon; and it can extend and compress time. It can also use fast- or slow-motion cinematography to alter the speed of time, while the freeze frame can make time stop. It is possible for black-and-white and color images to appear in the same scenes to indicate a shift in time. Nowadays, the rapid cuts and transitions used in some films to give a glimpse into thought and memory further reveal the freedom of time and space. Even when a scene is confined to a single space, shooting from different angles can enrich the limited environment.

The aforementioned techniques are used in many foreign films. A broad sphere is waiting for people to explore. Why should we stick with the limitations of time and space of the stage?

Some people cannot depart from the habit of dividing drama into several scenes and acts. They think the difference between time and space in drama and film is only a matter of quantity — if drama can be divided into three or four acts, film can be divided into ten or twenty. Such an understanding is still drawn from the perspective of drama, without recognizing the basic difference between cinematic and dramatic time and space.

## DIALOGUE AND THE MONTAGE OF SOUND AND IMAGE

The expressive means of drama is dialogue. Film adapted dialogue into its means of representation after sound made its appearance, a change that brought film closer to drama. Dialogue is certainly a major device for expressing the thoughts and emotions of characters. However, if film relied entirely on dialogue, as is the case with drama, it would make the mistake of neglecting other means of cinematic representation, thus limiting itself.

Generally speaking, dialogue in film should be succinct, with much expressed through visual images. This is only one point. The key point is not to construct film on the basis of dialogue, but rather on that of synthesis. Furthermore, filmmakers should deviate from their concept of drama and adopt montage, which combines sound and image. That is to say, when conceiving a film, filmmakers should consider not only visual composition, but also the application of sound — to combine sound and image together organically so that dialogue, music, and sound supplement one another. The visual montage of silent films is obviously no longer sufficient; a montage of sound and image should be learned and used.

On stage, dialogue always goes together with performers. Sound comes whenever characters speak. But since its sound track is separate from the images, film has a distinct advantage. The significance of the separation of sound and image is immense. It not only releases film from the mechanical combination of sound and images, but provides a new means of cinematic representation. Such devices as showing a character speaking in one instant, then cutting to a character listening, or a monologue or voice-over narration in the next instant are in common use. One new method is the juxtaposition of sound and image in which the image on screen is unrelated to the sound. Image and sound are completely separate. The parallel of the two creates a new meaning. If, for example, the image on the screen is a crowded street, while the sound reveals the dialogue between two characters, the combination produces a kind of special effect. In short, the separation of image and sound is a special cinematic device and its potentials are yet to be explored. Aside from dialogue, sound effects themselves are another important factor. Sound can not only serve as a foil to the situation, but can function independently to play a role that cannot be substituted.

It is time that we throw away the walking stick of drama that we have used for so long. We should let ourselves go and make great progress in our filmmaking.

**Author's note:** This brief chapter is only part of my unsophisticated thoughts, and the subject needs to be studied further. I wrote this to encourage people to discuss these problems.

# 2 THE MODERNIZATION OF FILM LANGUAGE

Zhang Nuanxin and Li Tuo

translated by Hou Jianping

When we attempt to analyze the reasons why the development of our film lags behind the rest of the world, we can approach it from a different (and often neglected) point of view: what is our position on theoretical research into film art? Do we have a comparatively systematic and advanced film aesthetics that develops out of our own culture? Is our filmmaking under any explicit aesthetic guideline, or is its development quite blind? Do we have a clear knowledge of recent developments in film theory and filmmaking internationally? Should we, or should we not, learn and absorb ideas from foreign art? Is it proper to separate our film theory and production from the rest of the world and to close the country to international discourse? Will it promote the development of our film art if we do so? Such questions cannot be avoided. We should put more effort into facing and resolving these problems both theoretically and practically, especially now, while our film is backward.

In this chapter, we shall explore them from a single perspective: how to bring our film to catch up with the development of world cinema and the modernization of film language. The exploration of cinematic language in this chapter has been done exclusively from the perspective of the forms of representation in film art. For instance, when we trace the history and present situation of cinematic language internationally, we do not concern ourselves with the issues of film content in each era, nor with political or economic aspects that may stimulate (or delay) its development.

## WHY EMPHASIZE CINEMATIC LANGUAGE?

The answer to this question is quite simple: the cinematic language we have used in many contemporary films is cliché-ridden. As a matter of fact, the audience and many filmmakers have long sensed this problem, but seldom have had the opportunity to express it, not to mention to discuss it openly in newspapers or magazines. Why? There are two possible reasons: first, there are steps to follow between perceptual cognition and the conceptual; second, much resistance exists.

What kind of resistance? Did anyone forbid people from raising these questions? Of course not. On the contrary, if that were the case, the problem would have been easily resolved. The point here is that because of the repression and havoc of cultural anarchy wrought by the Gang of Four, and because the task of eliminating their pernicious influence is far from accomplished, a serious neglect of research into film aesthetics and the exploration of production techniques still exists among filmmakers. We should point out that such policies as considering politics but not art, considering content but not form, and considering the philosophies of artists but not their artistic techniques did not originate from the time of the Gang of Four. For a variety of complicated reasons, certain notions about the reflection of leftist ideas in art and literature and the infantile chaos of the petite bourgeoisie's left wing have been constantly growing and corroding our art theory, ruining the circumstances of artistic and literary work. For example, the Marxist principle that content determines form (and that form exerts an important counterforce on the representation of content) is frequently misrepresented as meaning that form is nothing as long as content is good, or that form would be naturally beautiful if content were sufficiently good. Such opinions have seldom been seriously denounced and criticized in theoretical circles. On the contrary, many people accept them as Marxism and never question them.

The Gang of Four has long been thrown onto the historical garbage heap. However, the thinking of many has not yet been liberated. There are some who are not sensitive enough to literary and artistic thoughts and ideas, which reflects the leftist tendency and the petite bourgeoisie's frantic disorder. It is under such influences that our film circles, even to the present day, cannot create an atmosphere in which people can speak securely on a large scale about the artistic quality of film, its representative techniques, aesthetics, and language. On the contrary, until now, among the film criticism we frequently read, most emphasize an analysis of the ideological content of film; even those few articles that examine the artistic quality of film are often superficially addressing it from the view of how form should serve the purposes of content. As to film form itself, few have made any profound research.

At the present time, in order to meet the demand to develop our film art rapidly, we can no longer avoid these problems. We should begin immediately our research into the representative forms of film, both theoretically and practically. A key point from which to start is to analyze, study, and summarize carefully the changes and development of international film language, and to recognize specific regular patterns so as to assimilate them and to stimulate innovation and progress in our own film language and a more rapid development of our film art.

## THE RAPID AND SUSTAINED INNOVATION OF FILM LANGUAGE

Film is the youngest of all the arts; however, no other art can compare to it in terms of its rapid innovation and development. It has been only about eighty years since the Lumiere brothers invented the cinematographe, but since film is an art that relates most closely to contemporary industry, science, and technology, their tremendous rapid development in this century made it possible for its rapid growth. Film has made the great leap from infant to giant within a few decades. Such rapid development naturally makes film's content and form constantly change. Film's development is frequently divided into twenty-year segments, a few decades, or even only a few years. Thus the supercession of the old film language by the new has been quicker and more acute than that of any other art. This is one of the most significant characteristics of film art.

The first person who could be called a director was George Melies. In many of his stage dramas (most of them fairy tales), by combining techniques of the stage with the special effects of photography, Melies created a number of cinematic techniques that heavily influenced the development of film art. It is because of its adaptation of representative forms from the ancient and already mature art of theatre that film was able to grow out of infancy. Yet because of this, for a long time film could not get rid of the traces of theatre in its process of becoming an independent art.

The milestones marking film as a mature art appeared early in the century, during the 1920s and 1930s, when silent film flourished. At that time, great film artists like David Griffith, Sergei Eisenstein, Vsevolod I. Pudovkin, and Charlie Chaplin made their appearances. They created such films as *The Battleship Potemkin, Mother, City Lights,* and *Modern Times,* which are highly sophisticated both in art and ideology. The development of film language at this time was most represented by the study of montage both theoretically and practically. At first, it was Griffith who transformed the sequence, which then consisted of the plain composition of a single shot, into several long, medium, and close-up shots. His techniques were further developed into the mature theory of montage by Russian artists like Eisenstein and Pudovkin. In short, they laid the theoretical foundation for film as an art, and for the first time since its appearance, modified the filmmaking experience into theoretical patterns that became film aesthetics. No matter how glorious the achievement of silent film, it only lasted about twenty years. The appearance of *The Jazz Singer* in 1927 marked the end of the silent period and the advent of sound.

After the application of sound to film, film remained basically a visual art, but was no longer pure. It equipped itself with the most expressive means of human thought — language — and made possible limitless potentials for reflecting the depth and breadth of life. It would lead to one change in film language after another.

During the period when silent film became fully mature, though, film learned much from theatre. The medium gradually became independent by applying its unique ability to "speak out" with visual images through the use of montage. However, after the appearance of dialogue, that phenomenon decreased and the influence of theatre suddenly increased. It should be noted that at the beginning of sound film, film language retrogressed temporarily because of this. However, through the efforts of many film artists, this temporary retrogression became another opportunity to learn from theatre, and created its own mise-en-scène, which some people called montage within the shot. While this mise-en-scène had certain similarities with that of theatre, the difference is crucial. The central issue is the camera movement in silent films. Movement of the camera makes it "see" in motion with the same positive and interesting point of view as that of the audience. This enriched and developed the language of the sound film, and moved it into a more advanced stage.

Italian Neorealism, which appeared after World War II, and the French New Wave, which appeared early in the 1950s, broke through the restrictions and made many explorations from various viewpoints and in various modes. Equally important was the development of color film, which greatly influenced the development of film, though not as heavily as did sound. In the earliest color films, color was used primarily to amaze the audience — color for color's sake — or to depict the hues of nature. But with the further development of film art, color became a mode of representation, a new and powerful means in cinematic language. Film assimilated much from painting for lighting, tone, and composition, but it was more closely related to photography. Since the development of color stocks, the design and form of film established an inseparable relationship with painting. To a certain extent, we can say that a color film is a painting moving in time and space. Many film artists were able to adapt principles of painting to the needs of film, making them into the technique of cinematic design. Color and the art of painting became major components of film language. Because color in cinematic design complicated construction and lighting, some have studied it as color montage.

We have given a brief retrospective of a few important innovations of film language, and the debates between the innovators and the conservatives around those issues in film history. The reason to review them is to indicate that innovation in film language is frequent. Furthermore, the process through which old film language is replaced by the new is more acute than in any other art. After Jiang Qing controlled our film circles under the signboard of cultural revolution, our film art had not only become stagnant, but had seriously retrogressed, moving in a direction opposite to the rapid developments in international film art. Until the present, in terms of film language, our film has continued to follow the aged patterns of the 1950s, 1940s — even the 1930s. Some of the most recent films that reflect the life of the Chinese people in the 1970s still use outdated representational techniques. By so doing, they certainly will not meet the demands of the people for an aesthetics of film art in the New Era that can realize the four modernizations.

## NEW EXPLORATIONS ON FILM LANGUAGE STIMULATED BY CONTEMPORARY FILM ART

Since the 1950s, and especially after the 1960s and 1970s, the features of world film art have been changing dramatically. Not only have there been rapid innovations in film language, but different schools have continued debate. There have been progress and retrogression, and the situation has been quite complex. Our film scholars have had little chance to learn anything about recent foreign films due to the blockade brought on by the cultural tyranny of the Gang of Four. Most recently, when we at last came to know some foreign films and theoretical materials, we signed with relief, "One day in a hole, a thousand years in the world." In this section, we shall study a few trends in the development of contemporary film language based on the materials and films we have seen.

One tendency in the development of contemporary film art is that the narrative mode of film language (or the structure of film) has moved further away from the influence of theatre, and is becoming more cinematic. As mentioned earlier, theatre had a heavy influence on the development of film. For years, film was structured in basically the same way as theatre; that is, the story was revealed by way of dramatic conflict. Such structuring continued until the 1950s (as in Hollywood mainstream films from the 1930s to the 1950s that "conquered the world"). For decades, this was never questioned. When speaking of film structure, many film theoreticians unhesitatingly accepted the many structural laws of drama.

The appearance of Italian Neorealism early in the 1950s and the French New Wave, which stunned the world at the 1959 Cannes Film Festival, expounded the development of film language. In terms of the forms of cinematic representation, many aspirations of Neorealism and the New Wave are important and useful. Among them, these films broke from the limitations of dramatic structure and made a bold attempt to structure film according to its own characteristics, bringing innovation to the narrative in film. In Italian Neorealist films, life was represented with ordinary and detailed events, which made them quite different from those whose structures were based on theatrical laws. In the Neorealist films, there were no complicated turns, no surprising situations, and no exaggerated conflicts.

Likewise, the French New Wave claimed that "plot — the dramatic structure which screenwriters like best — is no longer of importance in contemporary film. The popular means of stylization such as 'dissolves,' 'crosscutting,' and 'flash-backs,' like those of traditional modes, have gradually disappeared." "New cinematic language is of course to meet the need for expressing new ideas. Its main function is to express meanings, not to tell a story; it directly attempts to make a redemption of physical reality, thus restoring the real essence of life — the essence of visual art" (André Labasse).

The point of view presented may not be entirely accurate, but we can get to know certain characteristics of the structure of these films. Under the influence of Italian Neorealism and the French New Wave, young filmmakers in various countries explored cinematic structure in their works and made their contributions. Until the 1970s, it can be assumed that many films found their own unique mode of narration, basically extricated themselves from the influence of the dramatic laws of conflict, and went their own way of development. Based on films we have seen, such as French and Italian "political films" like *Milan Incident, Z, The Confession of the Policeman to the Prosecutor,* which shake off all concepts of dramatic conflict, they broke the cliché of telling a story in a few acts, and applied a documentary mode from beginning to end. This gave their narratives a strong documentary style, which tells us that what we see is not faked, but a truthful record of actual political events. We are not claiming there is no dramaturgy in these films. Film is a synthetic art. It would not be right, nor would it be possible to deprive it of the elements of drama, any more than those of literature, music, and drawing. But we must emphasize that contemporary film has been able to break through the limitations of conventional narrative and to explore cinematic means, which can bring it closer to reality and enable it to express the ideas of the artists more naturally.

Another development in contemporary cinematic language is a breakthrough in the use of shots, both in theory and in practice. The principle of montage invented by Griffith and Eisenstein in the early period has long been regarded as the basis of film art. The position of this aesthetic was so solid that it seemed impossible to change. For decades, even to the present, Chinese filmmakers have taken montage as the only principle by which to connect shots. Filmmakers in other countries not only have developed it further, but have gone quite far.

Early in the 1950s, a group of film critics and directors led by French film critic André Bazin began to challenge the montage. The theory they proposed was that of the "long take." Bazin criticized Eisenstein's theory that took shots as primary materials into which montage alone could generate life and turn them into art. He pointed out that montage theory put too much emphasis on editing. Actually, he argued, a single shot in itself is a forceful representation that possesses the power of intense artistic compression. To Bazin, if elements within the composition of shots are brought effectively into play, a film can be completely constructed of long takes. Of course this is not the sole idea behind Bazin's aesthetics and theory. We should point out that Bazin's theory influenced the art of world film enormously, especially after the 1960s when directors who applied the principles of the long take in their filmmaking appeared in a number of countries.

As a matter of fact, since the appearance of sound in film, montage had long been challenged because of the use of the moving shot. Even in the USSR, the birthplace of montage, filmmakers have long broken the limitation of montage and made new explorations. For example, the concept of "multiple compositions," which recently emerged in the USSR, is similar in so many ways to the long take. Multiple compositions refers to shooting from various levels and angles, using diverse camera movements, and creating many different compositions and scenes within a long shot. The filmmakers claimed that multiple compositions was a new method of montage that fit more effectively into the essence of contemporary cinema. Multiple compositions is a form of montage that restores the highly active movement lost in the long dialogues of the early period of sound film, and brings new meaning to it. It is worth noting that Brian Henderson, an American theoretician, reexamined the two opposing film aesthetics in "The Long Take," in *Movies and Methods,* published in 1976, saying both are one-sided. He further explored the possibility of combining the two and creating a sequence of structure. It is a pity that Chinese filmmakers know little or nothing about the debates on cinematic language and the new development of film theory.

Another important tendency in the development of film language is the exploration of the new means of cinematic representations as plastic arts. There has long existed a dispute between theatrical film and literary film. In addition, there have been the poetic film and prose film. The rapid advancement of science and technology made it possible for the cinematic techniques of representation to change continually. Thus contemporary film quickened its separation from drama, the novel, and poetry, and increasingly revealed its own uniqueness and independence.

Many films of the 1970s presented their content and artistic appeal through synthetic use of such aural and visual means as lighting, color, performance, combinations of sound and image, and changes in rhythm. Consequently, film can at times become a visual symphony of art. The use of color as a means of the plastic arts was mainly based on principles of painting in the past, but in modern cinematic language, its use is based on principles of cinematic representation. The basic use of color in painting has been broken. The rhythm of film has long been a key element in film. However, in contemporary cinematic language, rhythm is more prominently used as a means of the plastic arts — its importance is increased and it becomes a new characteristic of contemporary film language. For example, variable speed cinematography was applied in film long ago, primarily in scientific and educational films. Now, in contemporary film language, such shooting, especially high-speed shooting, is also applied in feature films in order to create different rhythms and artistic effects. In recent years, the split screen emerged, providing film with more freedom in the manipulation of time and space. At times there can be as many as twenty images on the screen, giving more prominence to the characteristics of high compression and intensity in film.

Sound film, which long explored the relationship between sound and image, has gradually elucidated the principles of the combination, opposition, and separation of the two, and increased the expressive power of both. Today there is a tendency toward more frequent use of the separation of sound and image. There are new cinematic techniques of presentation such as the microzoom, tilted shots, and others that also continue to make fresh appearances.

Another tendency worth noting is the constant exploration of new spheres of representation such as direct depiction of the psyche and emotions. Unlimited freedom with time and space in film allows it to depict directly the psychological world. Experimentation with the presentation of the psyche is a tremendous breakthrough in cinematic language. Such experiments began with the French New Wave, and have become increasingly mature. Thoughts, fantasies, memories, ideal, wishes, and even the subtle and complicated subconscious can all be reflected through visual images. These representations are more direct, vivid, ardent, real, and more emotional than in speech or the performances of dramatic actors. There is a good example in the French film Z. The wife of the congressman sees her husband die on the operating table after the attempted murder. The white sheet drawn over his body is etched deeply in her mind. Later, the director cuts back to this scene several times, emphasizing the wife's suffering when recalling this painful moment. Because film can so powerfully depict psychological activities, the rush of ideas, and shifts in feelings, it has an advantage over all other arts in presenting profound social issues and complicated characters.

## LEARNING FROM FOREIGN FILMS AND STIMULATING THE MODERNIZATION OF CINEMATIC LANGUAGE IN CHINA

We have discussed the history of cinematic language in which the new has continually superceded the old, and recent explorations and developments internationally. We can only conclude that in order to hasten the development of our own cinematic language, we must consciously and quickly bring about a transformation of it. In the process of so doing, we should pay close attention to recent improvements in cinematic language internationally, and bravely assimilate and utilize them.

The distance between Chinese film and the rest of the world was shortening at the end of the 1950s and the beginning of the 1960s. By the time such outstanding films such as *Early Spring* and *Stage Sisters,* which revealed an obvious national style, made their appearance, the level of Chinese film art was not far from that of the rest of the world. However, because of the stagnation and retrogression created by the Gang of Four, the artistic level of contemporary Chinese film has moved further away from that of the international cinema. This backwardness is especially revealed in our film aesthetics. For example, most of the recently produced films still basically follow the so-called model of theatrical film.

While examining the development of cinematic language and studying new trends in the development of contemporary cinematic language, we have put our emphasis on addressing the influence of drama on film and how film gradually broke away from this to become an independent art. This approach was taken because many Chinese filmmakers can never escape drama, the contradictions of drama, dramatic conflict, and dramatic situations whenever they think of film. It seems film can hardly take a step without the walking stick of drama. Consequently, screenwriters search hard for drama, directors go all out to produce drama, and performers do all they can to act it out. The result is often merely canned drama instead of films that honestly, naturally, and vividly reflect real life. A common criticism given these films by their audience is that they are artificial. Aside from their false content, a major reason is their strongly dramatized representation.

The basic need to change and modernize cinematic language lies in the fact that China has already entered into a New Era. The realization of the four modernizations is a significant revolution — it demands an extensive and thorough change both in our economic base and superstructure, as well as in ideology and living conventions. All these changes, of course, demand that literature and art adjust accordingly, and film should be among the first to make them.

It takes a great deal of effort in many ways to raise the standard of film art. To achieve this, the most urgent step at the present is to learn from the art of world cinema. Of course, during this process, one problem must be solved properly, that of nationalization. We must learn from the good and progressive art of foreign film in order to turn it into our own element through the power of nationalization, and improve and develop the film art of our own nation. The problem we face is that some wrongly emphasize nationalization in order to oppose learning advanced artistic means from foreign film. We think this attitude is short-sighted.

China is a civilized country with a long history. People have a strong sense of self-respect and pride in their nation and rich cultural heritage. Every sensible Chinese should have this attitude. But if we examine Chinese history over the last millennium, we can easily see that it is because we constantly assimilated foreign arts with which to develop and improve our own that we created this significant culture, and that different peoples within the nation were also learning from each other. Currently, to develop our national film, we must also take this attitude. The national stylization of film is not something that cannot be changed and further developed once established. On the contrary, from the history of Chinese film, we can tell that while we were assimilating the film art of the world, we were also exploring and establishing our own national style. Film, originally an imported product, is not the result of Chinese literature and art anyway. If we use nationalization as an excuse for refusing importation, should we wait then for the appearance of our own Edison and Lumiere brothers to create our own national film?

Finally, we want to point out that although we emphasize the modernization of cinematic language, we needn't mechanically take over and thoughtlessly imitate foreign cinematic language. We should take a practical and realistic attitude toward foreign film. We should digest whatever we learn from the cinematic language of foreign films, integrate it with the real life of the Chinese people, and create a modern cinematic language of our own that can manifest the unique style of our nation. In short, we should learn first, then digest and ultimately assimilate. We would like to end this chapter with this quotation of Lu Xun: "Though it is Western civilization, if we can assimilate it, Western civilization can be turned into our own. It is like eating beef — it is impossible to transform us into beef simply because we eat it. . . ."

# II    The Debate on the Literary Quality of Film

While the discussion about the ontology of film and how to raise the quality of Chinese film centeed around the major issue of drama and film, many elder film artists were dissatisfied and worried about the bold experiments into forms of representation as well as cinematic language in films like *Xiao Huar* and *Troubled Laughter*. They claimed that the low quality of Chinese film was not due to obsolete film form, but due to their low literary quality. This developed into another debate at the beginning of the 1980s.

The major figures who launched this attack consisted of directors and screenwriters, including Zhang Junxiang, at the time chief of the Shanghai Film Bureau. They were obviously against the current situation in film circles in which the middle-aged directors had again proposed the auteur theory and discussions of the modernization of cinematic language (which by the time had gone on for about a year) continued.[1] In an article published in February 1980 Zhang Junxiang, reversing his original position on the characteristics of film expressed in his book, *On the Means of Representation Unique to Film,* published twenty years earlier, claimed that "film is literature — literature written with the filmic means of expression." And he repeated this idea in two articles, "My Basic View of Film" and "Again on Film Literature and the Literary Value of Film" published later. He believed that "the director's task is fully to represent literary values in films through the cinematic techniques he commands."[2]

In response to this confirmation of "literary value," Chen Huangmei stated again in 1982 "don't forget literature"[3] and soon got some positive answer from a group of well-known screenwriters including Wang Yuanjian, Lu Zhuguo, Ai Mingzi, Li Tianji, Meng Senhui, Wang Lian, and Yie Dan.[4] Tian Shen further argued that "any film devoid of literature is only a meaningless frame," thus to some extent, "literature should be the mother of film, . . . to deprive film of literature is to turn film into a flower without root, water without a source."[5] Song Jianbo also stressed that "literature is like blood flowing in the body of film, bringing true life. Without literature, there would be no film art." Thus the most important aim of filmmaking is "to make full use of the filmic means of expression to embody as many literary values as possible."[6] Most of the supportive ideas came from screenwriters, probably because their position in film was becoming less important. In contrast, the doubts and negative opinions were coming from the theory circles.

In contrast to the debate on the theatricality of film, which made great efforts to get film out from under the influence of drama and literature, this discussion tried by all means to bind film to literature. Since to do so means the loss of film's own identity, it naturally evoked an arduous response and debate. (Strangely, *Film Art,* the journal that shocked film circles with its appeal for the modernization of film language, kept quiet on this argument; the debate was basically carried out in *Film Culture, Film Literature,* and *New Film Scripts.*) Zhong Dianfei was the first to talk back: "I don't agree with the assumption that the major problem with Chinese film is that of its 'literary' values." He emphasized that "the feeling of putting one's feet in one's own boots and going his own way is becoming stronger for me. Poems should be poems, and film should be film."[7] He argued "the connection of one [art] with the others is temporary and conditional, and the development of itself is eternal and unconditional."[8] The idea of judging film according to its reflection of literary values "won't do any good to the improvement of Chinese film."[9] Zhang Wei, a young film scholar, sharply criticized Zhang Junxiang's view, saying Zhang's point was to show that "the artistic manifestation of film is objectively the absolute negative embodiment of the literary phenomenon, the director's work is the negative translation of the scenario, the process of script to screen is a transformation process from one art to another. . . . That means Zhang severed the unity of creation in film."[10]

Film theoretician Zheng Xuelai almost completely denied the idea of literary value from the aspects of methodology and asethetics. He argued that "the literature of film and the 'literary' value of film, strictly speaking, are not scientific concepts, but a creation of Zhang. And to put literature above every other art is not in accordance with the laws of art, nor with its historical development." Film is not literature, it is an art form with its own aesthetic characteristics. Furthermore, "it is impossible to talk about the essence of film without addressing film aesthetics and the special means of cinematic representation."[11] Yu Min basically agreed with him in his article, "Diversification, Not Prescriptions," saying that "different forms of art have different means of presentation . . . the one presented by means of literature is literature, and the one presented by means of film is film." Literary quality shouldn't be used to replace the characteristics of film art.[12]

If we consider the two debates from the viewpoint of their intention, we can say that there is no contradiction between the two — both meant to improve Chinese film. One pointed out that film was short of its own quality from the aspect of film form; the other noted that film was short of literary quality (referring to the profundity of film themes) from the viewpoint of film content. Both exposed the same problems in Chinese film. Yet if we examine them in terms of the concept of film, we can see that the two were obviously opposed to each other. Whereas one tried to defend the purity of film, showing film was neither drama nor literature — film was simply film — the other argued that film belonged to literature, and sought to replace film quality with the literary quality of film.

This debate, which lasted about four years, ended without a conclusion — neither side surrendered its opinions. Though Zhang Junxiang repeated and further developed his idea four years later in "Again on Film Literature and the Literary Value of Film,"[13] the issue was ignored by the theory community, which invariably "loathes the old and favors the new." At the time a more interesting and tempting issue was being discussed: the "new concept of film."

## NOTES

1. Shen Yiaoting, Wu Yigong, and Song Cong, "Film Art Is Directors' Art," *Wenhui Daily,* November 2, 1980.

2. Zhang Junxiang, "Essay Done in Film Terms," *Film Culture,* February 1980.

3. Chen Huangmei, "Don't Forget Literature," *Film Scenarios,* January 1982.

4. Wang Yuanjian, "Film: A Visual Form of Literature," *Film Literature,* September 1980; Lu Zhuguo, "Strive to Strengthen the Literary Quality of Film," *Screen and Audience,* August 1982; Ai Mingzhi, Li Tianji, and Meng Senhui, "A Subject Never to Forget," *New Film Scripts,* February 1982; Wang Lian, "I'm All for

'Don't Forget Literature,'" *New Film Scripts*, February 1982; Yie Dan, "Film Can't Separate from Literature," *New Film Scripts*, February 1982.

5. Tian Shen, "Film Should Belong to Literature," *Film Literature*, September 1982.

6. Song Jianbo, "Thoughts on the Literary Value of Film," *Film Literature*, December 1982.

7. Zhong Dianfei, "Notes on Film Awards," *Popular Cinema*, June 1986.

8. Zhong Dianfei, "Film Form and Film's National Form," *Film Culture*, January 1981.

9. Zhong Dianfei, "Film Literature Should Make a Fresh Start," *New Film Scripts*, January 1983.

10. Zhang Wei, "Query on the Literary Quality of Film," *Film Literature*, February 1982.

11. Zheng Xuelai, "On Film Literature and Film Characteristics," *New Film Scripts*, May 1982.

12. Yu Min, "Diversification, Not Prescriptions," *New Film Scripts*, February 1983.

13. Zhang Junxiang, "Again on Film Literature and the Literary Value of Film," *New Film Scripts*, April 1983.

# 3

# ESSAY DONE IN FILM TERMS

Zhang Junxiang

translated by Hou Jianping

I would like to give my personal views on directing. The work of film directors is indeed very heavy and difficult. Directors must be responsible for the political and artistic qualities of their films. In China the interface of the left and the right will likely continue; however, an absolutely secure situation may not produce outstanding art. Certainly directors and scriptwriters want to have a sense of security, but on the other hand, we must also acquire a sense of responsibility — a responsibility to sing the praises of advanced persons and events, and to expose and criticize backward thoughts and events. Aside from these political issues, directors should also be responsible for the artistic quality of their films. For years political criteria have had primary emphasis. This situation has given us many lessons — many filmmakers would rather remain politically safe than seek artistic pursuits; this consequently has led to many mediocre and formula works. Directors should be responsible for the artistic quality of their films in two ways: one is by representing the literary value of the work, the other is by using cinematic means of expression appropriately and creatively. In other words, the director's task is fully to represent literary values in films through the cinematic techniques he commands. We often talk about literature and art. Art includes painting, music, dance, sculpture, architecture, drama, and film. Film is considered the seventh and youngest art. The first five have nothing to do with literature, but drama and film are not only art — they are a synthesis of art forms, and also are literature — the literature of drama and film.

What is film literature? Generally, the term reminds people of the written script, referred to as the basis of filmmaking. This is no misunderstanding. In the USSR there is a highly inappropriate saying in which the script is regarded as merely a "container" — a "box" to be temporarily used for a soon-to-be-finished film. The complete form is what is represented on the screen. The written script is a necessary foundation, but not a complete work of film art, nor a complete film literature. This actually puts a higher responsibility on screenwriters, though it is the director who will complete the visual images, and at the same time ensures that the literary value of the script is best presented. The glamor of a script cannot be fully cast unless it is represented on the screen.

I am not in the least downgrading the role of the screenwriter by saying so; on the contrary, I mean to ask screenwriters to command a better knowledge of the cinematic means of representation so as not to have their work misunderstood or distorted by a director. I believe that the prosperous future of film depends on the appearance of great screenwriters, not only in China, but worldwide. The glamorous era of film has not come yet. The reason is that in comparison with narrative, theatrical, and lyrical literature, that is to say, in comparison with the works of Shakespeare, Tolstoy, Li Bai, Du Pu, Cao Xueqin, and Lu Xun, film literature lags far behind. However, the glamorous time for film will eventually come. It is true that film to a great extent depends on industrial technology, but the development of cinematic technology has reached such an advanced stage that the tools and technical means a director commands are quite mature. It means that the material condition for the appearance of great screenwriters and great cinematic literature has already been founded. If screenwriters can realize the popularity of film among the masses and realize that film is a most capable medium for communicating thoughts and feelings and that film will inevitably become a major event in the cultural life of people, if they will consequently make great efforts to command this form of literature — to apply cinematic representation skillfully and maturely in the same manner that Shakespeare, Tolstoy, Cao Xueqin, and Lu Xun used words — the magnificent era of cinematic literature will eventually come.

I want to encourage film directors to give more attention to the literary value of film. I wrote a booklet, *On Special Cinematic Means of Expression,* intending to point out that film has its own special means of representation. These are not mysterious; they should and can be commanded with some extra effort. Of course, I still urge filmmakers to command the cinematic means of representation, but at the same time I want to stress that they pay close attention to the literary values of film. Why? Nowadays, it seems that while the auteur theory has persisted, a tendency to ignore the function of screenwriters has appeared. I don't agree to change "screenwriter and director" to "director and screenwriter," nor do I agree that film is the director's art. It is true that now the director often helps to adapt the script, "cinematicizing" it; however, no work lacking cinematic quality can be turned into a film merely by being cinematicized.

There is a tendency now to judge the artistic quality of a film according to its techniques, or to believe that if the foreign cinematic techniques of the 1970s are applied to our filmmaking, the quality of films will improve. I am not against learning from the 1970s' techniques, but faced with the fact that the form of film is being emphasized, I'd like to make a loud appeal: *Don't ignore the literary value of film!* To me, the low artistic quality of many films is not because their means of representation are clichés, but because their literary values are not high. Of course, primarily, screenwriters should be responsible for this, but some directors don't pay enough attention to the original literary value of the script, or don't even fully understand it.

On hearing the suggestion that we should learn from American films of the 1940s, European films of the 1950s, and Soviet films after the October Revolution, some people would strongly disagree, asking why we should learn from those antiques instead of from foreign films of the 1970s. First of all, it is not that we don't want to learn from the 1970s; second, there are indeed many things worth learning from the films of the 1940s and 1950s, especially in terms of improving our fundamental skills of filmmaking. For example, a film like *Waterloo Bridge* tells a vivid story by depicting the feelings among five or six people. Our films haven't reached that point. Some foreign films have as many as thirty, forty, or even sixty identifiable characters. It is not even easy to recognize the faces of so many people within a two-hour film. There are many things in European and American films of the 1940s and 1950s worth learning. Besides, to learn from the films of the 1970s doesn't mean only to absorb their structures and editing techniques; it is more important to see how those techniques are applied to serve the literary content and value.

What are literary content and literary value? First, I'd like to address the ideological content of film. Every film has its ideological leaning. Even modernist literature is concerned with philosophical ideas. Whether ideological or philosophical, every film has a central theme, an opinion of the filmmaker toward life. A two-hour film doesn't only relate a story, but also tells what the filmmaker thought about the characters, events, and life depicted. It seems people are avoiding talking about the theme of films. It is true that we took a detour in the past — many created characters for the sake of diagramming a theme. This habit of generally diagramming a theme in art has not yet been eliminated. We should avoid treating an artwork as we solve a mathematical equation, and avoid getting down directly to the theme, but at the same time, we should take measures against another tendency, that is a belief that film directors do not have to consider the themes of their work at all. Some pointed out that nobody could clearly elucidate the theme of *The Dream of the Red Mansion*. It is true that there are various views of it. But *The Dream of the Red Mansion* is a novel. If it were to be adapted into film, one could not include all its content. The opera, *The Dream of the Red Mansion,* only depicted the love among Baoyu, Daiyu, and Baocai, and omitted the rest. I have seen *War and Peace* made by Americans. To me, the major flaw in the film is that the filmmakers tried to put everything Tolstoy wrote into it yet articulated nothing clearly. A film is different from a novel, and it is necessary to present the ideology or the philosophical ideas clearly, though we are against making diagrams.

There still exists the problem of theatrical effects. Films are still being shown to thousands in the theatre, and usually not in repeated viewings; thus the articulation of ideology should be crystal clear. There is a principle in theatrical theory that emphasis should be put on the average audience, that is, what we usually call "a combination of elegance and popularity." Therefore, it is better to articulate clearly the ideological intention. The theme of *Anxious to Return* is very clearly presented. Director Li Jun says that his emphasis is on the conflict between Wei Desheng's leaving and staying throughout the film, focusing on Wei's confrontation with money, death, and love. In his summary of directing, Xie Jin, director of *Ah, Cradle,* says that to love children is to love the future; the focus should be on the fate, feelings, and personalities of human beings. He says what is addressed in the script is humanity, a theme that no one dared touch upon in the past. Isn't this crystal clear? What he wants to depict is that the revolutionary proletariat best understand humanity and the future. Modernists claim that they want to depict life as it is. But what to depict and how to do it is not a matter of causality. In short, we should not diagram the theme in generalities, but at the same time, we should not ignore its clear representation.

Second, let me address the depiction of representative characters. The most important issue of literature is to present people — people as flesh and blood human beings, not as mere concepts. What is more, these people should be presented within the complex of social relations; their inside world and psychological state should be revealed. There is no exception for any form of literature. On this point, it seems there is no disagreement among realism, romanticism, and modernism. Whether or not they are capable of depicting well the images of people is a good test for film directors. Wei Desheng and Yuzhen in *Anxious to Return* and Shen Duoyu in *The Big Dipper* are examples of outstanding representations. Techniques are used, but they are well hidden. Many films use cinematic techniques, but they are used so awkwardly that it is not difficult to tell that the filmmakers are playing with them. An experienced director does not constantly think about what techniques should be used at what point in his filmmaking. He confronts a situation, responds to it, and finds the most powerful and vivid way to present it. It is a matter of artistic accomplishment and experience. In sum, there is no shortcut but to have a deep understanding about a given situation and the characters. Now many scripts are very artificial. It is true that scripts cannot be written without applying techniques, but we should not rely heavily on them. Without a foundation in life, written techniques can achieve nothing.

The examples mentioned reflected the rich thought and feelings of characters and revealed their psychology. *Li Siguang* is a good film, but we wish to see more about Li's inner activities. What we see on the screen is what and how Li works, but we are not clear about his intention. I am not asking to present every detail of the character's inner activities. The realistic cinematic means of expression is to present characters' actual behavior, through which to reveal their spiritual world. Modernist films or stream of consciousness films always concretely present a character's psychology in detail. I wonder if this is the right way. Films remind their audience of the indefinite and rich spiritual world through limited concrete images. If everything were concrete, the audience would lose the pleasure of being cofilmmakers. Of course, dreams and the stream of consciousness exist and can be presented in a film, but they should be based on analogous experiences of the audience or they will not understand it. Subconscious activities and dreams usually do not follow any logic. When these become abnormal, they are beyond the understanding of the average audience and their viewing pleasure is destroyed, for they can only guess what the filmmaker is trying to express.

Another issue I'd like to address is the images of characters. There is voice-over narration at the beginning of *Troubled Laughter,* saying the film is not about a saint or a ghost, it is about people. Some say this is a new principle. Actually, it is a basic rule of realism. Because some artworks are against this and the Gang of Four completely threw truthfulness out of art, it is ignored. I still hold with the idea of presenting ordinary, everyday people. We need to write about ordinary people, but they are not actually so ordinary — there is much we can learn from them. Characters in many foreign films are presented as incapable of being understood, as being pessimistic about contemporary material civilization, or even as reaching the point of irrationality and abnormality! We certainly cannot agree with that.

Third, let me consider the means of literary expression. Film art certainly should apply cinematic means of representation, but since film is also literature, directors cannot ignore literary means of expression and techniques. Film directors should learn all kinds of literary techniques in order to maintain and develop the literary value of the script. Film literature should be and can assimilate the merits of narrative literature, drama, and the prose poem. For instance, when, in *Anxious to Return,* Wei Desheng tells Yuzhen of his past, concentration is on his speech, which is a method of narrative literature. There is no flashback depicting his father's being bitten to death by mosquitoes. In *The Flowing River,* Li Mai also tells her story merely by narration. Films don't always resist narrative methods. When Li Mai tells her story, it is better to listen than to look at her husband's encounters, for what the audience wants to see is not what happened in the past, but her excitement while speaking and her strong, rebellious spirit. Therefore, it is wrong to maintain the general notion that in order to be cinematic and have a good visual presentation, narrative modes must be discarded and flashbacks must appear whenever there is recall of the past.

In *Anxious to Return* there is a long sequence in which a thief who has stolen gold is tied to a tree and Wei Desheng pleads mercy for him. The whole sequence could be performed on a stage in exactly the same way. The representation of emotion is also an important issue in film. Wei Desheng looking repeatedly at the passing geese and Shen Duoyu playing his flute in *The Big Dipper* are cinematic equivalents to prose poems. Songs in film are also included to express feelings.

In short, film should not reject the advantages of narrative literature, drama, and prose, but should absorb them. Of course, they should eventually be transformed into being cinematic, not just mechanically adapted. Thus, on one hand, film directors can neither emphasize the cinematic means of representation alone nor ignore film's literary value; on the other, they must be good at using cinematic means to fully present literary value.

I would like now to address the issues of "throwing away the walking stick of drama" and "the need to divorce film from drama." To me, it is right to oppose lengthy dialogues, exaggerated or even generalized performances, and the confinement of the stage. As Zhong Dianfei articulated, the audience should not be restricted to one seat in the theatre. That is, film directors should be adept at shooting from different distances and angles, structuring time and space, and using montage. But we should not resist dramaturgy at the same time we oppose staginess. Films are still shown to mass audiences in theatres, and theatrical effects should not be ignored. Therefore, the crutch of drama will most likely continue to be used. There is a current statement that condemns film literature as being led by dramatic situations. It seems that every basic means of drama such as conflict, suspension, and climax should be all put aside. This needs to be clarified. In his notes on directing *Tearstain,* Li Wenhua articulated how he stuck to suspense. How did Cao Yi die? Is Kong Nina crazy or merely pretending to be so? Can Zhu Keshi solve this case? Li said he tried to capture attention by frequently reminding the audience of these questions. This is at least one of the reasons *Tearstain* succeeded.

What is theatricality? This is worthy of further discussion. There is a tendency to understand theatricality simply as conflict. Life is filled with contradictions and drama with conflicts, but we should not simply consider dramatic conflicts as opposing views and a few confrontations. The representation of conflicts is dramatic and a moment of suspense can catch the viewers' attention. Theoretically, there are three definitions of dramaturgy. One is based on conflicts. Dramaturgy results from the conflicts between opposing forces. These can be between individuals and society, or among or within the heroes. The second, based on strong will, claims that heroes have indomitable wills and do not yield to any kind of difficulties. The third is based on crisis. Dramaturgy occurs whenever a crisis and turning point in life takes place. However, whether based on strong will or crisis, conflict always involves two or more opposing sides. In most cases, dramaturgy is produced in moments of quiet and peace, but when life reaches a crossroad, it comes from the suspense of achieving success or going down to defeat. Therefore, the theatrical principles such as suspense and climax cannot be thrown away. In my understanding, Zhong Dianfei's proposal to divorce film from drama means to discard the restrictions of the stage, but not all means of theatrical literature.

Let me emphasize again that film literature should incorporate matters of narrative and theatrical literature, and lyrical prose — it is a "polygamy." Ever since film appeared, debates over the relationships between film and drama have existed. For decades, on one hand, film submitted to stage drama, but on the other hand, its resistance to drama has never stopped. Wasn't there a debate on the "prose film" and "poetic film" in the USSR? The so-called prose film intended to incorporate narrative literature, while the poetic film tried to move closer to lyrical literature. Both tended to resist drama, but neither succeeded. It is difficult to predict the future. Perhaps, with the technological development of television, films could be viewed individually and repeatedly in a living room. Then we would not worry about theatrical effects or dramaturgy.

The literary values of film — its ideology, images of characters, divergent techniques of narrative representation, theatrical and lyrical literature — will eventually have to be represented by cinematic means. However, generally speaking, the cinematic means can only enrich literary values, not create them. If scripts do not provide these values, no matter how competent their directors, they simply will be unable to fabricate them with montage and mise-en-scène. At the same time, if a director does not thoroughly understand the literary values of a script and does not consider their representation as his priority, then all applications of cinematic means will be nothing more than a display of techniques.

Actually there are many methods available that allow directors to represent literary values. First is performance. Without performance, the major part of literary values can only exist on paper. I was very pleased to see the appearance of young and talented actors and actresses like Zhao Erkang and Siqin Gaowa in *Anxious to Return,* Ma Xiaowei in *Ah, Cradle,* Sun Daolin in *Li Siguang,* Chen Qiang in *Look at This Family,* and Wang Runshen and Du Defu in *The Big Dipper.* The characters they performed made a deep impression on us. I think we can learn much from the final farewell in *Anxious to Return.* Yuzhen agrees to let Wei Desheng leave for his army. The two walk slowly and silently in the forest. Yuzhen carries his bag. When he wants to take it from her, she refuses — it seems to comfort her the longer she can hold it. Eventually she puts it on his back, but when he stares at her, she avoids his look. These are simple gestures and the lenses used are ordinary. But through the detailed performance, Yuzhen's contradictory emotions — she doesn't want him to leave, but has to let him go — are well represented. This is a fine collaboration of director and cast. Some claim that if the right cast is chosen, half the work is done. This is reasonable. In other words, if the wrong people are cast, what is lost would be more than half. Of course, even if the best are chosen, the director still has half his work to do — enlightening the cast on how to create the best images for their roles.

Lenses, mise-en-scène, sound effects, and music are special means film directors have at their disposal. In using them, they need the cooperation of cinematographers, art designers, and sound recordists. Camera distance, angle and movement, and different approaches to editing are the major expressive methods directors command, which enable them to turn the narrative, theatrical, and lyrical means of expression into those of film. The eleven films we have discussed here have accumulated many new options.

Ever since the discovery that film could be cut and glued together, the technique of putting different scenes shot at different times and places has been used, and montage was created. The manipulation of time and space is not new. When American director D. W. Griffith made *Intolerance,* he created a powerful impression by editing scenes of different eras together. In the early American Western, the cliché of the hero's last-minute rescue of the beautiful woman was also a manipulation of time and space. Therefore, we shouldn't mystify this technique. At the same time, we should also realize that such manipulation is open for further development. It is a technique that enables the structure of film literature to go far beyond the sphere of theatrical literature and enriches the means of cinematic representation. Contemporary filmmakers have made many breakthroughs in this respect and young Chinese filmmakers have also made some satisfying experiments in films like *Xiao Huar* and *Troubled Laughter.*

The expressive power of mise-en-scène, which includes cinematography, art design, makeup, and costume, is another method at the director's disposal. Art design, which provides a typical environment for typical characters, should enlighten the atmosphere and reveal characters' mental attitudes, ideas, and emotions. The battle on the ice in *Anxious to Return* gives the audience a strong impression of the harsh circumstances faced by the Allied Anti-Japanese Army. If the location were a forest or hillside, the effect would not be the same. In *The Guide,* Xingjiang's street fair, desert, and strange-looking trees are all well chosen. Some complain that the mountain region where Yuzhen lives in *Anxious to Return* is too pretty, too much like a peaceful haven. To me, the director's selection of such a colorful land, with its peaceful spring, was appropriate, for he may well have intended to give an impression of serenity. Wei Desheng could easily enjoy a peaceful life in this place, but he insists on leaving — he wants to look for the Anti-Japanese Army, an army that will "exist until the death of its last soldier." Recently I took another look at my own film, *The Prairie Fire*. I regretted that when Mengzhi and Qiuying discuss their marriage, the setting is under a tree, for no such tree exists near the mine. It would have been better to set it on a slag heap, probably, for this could have conveyed their feelings and circumstances. In other words, selection of design and location is as important for a director as for his cast.

I would like to address briefly location shooting. To shoot on location has its own advantages. It is economical and realistic. But from an artistic perspective, it is difficult to find a location that can provide a representation of the inner world of the characters. Italian filmmakers use a lot of location shooting, but they must in order to save money. British filmmakers don't like to use location shooting. They pay more attention to art design, as can be observed from adaptations of Dickens' novels. Thus we should not consider location shooting the best approach. Art should be superior, more condensed and representative than real life. Why would some of our directors rather shoot on location? Probably because our designed settings often look unreal. In terms of representing literary values with mise-en-scène, we need to put more effort into further explorations.

The last subject I want to discuss is sound effects and music. These should be among a director's most important methods, but there has not been enough emphasis put on them. When we speak about montage, more often than not we mean montage of image. Little consideration has been given to the montage of sound, and the montage of sound and image. We can even say that there is an area in the use of sound that has yet to be opened. Even if a film uses a large orchestra, that doesn't guarantee a good effect. The truth is we would sometimes achieve better results with a smaller orchestra. Another issue we all agree upon is the need to use songs in films more effectively. Songs should be used to stimulate situations and express emotions. They should not be independent. When at the college entrance examination in *The Loyal Overseas Chinese* Huang Sihua sings "I Love You, China," the song is effective, but why let her sing an entire song on the deck at the beginning of the film when the audience has no idea who she is? This song is nothing more than an isolated performance.

In short, by summarizing experiences in these films, we once again realize that directors should be good at depicting the literary value of a work with their cinematic means of representation.

Finally, I would like to address briefly the issue of national form. The Chinese way of thinking and feeling must be of Chinese national style. It cannot be replaced by that of foreigners. The living habits, language, and ethics of characters should also be national. No one debates this. What currently evokes debate are issues about the use of lenses and montage of sound and image. After the overthrow of the Gang of Four, we had the opportunity to see many recent foreign films in which there were a number of new techniques. Some young Chinese filmmakers began to experiment in their own films. They believed that these were new film languages and were positive that these new forms would affect the content of our films. Meanwhile, many audiences as well as people in film circles could not get used to these techniques; therefore, they doubted them. To me, film is an important art form. Dissolves and multiple images are nothing more than techniques of representation. The issue is not whether or not we can use them, but whether or not we can use them properly. Of course, it takes time for people to get used to them. Some foreigners don't know of the closed and isolated situation under the Gang of Four and worry about the mechanical imitation of techniques by some young filmmakers. This is understandable. But we ourselves should have a bit more patience and not strangle them in the cradle. I do believe that these young filmmakers will soon learn to use these new forms and techniques properly and creatively. At the same time, I hope these young filmmakers will not accuse older directors who don't use them of being outmoded and conservative. Various styles should be permitted. *Xiao Huar* and *Troubled Laughter,* which used these techniques, are good films, but *Ah, Cradle* and *Anxious to Return,* which didn't should also be acknowledged as good. At this time, I believe we should have circumstances in which various styles or schools can coexist and develop freely. As Xie Jin said, it would not work out if we only knew one set of boxing.

Another issue of debate is the manipulation of time and space. As discussed earlier, it really opens a new field for cinematic representation, but it contradicts the structures to which we have long been accustomed, so it is difficult to accept. As mentioned, the interaction of time and space has long been used in film, but its popular usage didn't occur until the representation of the stream of consciousness in Western films. Films of the stream of consciousness emphasize the interaction of time and space in order to present the subjective workings of characters. Narration of such films is not limited by plot, but only follow the subconscious activities of characters. Their directors have various theories, all of which are quite ambiguous, like their films. Briefly speaking, we can understand them this way: they believe that most dramatic structures are based on plot development, which they call exterior structures. Most films follow this pattern. They believe it is time to change this and base everything on the subconscious, which they call interior structures.

As a matter of fact, the behavior of characters, their relationships and shifts in relationships that form the plot are decided by their inner activities. Therefore, exterior and interior structures should be unified. We have always opposed creating situations arbitrarily without considering the psychologies and relationships of characters. At the same time, we are against depicting the subconscious discretely, without revealing relationships and promoting development of a situation. Thus the issue of whether exterior or interior structures should be selected or combined doesn't matter. Of course, there are things to learn from the structure of stream of consciousness. *Xiao Huar* has made a fine experiment with it. But such methods should not be mechanically accepted.

First, as discussed earlier, it is not good to present every subconscious activity of a character; second, in narrative literature this must be done indirectly through behavior, for one cannot directly depict the subconscious, and the only alternative is voice-over narration, which is not a good way either. Finally, works of the stream of consciousness often come out of the subconscious, out of dreams and abnormal psychology and are presented through many disconnected and illogical images. We know that memory and imagination are not restricted by time, space, and order. One may recall what happened three years ago and then what happened twenty years ago. However, since memories are events that actually took place in one's life, they more or less must be logical. Fantasies, also based on life, must also follow its logic. But when it comes to the subconscious and dreams, the logic of life is of no concern at all. Therefore, on one hand, we admit that the free interaction of time and space opens a new road for film structure. Although it gains from films using the stream of consciousness and contradicts the dramatic structures with which we are familiar, it can be accepted once people become accustomed to it. On the other hand, we should not be led astray by the mysterious methods of the stream of consciousness and imitate representations that need additional notes to understand. We should learn to make good use of the free movement of time and space in film, but should not be obsessed by it. The truth is, in Western literature, the stream of consciousness is already out of date and was never very popular in film. Like many other schools, it left its impact and eventually disappeared.

We don't oppose learning from foreign experiences, but we should not ignore our own traditions. We should inherit them and, at the same time, continue to make our own innovations. It is to create our own new forms and means of representation that we learn from foreign countries. I don't agree that "our film is for the four billion people of the world, not just the one billion of China." I firmly believe that our film can be open to the world only if it is first open to Chinese audiences.

The task of the film director is heavy, but each of us is willing and competent to shoulder it. We should constantly draw from our experiences, including those of the seventeen years before the Cultural Revolution, and use them to direct our filmmaking. At the same time, we should critically assimilate foreign experiences. Let's put our efforts together and strive for even further achievement in our films.

# 4 FILM LITERATURE AND FILM CHARACTERISTICS: A DISCUSSION WITH ZHANG JUNXIANG

Zheng Xuelai

translated by Hou Jianping

In recent years scriptwriting has been in a period of unprecedented progress. Based on such problems as a lack of ideas, the neglect of content, a biased emphasis on form, the poor representation of characters, and overemphasis on expressive techniques in our filmmaking, Zhang Junxiang proposed that scriptwriting be given more attention. There is nothing wrong with this. The problem is that in all the articles he has written over the last three years, he has articulated such ideas as that film should present literary values, that film is literature rendered by cinematic means, and that film is literature. I believe these ideas need to be discussed. Is film an independent art form, or a branch of literature? The application of basic film theories is required to answer this question.

## ON THE VALUES OF LITERATURE

Zhang Junxiang divides literature into four categories: narrative, lyrical, dramatic, and filmic.

As far as I know, the term *film literature* was initially used by Soviet film theoreticians. *Defending Significant Film Literature* written by Friederich M. Ermler, a well-known scriptwriter and theoretician, heavily influenced Chinese film. However, as a term, film literature was rarely used by the Soviets or Ermler himself. Instead, *film script* is the term frequently used in foreign film theoretical circles. In a country like the USSR, which put significant emphasis on the function of the script, only a few theoreticians used the term film literature for purposes of debate, while the term film script appeared in their formal theoretical writings. No such term as film literature appears in their encyclopedia. Thus, to a great extent, film literature used as an artistic concept was the unique creation of a few Chinese. If film literature referred only to the script, there would be no debate. The question is whether or not film as a synthesized art form is literature or "also literature."

The close relationship between film and literature, the important role literary writers played in improving film, and the significance of the script as the basis of ideas and art in film have all been accepted in filmmaking practices internationally. However, to admit that film is closely related to literature and to remind others "not to forget literature" is different from the idea that film is literature or film is literature by means of cinematic techniques. At the same time, the concept of the value of literature also needs further discussion.

Zhang Junxiang states that the value of literature includes three factors: the idea and philosophy or theme of the work, the portrayal of typical images, and the expressive devices of literature.[1] I wonder whether or not "the value of literature" as an accurate concept of art and literature exists or can be defined in this way, for not only literature, but every art contains ideas and themes, and has the task of presenting typical images. Furthermore, not all literature (i.e., aestheticist literature and modernist literature) presents typical images or contains philosophical ideas. All literature and all art contain an ideology and an art form, and face the task of depicting images. But as to whether or not the images presented can be said to be typical requires that each case be analyzed independently. If the term *value* has to be used, what all the arts intend to convey can be called the value of aesthetics, not the value of literature. To put film above all other arts is against the laws of art and is not in accordance with art history.

Generally speaking, literature is also an art form — the art of language. According to the accepted concept of art and literature, the components of art can be divided into five categories: language, modeling, sound, performance, and real objects. Ever since primitive society, they have been reflected in the artworks of various peoples and times. In different historical eras, different categories have dominated. Literature is merely the art of language; that is, it uses words to express aesthetic tastes and feelings toward objective existence. Like the other arts such as dance, sculpture, music, and painting, which use different representative devices, it also contains aesthetic value.

Among all the arts, film is the youngest and most recently developed. Film is most closely related to drama in terms of behavior, and most closely related to painting in terms of the visual arts. However, even in its infancy, film began to rebel against being dramatized, and the traditions of painting did not take root in the medium either, for its effects can only be observed from the surface of composition. Anyway, in terms of their influence on film, neither drama nor painting can be compared to literature. The mature and special poetry of film is closer to that of language, especially in contemporary films, whose poetry is very close to that of lyrics. On this point, "means of literature" has many points in common with cinematic devices. But film is not a duplication of literature, nor is it a deviation or branch of literature. Film has its own law of art.

As early as the 1920s, debates on what film actually was were initiated. One opinion argued that film was literature, another said it was drama, and yet another claimed it was painting. Consequently, when people discussed the features of film, they addressed them from three viewpoints: the features of literature, those of drama, and those of painting. Such debates lasted into the 1930s and 1940s. Though film in various ways has many similarities with drama, painting, and literature, it is, after all, not drama, painting, or literature. After the 1950s, with the development of cinematic techniques, the synthetic quality of film was recognized through filmmaking practices, and people seldom have argued over this issue since.

Zhang Junxiang, on the one hand, admits that film is a synthetic art form; on the other, he argues that "film is also literature," "film is literature," or film is "literature by means of cinematic techniques," and its a priori task is to present the "value of literature." Such arguments inevitably evoke a confusion of basic theoretical concepts. Sometimes, he even opposes "special cinematic techniques" with "the value of literature," saying the former is "nothing profound and not difficult to command."[2] On this point, the idea that film is literature reaches its extreme — film is turned into literature that no longer needs to follow the aesthetic features of the medium.

I don't believe we should talk about the quality of film without addressing its aesthetic features and its special representative devices. Even Zhang's concept of "literary value" brings us to the sphere of the content of all art. It cannot be used to distinguish between the aesthetic and poetic features of different arts. The special feature of film does not lie in the composition of shots, but in the movement between shots; that is to say, it lies in montage. All the other arts, such as literature, drama, painting, music, and architecture, which preceded the existence of film, lack the narrative and representative devices of film. The synthesis of film does not mean to combine mechanically all the elements of the arts together; it is presented through the aesthetic features of film itself. This is the essence of film as a comprehensive art and the reason why film is different from literature.

Although literature played a very important role in the development of film art and film is very similar to literature, yet film after all is not literature. Film is not an "art of language," or we can say film is not primarily an art of language. Film combines the art of time and space and makes use of all other art forms according to its own characteristics. Film is an independent art with its own specific aesthetic features and it holds an equal position with literature, drama, the fine arts, music, and dance. To regard film as literature may seem to heighten the position of film, but actually it denies the existence of film as an independent art.

## ON THE QUALITY OF LITERATURE
## AND THE QUALITY OF FILM

There is an ongoing debate within film circles over the literary quality of film. To me, the concept of the literary quality of film and the literary quality of scripts is different. Someone has divided the literary quality of film into five parts: typical characters, profound ideology, reasonable plots, characterized dialogue, and complete structures. I think this is nothing more than the continuation of the literary value mentioned earlier. In some essays, we can observe that the concepts of literary quality, content, ideology, and philosophy are used interchangeably, probably because people accept the idea that literary quality refers to the same thing as literary value.

The filmscript is a kind of literature (or "the fourth category of literature"), but film is not literature. A script may provide the future film with an ideological and artistic basis, but this does not mean that since a film will present the literary value of a script that film, therefore, should be subservient to literature. I believe that this issue provides the initial theoretical basis for a discussion of the literary qualities and ideology of the film script. Two related questions here need to be properly addressed:

Is the filmscript only a kind of literature, or is it both a literary work and a cinematic work?

Conceptually, what is the difference between "ideological and artistic basis" and "literary value"?

Such matters as whether or not the filmscript is the fourth kind of literature and whether or not film can be an independent genre of literature have been major issues of debate in foreign countries, especially in the USSR, since the 1930s. Among scriptwriters and theoreticians, those who argue that the filmscript is an independent genre of literature, or has equal rights with any other literary forms, believe that the filmscript deserves to be labeled a fourth kind of literature. However, they still adhere to the basic idea that the filmscript, at the same time, is a work of film, or is primarily a work of film.

The reason for this is obvious. Why are filmscripts written? To produce films, of course. Without the production of a film, it is pointless to write a filmscript. Writers might just as well express their ideas through novels, poems, prose, or feature articles. The reason for us to admit that the filmscript is an independent literary genre or the fourth category of literature is that the filmscript is different from narrative literature, lyrics, and drama with regard to its poetic principles and writing devices. However, the filmscript, unlike the poem, novel, or prose piece, is not after all a complete work by itself. A script requires the collective efforts of directors, actors, cinematographers, art designers, and musicians in order to be depicted by cinematic and artistic devices, and it is eventually completed at the editing bench. The case is quite similar to drama. As Alexander Ostrovsky pointed out, "A work of drama can only obtain its formal existence on the stage." By the same token, the ultimate completion of a film is done on the screen. Can we not say that unless it has been written to be made into a film and meets the basic requirements of the medium, a filmscript has no aesthetic value, or that even if filmscripts form an independent literary genre, they have no aesthetic values until they are turned into films?

The filmscript is both a work of literature and a work of film, but it should be primarily a work of film. Only when it is based on the artistic principles of film is a script capable of providing us with the appreciation of the beautiful. Why do foreign scripts (mostly scripts with scene descriptions) have a large number of readers, especially young people, in China? The main reason is that Chinese audiences do not have opportunities to watch these films, and reading the scripts helps. At the same time, many amateur scriptwriters also try to learn something from these scripts so as to make up for their lack of watching foreign films. Otherwise, foreign scripts would not have so many readers. The public would rather read real literary works such as novels. In foreign countries, scripts as reading material have few readers.

Although the filmscript has become a kind of reading material, its existence is still for the purpose of film production. There is no historical position, either in film or in literature, for those scripts that are not made into films. On one hand, scripts form a branch of literature; on the other, they provide the ideological basis for film art. It is this duality that evokes the long-standing and intense debates around film and script, with one argument claiming that the script is the basis of film, and the other insisting the script is an unfinished work. The truth is, "the basis of film" and "an unfinished work of film" are not substantially different. Basis means foundation. The script is the foundation for the film, which is the building. Only if it has both parts is a cinematic artwork complete and a building fully established. At the same time, the unfinished work already predicts the completion of the whole. A script, by itself, is already complete. Only with regard to the completed film for which it is the base can it be considered unfinished and in need of further work. This duality actually reflects the special discipline of film art and the dialectical relationship between script and film.

Why do we consider the two concepts — filmscript as the ideological basis for the future film and film as the portrayal of literary value and literary quality — to be different? Since the script is the ideological and artistic basis for film production, it first of all should echo the principles of film art and the aesthetic features of film as a synthetic art. Because filmscripts are also a kind of literature, during the writing process as well as after the film is completed, they should possess the features of literature. The literary quality and cinematic quality of a script supplement each other. They should not be unbalanced. If only cinematic quality is emphasized, the script will probably be nothing more than written scene directions, whereas if the literary quality is overly stressed, very likely the narration and description will be written in a prose style that will not provide a solid basis for the forthcoming film. The lack of balance between the two aspects will result in a script that will not have true aesthetic value. This is perhaps the secret of most successful foreign film scripts.

The literary quality of a filmscript should also differ from that of narrative, lyric, and dramatic literature. It should follow the principles of cinematic montage. When the well-known director I. E. Heifitz said, "Montage is the art of screenwriters," he was not trying to be modest. To mention montage does not mean to ignore the portrayal of characters, the development of plot, and the completeness of structure for the sake of "pure film." Sophisticated films should certainly pay much attention to images, plots, and structures, but these are different from those of literature. Currently, Western modernist film directors enthusiastically propose plotless, unstructured, and anti-imagistic works. However, we should not refrain from the application of montage for fear of falling into their pattern, believing that the use of montage will inevitably lead to the denial of the literary value of film. As a matter of fact, these modernist film directors are the ones who most vigorously oppose the principle that montage thinking is dialectical thinking.

The reason for maintaining the distinctions between the literary quality of the filmscript and the literary quality of film is that filmscripts as a genre of literature must possess literary quality, while film can emphasize the qualities of any of the following: literature, drama, music, or painting, either stressing a particular one or combining them all together. For the most part, this is decided by the genre and style of the film. Thrillers, for instance, have no need to strive for literary quality; comedies must pay special attention to dramaturgy and comic effects; musicals must make the best use of music; and kung fu films such as *Shaolin Temple* and *Pride's Deadly Fury* need to present true kung fu for their audience.

With the development of the representative potentials of film, our understanding of cinematic quality goes far beyond the limitations of the original concept. Many of our filmmakers still constrain themselves within the concept of the drama film of the 1930s and 1940s, believing that the poetic film and prose film are heretical and even reproach them as modernist. They do not know that Sergei Eisenstein and Alexander Dovzhenko have long been representatives of the poetic film, while Eugeny Gerasimov and I. E. Heifitz are well known for their sophisticated use of the style of the prose film. Obviously we cannot put these film artists into the modernist school. In truth, the prose film has become a quite popular style in contemporary filmmaking. Because it is closer to narrative literature — the poetic characteristics of prose — it brings film and literature closer. From this point of view, we may say that the literary quality in contemporary film has greater emphasis. Of course, this is not the only style that is acceptable.

In terms of the effective integration of the literary quality of script with that of film, I still believe that Dovzhenko's *Song of the Sea* is the best work. The reason I think so is not because the script won the first Lenin Award or because I translated it into Chinese and have a special preference for it. When the style of *Song of the Sea* is addressed, it is referred to as a prose film, an epic film, or a poetic film, but Dovzhenko himself called it a "long, dramatic film poem." He meant that the script contains not only elements of prose, poetry (lyric), and epic (narrative), but also elements of drama. It is highly synthesized film art and, without doubt, also has literary power. His premature death made it impossible for him to turn the script into a film himself. To me, the film falls far behind the script in terms of quality. This means that a wonderful script, no matter on what scale its literary quality or literary value, cannot be turned into a wonderful film without a talented director. The script is the basis and the director is the key. This certainly reflects the law of film production. I am not saying that if a filmscript provides literary values it alone is capable of functioning as an ideological basis, and that accordingly the sole task of the director is to realize these values by means of cinematic techniques. In other words, it is wrong to think that screenwriters are solely responsible for literary quality while directors alone are in charge of cinematic quality, and to believe that this is the solution to the relationship between the literary quality of a script and its cinematic quality.

One mark of the development of our film in recent years is the various directions of development in film style, genre, and structure, and the broadening of our understanding of film. The appearance of films such as *Sha'ou, Narrow Lane, Country Couple, Love-forsaken Corner,* and *The Herdsman* let us see the promising future of our film. I do not agree with those who think our films to date have not reached the high level of films such as *Waterloo Bridge* and *My Land, My People*. These films are not the most representative of American film, not like Chaplin's films, Griffith's *Intolerance,* or Welles' *Citizen Kane,* which represented the peak of film development in a certain historical era. We would lag far behind the rest of world cinema if we thought the Hollywood dramatic film should be our only model and the drama film of the 1930s and 1940s should represent our only style. The practices of our filmmaking, which have made such progress, are not in accordance with this opinion either.

The fact that I question the values of literature does not mean I do not think the achievement of screenwriters important, nor does it mean that I suggest writers do not need to have more experiences in life, to explore themes and to portray characters. All these are the primary problems writers need to resolve. Actually, for screenwriters, not only is achievement in literature and the accumulation of life experiences necessary, but knowledge of all kinds of arts and theories is also very important. The development of taste and the ability to appreciate art are decided by various elements, among which the correct philosophy of cinematic aesthetics is utterly important.

The theory of scriptwriting as one part of film aesthetics is a subject that urgently needs to be studied. We have to admit that, thus far, this is a weakness in our theoretical work. Many basic problems need to be discussed and clarified. It is with this in mind that I write this so as to ask for advice from Zhang Junxiang and others.

## NOTES

1. Zhang Junxiang. "Literature by Means of Cinematic Techniques," *Film Culture*, February 1980.
2. Ibid., p. 4.

# 5    DIVERSIFICATION, NOT PRESCRIPTIONS

Yu Min

translated by Fan Yuan

For the past two months, two newspapers [*Chinese Youth Journal* and *Wenhui Daily*] have been debating Chinese movies. Movies never fail to attract your attention once various comments are voiced about them. There has been, however, more criticism than praise in recent days, since people are trying to set a high standard for this particular form of entertainment. The primary source of the criticism, after all, is the existence of a large number of mediocrities. In recent years, a number of people have proposed prescriptions for curing the ailments from which Chinese movies suffer. Their efforts, indeed, should be appreciated. However, these prescriptions, from my point of view, are almost exclusively concerned with the alleviation of the symptoms rather than a fundamental solution. I believe that a fundamental solution lies not in prescriptions but in diversification of the ways of artistic creation.

First of all, I'd like to say a few words about the three most commonly known proposals. The first calls for a divorce between film and drama or for "throwing away the walking stick of drama." The proposal is not groundless, and is well targeted. I agree that many Chinese movies are not true movies, but what people call canned drama. As far as their structures and montages are concerned, they are all stereotyped, with the beginning offering either some kind of insinuation or knot before a major conflict unfolds. The ending usually features a climax in which the knot is untied before the whole drama comes to a close. In addition to their stereotypical structures, endless lengthy dialogues or monologues in these screened dramas also suffocate their distinctively filmic features.

Then what are true movies? They are made through visual images. Strictly speaking, all filmmakers are supposed to use their cinematic eyes rather than literary or dramatic eyes to seek out and then process source materials. That is, from the very beginning, every element in the whole process should already be that of a movie before it develops into integrated cinematic images. Besides visibility, mobility, and continuity, the characteristics of a movie also include synthesis, which appears in and is embraced by the other aforementioned cinematic features. Every image in motion is synthetic, as are all images in continuity, in which a variety of artistic elements, including acting, design, music, and photography, are combined to embody the general ideas of the film.

The various artistic forms that are synthesized in a film sometimes represent themselves, and sometimes do not. When we say they do, we mean they all play a role in accordance with their inherent characteristics. When we say they do not, we mean they are somewhat connected to the film but at the same time are transformed in ways required by the film. These various artistic forms are independent because they have their own characteristics, but their independence is conditioned by their connection with the film that combines them. Of course, when they are synthesized into a film, what is needed are their best parts, or those that best demonstrate their unique features.

A good movie can be compared to a meandering creek or a surging river. Though they may follow a winding course, they flow on ceaselessly forever. Or it can be compared to a good poem with fine rhythms that are both narrative and lyrical. What I hate most in a movie is endlessly long, clichéd dialogues. A distinctive language constitutes the best part of a drama, so dramas are not to blame when the best parts fail to be synthesized into a film and instead the audience is bombarded with drab, undistinguished speech that bores them to death.

Actually, theatrical movies are not necessarily bad. Since films have been recognized as art, there have been many excellent theatrical movies. Such was the case in countries like the Soviet Union, France, Italy, and the United States between the 1930s and 1950s. Even in the 1970s and 1980s, some good theatrical movies have been made. However, many poor theatrical movies exist, which is especially true in China. It is on this basis that some have proposed a divorce between movies and drama. This proposal seems reasonable as far as poor theatrical movies are concerned. When it comes to good theatrical movies, however, it can hardly be justified.

I love true movies, but this does not necessarily mean that all true movies are good. You can call *8 1/2* and *Last Year at Marianbad* true movies, and I agree they are representative as some people say. The former represents chaos and the latter, emptiness.

Just as there are both good and bad theatrical movies, there are the so-called true movies. The call for more good true movies is justifiable, and meets the demand of true cinema, which uses the process of synthesization to absorb the strong points from various artistic forms, including drama. However, the proposal for a divorce between drama and movies, though not totally groundless, can hardly produce a fundamental cure for what plagues the cinema. If logic were to be followed, we should also call for a divorce, say, from music, the fine arts, and photography, because these things can become scourges, too, if not properly applied.

The second prescription concerns improvement of the movie's literary quality. What is literary quality? It refers, some say, to the profundity of the ideological content, the depth of the characterization, and the perfection of language. True, a lot of our movies are poor because of their shallow ideological content, stereotyped characterization, and dull, redundant language. But why literary quality instead of cinematic quality? Does literary quality constitute a standard? If literary quality really refers to what was just described, then don't good dramas also call for things like profound ideological content, vivid characterization, and perfection of language? Should we not urge that literary quality be raised to improve poor dramas? And what about poetry? The idea of literary quality is highly ambiguous and hard to define.

Some people claim that a movie is the realization of literature through cinematic means. This is equally difficult to understand. Movies, after all, are movies, and they are an artistic form with distinctive features, independent of all other artistic forms. A movie is based on a screenplay, which is different from other literary works. A good movie requires a good screenplay. To advance the artistic level of a movie, the screenplay must have a dual nature. It should be independent literature that can be printed to be read and its aesthetic values should be as high as that of any other form of literature. On the other hand, however, it must be dependent literature, designed to meet the demands of a movie. A good screenplay should combine vivid language with profound ideological content and should be able to "project" a movie on paper. What I want to stress here is that there is a difference as well as a linkage between movies and literature. As far as their difference is concerned, literary quality is not equivalent to cinematic quality. Consequently, it simply would not work to improve a movie by raising its literary quality. In terms of their linkage, however, one might correctly try to increase the literary quality of the screenplay, even though the term "literary quality" still does not sound very clear.

The third prescription deals with the renewal or modernization of cinematic language. Since the first day movies came into being, the means of expression have undergone periodic changes, some of which were due to the emergence of new techniques. However, artistic means and technical means are two different things. Modernized technical means inevitably lead to advanced productivity, but artistic means, modernized or not, can be of great value, so long as they are properly used. New things usually evolve from the old, and sometimes things that look new are actually quite old. To depict new lives, new people, we should be expected to use new means and techniques, but at the same time, we should also speak rationally about the modernization of artistic means. On the other hand, it is also difficult to judge the advantages or disadvantages of the means of depiction without making clear the nature of the things to be depicted.

All artistic means, ancient or modern, have their strengths and weaknesses. What we should do is to discard the dross and select the essence. Of course, it is up to the artist to decide what to select and what to discard, but this does not mean that universal standards do not exist. Many artistic means, such as high-speed cinematography, flashbacks, and color–black and white alternations, unheard of in the 1950s, are now widely used. However, the excessive indiscriminate use of these new means by some of our directors causes their products not only to be much sneered at by the Chinese audience, but also makes them the laughingstocks of their foreign counterparts. A good many Western movies were successful not because of their breakthroughs in artistic means. In *Kramer vs. Kramer,* for example, there is actually nothing new in terms of cinematic means and in some scenes, like the courtroom debate, the depiction is almost the same as that of a drama. We can find similar examples in Chinese movies. *Happiness at the Door* did not involve great effort in this regard either, but it moved millions of people. *Call of the Sea,* on the other hand, played all kinds of new tricks, but ended up laying itself open to ridicule.

In summary, none of the three prescriptions discussed can really provide a fundamental cure for the illnesses of Chinese movies, though they can help improve them in one way or another. Therefore one might ask: "Is there really a fundamental cure?" My answer is: "Yes!" It lies in diversification of the ways of filmmaking.

In the early 1960s I advocated pluralism in literary and artistic creation, but was attacked by leftist elements for my position. My advocation was not groundless. The entire history of literary and artistic creation can prove me correct. Unless you can show me that Lu Xun, Cao Xueqin, Tolstoy, Guan Hanqing, Shakespeare, Du Fu, and Shelley all wrote the same way, you cannot make me reverse my position. These literary giants not only differed in their approaches to writing, but belonged to different schools in the first place. It is precisely these different schools that created a variety of genres and styles. Let's diversify the ways our artists go to the grassroots and touch the day-to-day lives of the people. Like the energy resources buried deep in the earth, profound characteristics and spirit are harbored in the grassroots. Whatever comes from these places can bring a new spirit, inspire new ideas, and bring fresh lives to the audience.

The most important and valuable thing in literary and artistic creation, I think, is to get first-hand material about life. Whoever wants to do something in this field should try to experience, to see and feel real life for himself. This is, in fact, a foundation-building process, which one will find extremely rewarding throughout life. By foundation, I mean two things. One is that any artistic tower built on such a foundation will stand firm and not easily collapse. The other is that because one's own experience is limited, one must understand, assimilate, and utilize the experiences of thousands of others in order to do good creative work. To achieve this end, one cannot do without such a foundation.

Now let's look at the common illnesses of Chinese movies today that result from their lack of such a foundation. First of all, I think, comes shallowness, the result of artists remaining on the surfaces of life instead of going deep to its bone. Then comes plausibility. What is more incredible than to arbitrarily let a young man from the mainland meet a Taiwanese girl on a deserted island after they have drifted separately on the sea for a long time? Who would believe it if you had a foreign seaman search every corner of the globe for his lost Chinese friend, or if you based the entire conflict of a movie on the shadow of a ghost? The third illness concerns making a movie at the expense of real life. One such movie tells of a model worker who suffers estrangement and isolation from her fellow workers. Hissed by a group of male workers when she comes to ask for help, she is told, the story goes, that she can get it only if she can defeat one of them at arm-wrestling. Who can imagine that in a well-run business she can be free to ask anyone she wants for help, particularly when she has few friends in the whole place? In another case, a young man is asked to climb a burning building to single-handedly extinguish the apparently uncontrollable flames, before he collapses, finishing the heroic deeds imposed on him. I am not convinced we really have fools like him in real life.

One might well ask: can these illnesses possibly be cured by the prescriptions already discussed? In fact, the use of any artistic means and the making of any smart artistic work can do very little to save a piece of artistic work from an acute deficit of real lives and thoughtful ideas.

The most difficult task facing us today is how to portray contemporary lives and people. We say it is difficult, partly because our own lives are in constant flux, making it hard to see clearly their movement and capture valuable materials without considerable social experience and a profound political conscientiousness. Our screen can become the mirror of our times only when all our filmmakers rid themselves of the airs of highbrow artists and take a step closer to ordinary people, and when they speak more frequently not only of the "secrets" of foreign movies, but also of the changing lives in Chinese society, the people involved, the conflicts they are facing, and ways to embody and depict their ideas.

Let's diversify our ways to raise more talented people. While working to cultivate young artists, we should continue to offer more opportunities to those already established. To produce first-class movies, we first need first-class filmmakers. The biggest obstacle to successful creative activities is usually the lack of experience and understanding of life, particularly contemporary life, on the part of artists. Without ample life experiences, not even the wings of the imagination can take one up into the sky.

Making a movie requires the mobilization of the means of almost all artistic sectors, a tremendous task considering a movie usually lasts no more than a hundred minutes. How many subjects should a cinematic artist command in order to make a good movie? My answer: the more the better. One should try to master and absorb all subjects in the field of art including literature, drama, and music, with a clear aesthetic orientation guided by Marxist-Leninist philosophy. It should be clear that one could make movies without having to meet these requirements, but to do so would be a standard of craftsmen, not of Chinese artists. Filmmakers must play a role that corresponds to the tremendous impact movies can sometimes create. The artists of our times, in other words, should strive to become the best of their contemporaries.

Let's diversify our ways to explore new areas and new themes. Many taboos and restrictions have been cleared over the past four years, bringing a variety of new products to the audience. This is healthy. A close look at current developments shows that there is an increase in movies focusing on contemporary lives. Many social ills, conservative ideas, and antireform forces have been attacked on the screen, while those devoted to reforms, scientific research, and services, to name only a few, have been commended. Literature and art must offer different images and characters of different times with deep impressions to show the true spirit of the present and differentiate it from other historical periods.

Despite the growth in variety, however, we film critics have not failed to find many movies that still suffer from serious stereotyping and, in some cases, with entire plots simply derived from wornout situations like triangular or even quadrilateral love affairs. We should admit that our film industry lags far behind in presenting abundant and rich lives and hardly meets the demands of the audience.

When we call for diversification in the making of movies, we should focus our attention not only on these tangible items, but also on the characteristics, styles, and integrity of the people we present. It is precisely these people and things that help nurture the minds of the audience, and give them true aesthetic feelings and indelible impressions.

The diversification of filmmaking is a task that rests wholly with the artists themselves. Without painstaking efforts, without taking some risks, no new trails can be blazed in the field of art. However, we must work to ensure that a favorable environment is created to give full play to artists, who in turn will then contribute the best they can for the cultivation of the masses.

# III The Debate over the New Concept of Film

In Chinese film circles, people refer to 1982 as the "Year of the Concept," for in this year, in film circles, both in film research and filmmaking, everyone was talking about the concept of film, a phenomenon brought on by a heated discussion of André Bazin. Early in its infancy, Chinese film adopted the Hollywood model, and after Liberation, it was heavily influenced by Soviet revolutionary film and Sergei Eisenstein's montage theory; thus the concept of film in China is a combination of dramatic conflict and montage. Furthermore, for years in Chinese film circles, as in any other field, the rapid changes and development of Western culture and art had been denied and criticized. The Cultural Revolution (1966–1976) and the closing of the country distanced its level of filmmaking, cinematic techniques, film theory, and aesthetics from the rest of the world.

When the door was reopened, the introduction of Bazin's realism and Seigfried Kracauer's "redemption of physical reality" brought great excitement and a new vision to Chinese film circles. Both were immediately taken over and used as theoretical weapons with which to attack dramaturgy (considered a source of clichés and artificiality) and to support nontheatricality (considered a symbol of contemporary film).[1] A "heatwave of Bazin" was begun that lasted several years. No matter what we think about this wave today, including our assessment of Bazin and Kracauer, we must recognize that the introduction and adoption of

Bazin's writings were, without doubt, very helpful in breaking through the traditional concept of film in China, and in facing the development of international cinema.

From the very start, the exploration of the new concept of film combined filmmaking and theory. Among the filmmakers, a group of young and middle-aged directors positively and consciously discarded devices that elevated reality and created stories. At the same time they opposed using artificiality to present and arouse emotions, and sought direct, internal, and representative truth. In 1981 Zhang Nuanxin, in the process of directing *Sha'ou,* proposed a "new concept of film," claiming that to reflect our times, one must "present a lively, ordinary person, maintain a truthful environment, and reflect on the beauty of life itself." Further, film "should reveal the personality and emotions of the filmmaker."[2] A number of other directors including Ding Yinnan,[3] Song Cong,[4] Han Xiaolei,[5] and Zheng Dongtian[6] stated similar ideas. Realism constituted the major part of the new concept at the time, and became the major feature of films made between 1981 and 1983. The adoption of Bazin's realism was not mechanical. According to Zheng Dongtian: "Initially it was technical devices such as the long take, natural lighting, location shooting, and realistic acting (*Sha'ou* and *Neighbors*), then it was documentary styles in lens use and nondramatic structures (*Lawyer on Probation, A Corner of the City, Backlit Picture*), and ultimately films appeared that resembled the works of the realist school in its late period, when it turned to psychoanalysis (*Narrow Lane, As You Wish*)."[7]

The subject of realism became a hot topic in theoretical circles. Furthermore, it became the core of the new concept of film in contrast to the traditional. However, while looking back at this period in which everyone seemed to be involved enthusiastically with Bazin's theory and the new concept of film, we rarely find an essay that thoroughly articulated this. As Shao Mujun later pointed out: "The 'new film concept' . . . is nothing but an adaptation of the theories of Bazin and Kracauer."[8] In such a confused situation, Yang Ni's "Film Is Film," one of the most systematic defenses of the "divorce" argument, became a powerful and influential article. She remarks that "I believe it a sign of innovation for film to set its narrative structure free from the constraints of dramaturgy . . . . [The New Era] requires that we discard the familiar yet improper concept of film and draw specific, unique principles out of the development of cinema proper." She proposes that "Film is film. It is not a visual interpretation of drama, nor is it a synthetic art."[9]

Confusion occurred in both film theory and filmmaking, partially because of traditional Chinese conformity in thinking and a limited understanding of the overdue admiration of realism, "desalination," and directors like Ingmar Bergman, Michelangelo Antonioni, and Federico Fellini. A few films reached the extremes of formalism. Wu Yigong's *Sister,* for example, and Guo Baocang's *Misty Border* are products of such influence. Confusion and controversy also appeared in theoretical circles, not only because these films failed badly at the box office, but also because people recognized that realism and desalination could not explain the diversity of world cinema, not even the best films.[10] Despite this, the debate did constitute an important part of film theory in the New Era. Previously, study and debates were concerned with external relationships: dramaturgical and literary values, film as a synthetic art. The discussion of the new concept of film focused on the study of ontology; that is, on what cinema actually is, thereby indicating an awakening of the cinematic consciousness in China.

Xie Fei, concluding that the new concept of film was the result of enlightened thinking, divided it into three aspects — aesthetic, ideological, technological — which he subsequently analyzed.[11] The change in the concept of film in China, he said, started with technical devices, then turned to content and ideology. The lack of content and ideology resulted in a number of films that merely played with formalist techniques, and contained only mediocre content. He argued that the order should be reversed, that ideology should precede content and techniques. From his point of view, filmmakers should first be thinkers and philosophers.[12] Thus Yang Ni, to a large degree, represents the understanding of the new concept within Chinese film circles; Zheng Dongtian quite objectively and thoroughly analyzes the changes and developments wrought by the discussion of the new concept, and Xie Fei calmly and accurately summarizes its characteristics and the limitations.

## NOTES

1. Zhou Chuanji and Li Tuo, "An Important School of Cinematic Aesthetics — About the Theory of the Long Take," *Film Culture,* no. 1, 1980. This was the first article to introduce and systematically assess Bazin's theory. Meanwhile, Bazin's "The Evolution of Cinematic Language" appeared in *World Cinema* and Kracauer's *Film: The Redemption of Physical Reality* and Bazin's *What Is Cinema?* were translated into Chinese (China Film Publishing House, 1985 and 1987, respectively).

2. Zhang Nuanxin, "Exploration of the New Concept of Film," *Exploration of Film Directing,* vol. 2, China Publishing House, 1982.

3. Ding Yinnan, "The Change of Film Concept and the Demand of the Audience," *Exploration of Film Directing,* vol. 2, China Publishing House, 1982.

4. Song Cong, "The Exploration of Contemporary Film Concept," *Film Art Reference,* August 1983.

5. Han Xiaolei, "An Experiment of Truthfully Presenting Contemporary Youth," *Film Culture,* August 1983.

6. Zheng Dongtian, "The Aesthetics of *Neighbors,*" *Film Art,* July 1983.

7. Zheng Dongtian, "Only Seven Years," *Contemporary Cinema,* January 1987.

8. Shao Mujun, "Notes on Film Aesthetics," *Film Art,* November 1984.

9. Yang Ni, "Film Is Film: A Response to Tan Peisheng," *Film Art,* October 1983.

10. Zheng Dongtian, "Only Seven Years."

11. Xie Fei, "My View of the Concept of Film," compiled by Xia Hong according to Xie's speech given at the Conference of Young and Middle-Age Directors, Beijing, China, and is published in *Film Art,* December 1984.

12. Ibid.

# 6

# FILM IS FILM: A RESPONSE TO TAN PEISHENG

Yang Ni

translated by Hou Jianping

If we admit that film is an independent art, we should not draw upon the other arts like drama or literature for its standards. If we admit that film form is constantly being improved, we cannot apply earlier film concepts to interpret contemporary film language. If we recognize that what determines the development of film form is an internal factor — its own artistic characteristics — not such external factors as its "synthetic" features, we should give concern and unbiased attention to all discussions about film both in and out of China. In short, film form is formulated and gradually improved through its inner drive in which technology and artistic characteristics constrain as well as stimulate each other.

Inevitably all arts decline after reaching an ideal stage in which form becomes fixed. The fading out of dramatic film and fading in of nondramatic film over the last forty years is an undeniable fact. However, the quality of a film is not determined solely by its structure and form. At a time when dramatic film was in its prime, outstanding nondramatic films (e.g., *Citizen Kane*) made their appearance, and similarly, good dramatic films (e.g., *Moscow Does Not Believe in Tears*) also emerged after nondramatic film became dominant. Nobody can tell whether or not the nondramatic narrative structure, which has been the mainstream for the last twenty years, will be replaced by another narrative strategy. But one thing is certain: the fact that obsolete representational methods are continually replaced by new ones symbolizes the vitality of film art. Thus

I believe it a sign of innovation for film to set its narrative structure free from the constraints of dramaturgy.

From the perspective of the historical development of the narrative strategies of the feature film, we can see that dramatic structure has never been a unique, inherited, and unchangeable device that has always dominated and that nonnarrative structures such as the interview, novel, and essay are not products of modernism. In contemporary films that take daily life as their theme and realism as their major device, a narrative approach appeared that introduced documentary structure to the feature. Such a strategy may be termed a documentary style, and the films, documentary features. As a trend in contemporary feature films, this documentary narrative strategy was created out of continuous explorations and considerations of the documentary nature of film. It breaks through the model of dramatic structure, enlarges (not constrains) the representative power of cinematic narration, and stimulates (not hinders) the perfection of film art form.

The study of narrative structure in the contemporary international feature takes place at the same time as the appearance of a large number of nondramatic films, including preliminary examples of this type in Chinese film. The New Era demands that we bravely face the realities of art and give an appropriate and scientific interpretation to these new cinematic phenomena. It also requires that we discard the familiar yet improper concept of film and draw specific, unique principles out of the development of cinema proper. Dramaturgy not only did not originate from film itself, but conflicts with the documentary nature of film and to a large extent weakens cinematic aesthetics based on the "redemption of physical reality" (Kracauer). Rather than lead Chinese filmmakers to invent dramatic situations, we should propose to them the recognition of the potentials of cinematic imitation and depiction of reality, and utilize these potentials in shooting, narration, and other representative devices. Film is film. It is not a visual interpretation of drama, nor is it a synthetic work of art.

## MODERNISM OR REALISM?

Mikhail Romm, director of *Lenin in 1918* and *Lenin in October,* is a well-known realistic film artist. *Nine Days of One Year,* another of his films, vividly reflected many social problems in real life in Russia and won him the Best Film Award at the Karlovy Vary International Film Festival in 1962. However, the aesthetic value of film is not limited to social content. If the 1960s can be considered a turning point for Soviet film, then this film can be taken as the point at which Romm consciously tried to get away from the narrative structure of traditional dramatic film. As the director remarked, this film was against "all principles" and "customs" he had been following for thirty years. "Its logic spoils the development of events and weakens association of the situations, . . . many events are set far from the central plot and the narrative line is interrupted many times." Romm later regretted the only narrative aspect of the film — the story of the "radioactive wave" — and said he was constrained by seeking a dramatic theme. The nondramatic narrative structure did not spoil the beauty of the film as a whole. In the same year, *My Name Is Ivan* (Tarkovsky, 1962), another film with a nondramatic structure, about the heroism of Russian children during World War II, won a major award at the Venice Film Festival.

The aforementioned examples are cited as a reminder that the nondramatic device was not used for the first time in China in the 1980s, nor was it the product of Western modernism. We should not generally take the adoption of this device as the blind imitation of Western modernists by Chinese filmmakers.

Actually, the Soviets were not the first to explore this nondramatic narrative structure and produce a few good films out of it. It was the Italian Neorealists who initiated it and left the world a rich and fascinating heritage. "Magazines printed on film" and "investigative strategies" were films like *Rome, Eleven O'Clock, Bicycle Thief, Rome, Open City, Paisa, La Terra Trema,* and *Umberto D.* Addressing this narrative methodology, Alexander Dovzhenko remarked: "Italian Neo-realist films did not use artificial dramatic means. They were exploring their own artistic way of presenting people's lives, a way unique to film." The trend of narrative structure in the international feature film reveals that in the late 1950s the position of the dramatic feature film was falling. In the 1960s, as one American film theoretician pointed out: "The dramatic formula of the 1940s . . . has become a useless cliché . . . in people's minds." Since the 1970s the narrative structures of most films, especially those that use daily life as their theme, are nondramatic.

One opinion puts forth a metaphysical formula that identifies nondramatic narrative structure with the plotless situations in Jean-Luc Godard's films, namely, nondramatic structure = plotlessness = Godard = modernism = antirealism = anti-Marxism/Leninism. Thus all films that use nondramatic narrative structures and their proponents are regarded as representatives of modernism. To me, such reasoning is groundless.

First of all, nondramatic narrative structure is not the same as plotlessness. Almost all nondramatic films, both in and out of China, have plots. The only difference is that diverse principles are used to organize them. Second, modernist films, whether from the perspective of film history or the personal filmmaking practices of modernist filmmakers, are an extreme or rare phenomenon. Godard's films are merely reflections of his personal modernist philosophical ideas, which have no ground to grow in China, nor do they by any means dominate world cinema. Since the time when the dramatic narrative dominated is past, and nondramatic modernist films cannot represent the present, why shouldn't our film critics enlarge their vision and seek arguments to support their point of view against international modernist and nondramatic narrative films? To face the existence of nondramatic narrative structure in realist film and the desire of filmmakers to explore the narrative potentials of film is the premise of our discussion about the relationship between film and dramaturgy.

Another formula put forward by those who oppose nondramatic narrative structure is that nondramatic narrative structure = nondramatic conflicts = nonsocial contradictions = nonrealism. As we all know, the conflicts in drama can never equal the social conflicts of real life. Dramaturgy and nondramaturgy refer to structural devices. Dramaturgy means to organize structure according to the laws of dramatic conflict; nondramaturgy goes against it. Furthermore, dramatic conflicts and the principles of dramatic conflict are not the same. Dramatic features constructed according to the principles of dramatic conflict do not necessarily exclude social conflicts. For instance, many Hollywood films of the 1940s used family contradictions to conceal social contradictions, and many glorified peace. On the contrary, it was Italian Neorealist films constructed not according to the laws of dramatic conflict that exposed to a great extent the poverty and ugliness of postwar capitalist society and reflected the severe and complicated social contradictions among different classes and status.

In the last few years in China, a number of feature films organized with nondramatic narrative structures appeared. Among them, many used realistic cinematic devices and reflected current social problems. Although, with regard to their overall structures or certain events, there still existed traces of dramaturgy, these films represented the efforts of coming cinematic narrative devices. The progress is revealed primarily in their attempt to be free from dramatic constraints in terms of handling such factors as plots and details.

## Nondrama in Plot Relationships

Dramatic plots in which closely related events, cause and effect relationships, and step-by-step developments lead to a climax are replaced by parallel plots. Dramatic plot is determined by the climax that results from dramatic conflicts. In order to make the conflicts intense, the plots of dramatic films must be closely interrelated, and events must be developed through cause-and-effect relationships. But in nondramatic films, there are few or no dramatic climaxes created out of highly intensified contradictions and "complete explosions," thus linkages of plot are not used to create crises and cause and effect relationships.

In *Sunset Street,* if we take the organization of the Coop as the central event, it would be very difficult to relate the emotional ups and downs between the woman doctor and Haibo, and the illness of the teacher to the major line; nor could we discern the cause-and-effect relationship between events like Erzi's selling doves, Shitou and Xiaona's quarreling, and the conspiracy between Wanrenxian and the Hong Kong Guest, with the collective movement of the neighborhood. In *A Corner of the City,* the narrative line — a journalist's interview with the model worker — is often interrupted by minor details such as opening a stall, a vacation, a wedding, childbirth, and dating, details that parallel the central event. The parallel plots present not only the experiences of people of different status and position (the journalist and his brother), but also the different attitudes of young people with the same status and position (the journalist and Xiao Yi), the psychology of the young with different experiences who have been treated differently than others (Ding Xiaoyia and Du Hai), as well as different attitudes toward the young of the same age and social status (Master Chen and Hu toward Ding and Du). It is like the use of the long take to lead the audience to penetrate the foreground of the plot to the depth of the social background. From the vertical and horizontal dimensions of real life, we can recognize the difficulties and confidences of contemporary young people as they progress.

## The Nondrama of the Film Climax

In dramatic films, the climax must be constituted by the dramatic situation and actions. For instance, Othello murdering his wife, Hamlet's duel, the quarrel between Nora and her husband before she leaves, the pursuit of evil in Hollywood films, and the repeated misunderstandings between male and female protagonists that precede the happy ending all lead to a climax. In nondramatic films, the climax is reached through the use of cinematic techniques and the nondramatic performance of actors and actresses. Wang Yian, a director with a clear conscience about narrative devices, deliberately avoided the dramatic climax in his film *Xu Mao and His Daughters*. While still maintaining the original event in which "the fourth daughter attempts to drown herself in the river," he took the following steps to "weaken" the climax: he cut off the artificially created events before the girl jumped into the river; he avoided such dramatic effects as a thunderstorm or loosely flowing hair when the girl jumps into the river; and he transferred emphasis from the act of jumping into the river to that of the "reactions of Xu Mao's other daughters" (*Film Art,* June 1982).

The reason why climax in nondramatic films can be handled by rejecting dramatic elements is that film has its own artistic means to express sudden changes in situations and the meaning of the theme. The expressive power of these devices is no weaker than dramaturgy. Strictly speaking, in film a climax not achieved through dramatic performance and plot should not be called a climax of situation, but rather an emotional climax, a visual climax, or a climax of sound and image. For instance, the theme of *My Memories of Old Beijing* is not revealed by in-depth exposure of the social contradictions of old China, but rather through the maturation of a child after she witnesses a series of ugly social events. The climax is presented through each unfortunate event and the effect it has on the child. Such a climax represented by a psychological change in the character is the emotional climax of the film.

The three emotional climaxes in the film are all rendered through a nondramatic presentation — the silent and staring face of Yingzi — but in each the cinematic language used to reveal the inner workings of the character is different. The first is presented by a close-up of Yingzi's face as she sits on a horse-drawn cart. The cut reveals that the bitter experience of Niuer and her mother has left an unforgettable imprint on Yingzi's mind. The second appears in the music class, when, with the chorus singing, the camera gradually focuses on Yingzi's thoughtful face, revealing that her mood is totally different from her environment, suggesting that the arrest of the "thief" has raised doubts in her about social morality. The hint is revealed in this transitional scene by the parallel of sound (the song) and image (Yingzi observing the arrest). In the final scene at a crossroad, intercutting the lingering eye of Yingzi with the back of the donkey, together with the highly expressive slow-moving camera, creates the emotional climax for the whole film: Yingzi comes out of her fantasy and bids farewell to hometown, relatives, and childhood, as well as to the audience. With a warm feeling toward her native land and friends, she gets on with the difficult journey of life.

At the end of *Country Couple,* three shots of the unpopulated, surrounding mountains, combined with the wheelbarrow and a train, create a cinematic climax of sound and image that hints of the theme: the collapse of the old economic system will naturally bring about a shake-up of time-worn tradition. This climax elevates the story of a peasant woman to a high philosophical level.

## Weakening Situational Dramaturgy with Background Details

In drama, aside from prescribing the personalities of the characters, details function to predict an oncoming crisis (for instance, Desdemona's lost handkerchief in *Othello*; the repeated "darning of his socks" in *Death of a Salesman*). Abundant details are not allowed to exist in drama. As Chekhov pointed out: "If you have a rifle hanging on the wall in the first act, you should fire it in the third." Clearly, the details in drama play the same role as plot in terms of intensifying conflicts.

A large portion of the details about daily life and surroundings represented in feature films constitutes a unique artistic expressive device. For instance, without the detailed depiction of the well, theme song, and folk song, is there any way we would get a strong sense of the period and native color in *My Memories of Old Beijing*? By the same token, in *A Corner of the City,* if details such as Master Hu drinking and listening to music, Du Hai trying to light the stove, and the old man with a bell in his hand announcing the weather along the street were omitted, how would we gain a sense of real life in the Peng Hu neighborhood?

In truth, to emphasize many details of daily life and its surroundings, to use the documentary nature of film, might weaken assumptions of the plot. Since changes of situation and emotions would be buried in large numbers of everyday details, a story would seem more like a documentary record of reality. With regard to structure, this simple and natural style would be one result of the rejection of dramatic plots. This documentary structure would relate, of course, to documentary devices. In *Country Couple,* the director made a serious effort to break with dramatic performance and structure to reveal theme. However, further improvement is possible. For instance, if the heroine was shown doing endless housework, with the camera patiently recording in documentary style her feeding the pig, selling it, and then buying more piglets, and her husband shown working day and night, ferrying people back and forth across the river, combining the background of the village and nearby town — its customs, ordinary life-style, and modes of production, details of rafting and activities at the local market — within the process of the developing situation, the theme of the film would be more distinct and solid and the climax more shocking.

## DRAMA OR FILM?

"Film is performance"; "Film is an art of performing." "While emphasizing cinematic characteristics, we should not forget that film is a synthetic art." These are reasons some have proposed that feature films be structured with dramatic plots. Tan Peisheng articulated this view most thoroughly in "Stage and Dramaturgy" (*Film Art,* July 1983). In his article, Tan proposed that "acting is the basis for dramaturgy, and film art also needs it." To him, acting is "directly visualized in the present tense." This not only "meets the demands of 'dramaturgy,' . . . but also reflects the nature of the redemption of physical reality on the screen." The dramaturgy of "screen representation" embodies in the flashback "how well events in the past combine with the present." An additional argument he makes is that "film needs a dramatic situation. . . . Drama and film have much in common in terms of handling conflicts." Thus he argues that film should combine dramatic performance and plot with the dramaturgy of conflicts into its own narrative structure.

To me, movement, acting, situations, the dramaturgy of conflicts, and the structures of plots are all concepts of drama. Though they reflect character and the laws of dramatic development, they have nothing to do with film art. It must be pointed out that it would be misleading if such a theory were applied to the study of film or filmmaking. I believe that the basis of film is not acting at all, nor is there any relation between acting and cinematic representation. In terms of the internal principles of plot organization, the narrative structures in many contemporary films reject the dramaturgy of conflicts in dramatic situations.

What is the foundation of film? The objective materials that make the existence of film possible — mechanical equipment such as the camera (including film) are the major components — constitute its roots. The technical ability to record actuality is the basis of cinematic representational strategies (including narrative style). The most basic artistic means of film is the use of the camera to present a documentary imitation of reality. In terms of the characteristics of filmmaking devices, we may label this as the redemption of physical reality. To emphasize the redemption — the actual shooting — we usually call this characteristic, documentary. I believe that among the many components of the cinematic medium, the prevailing element that most represents and determines its artistic features is its documentary nature. The narrative structure of film is formulated in the analogous yet contradictory relationship between the process of forming and developing the prevailing element and other artistic elements.

Drama, as we discussed it, is based on the theoretical system of Aristotle and represented by the European classics of Shakespeare and Ibsen. The major expressive means of these dramas is performance (including action and dialogue). Or we can say that performance is the major element of dramatic art. Performance shoulders the double function of imitating behavior and conveying the plot. To Aristotle, an action is one theatrical behavior. Dramatic performance and plot are almost synonymous, thus the plot must contain the dramaturgy of acting (including the conflicts produced from it). Performance is only one of the various elements of film. In terms of narration, the expressive power of performance is not only less than that of cinematography and editing, but performance itself is an expressive object of the narrative elements. Therefore, the narrative structure of film does not necessarily possess the characteristics of performance in drama.

I disagree with Tan over his understanding of the dramaturgy of acting. Tan remarks that "only when acting has both direct external visuality and internal expressive quality does it have theatrical value." I believe that "visuality" and "expressiveness" are external characteristics of dramatic acting. For instance, in *A Doll's House,* Nora converses with her girlfriend in Act I and quarrels with her husband in Act III. The role of Nora has both external visuality and internal expressiveness, but both of the situations cited can not be considered dramatic acting. The conversation only plays a supplementary role and has no dramatic quality, while the quarreling pushes the whole situation of the drama into a climax and is an action full of dramaturgy. Tan thinks that though drama and film have "a variety of ways of dealing with conflicts," they have a common basis in doing so, which is dramaturgy. Thus film should use the dramaturgy of conflicts in its own narrative structure. To me, there are essential differences in the structures of nondramatic feature films and dramatic feature films. These differences are not only reflected in the external form of dealing with conflicts, but, more importantly, revealed in the internal principles of plot organization.

Plot, in drama, consists of conflicts based on acting. The relationship between conflicts and plot is determined by the structural principles of dramatic conflicts. These principles require the plot to intensify conflicts, create crises, and lead directly to climax. Each plot situation should lead to the development of another and they are structured as cause and effect. The situations in dramatic film consist of cinematic visual language (originating with techniques of cinematography and editing in the silent period) and dramatic plots. Speaking of the adaptation of American classic scripts of the 1930s and 1940s, Archer Winsten says that films of that time had to "stimulate and foreground conflicts only hinted at in the original work. The protagonist had to make a choice between two purposes, values or women." Robert Brustein labels such films, in which "all the elements — settings, dialogue, and characters should serve the plot," as "Hollywood-style Aristotle."

Conflicts in nondramatic film are not represented through moral confrontations between characters. They are only suggested in the reflections of the characters toward all events encountered in daily life. The plots are not intensive and nothing takes place suddenly; instead, as in novels, everything develops slowly. Plot situations are not closely related and based on one another. Events are selected, synthesized, and presented with equal emphasis. For instance, in *My Memories of Old Beijing*, the three stories have no cause-and-effect relationship, are not developed on the basis of one another; thus there is no dramatic climax. The film breaks through the constraints of dramaturgy as a whole, but the handling of certain sequences (the encounter with the thief), insignificant events (the madwoman praising her daughter), and some dialogue (between the thief and Yingzi) is also influenced by dramaturgy. By the same token, the fight in the hotel in *Sunset Street* is an artificial and anticinematic climax, and the many coincidences in *A Corner of the City* force the relationships among characters, one to another, and a single accident fundamentally resolves the deep confrontation of ideologies. These are all remnants of dramaturgy in Chinese nondramatic films. However, we should acknowledge that these explorations of narrative structure are valuable. A combination of narrative devices during a period of exploration should be accepted. Even the narrative structures of the nondramatic films of the Neorealists in the 1940s were not perfect.

## THEATRICALITY OR REALITY?

Drama is produced out of the "desire" to "listen to stories" (Bernard Shaw). Since the major factor in the art of drama is performance, it is reasonable to label drama as the art of performance. Because time, space, and the condition of actors on stage are limited, how people behave as well as the revelation of the situation has to be an imitation of reality.

Imitation, then, is the artistic characteristic of drama. In order to create theatrical effects with the staged situation so as to attract the audience, the plot of a drama must be intensive, the scenes condensed, contradictions sharp, and the relationship among situations must be closely linked. So-called theatricality refers to all those expressive devices that are in accordance with the principles of dramatic conflict. In Tan's article, the concept of theatricality (that is, "to directly reveal visual performance in the assumed situation and to maintain and solve the suspense through the process of cause and effect") only includes the external characteristics of the dramatic laws of conflict. Not accurately defined, the confused concept is self-contradictory.

Since the situation constrained by the principles of dramatic conflict overly modifies materials collected from real life (for instance, highly condenses the natural flow of daily events and overly intensifies the contradictions of life), the art of drama is further distanced from reality. The assumption of the plot can be regarded as a sideline product of the principle of conflict. However, the audience, which comes to the theatre to "listen to stories" and readily accepts the art of drama as well as its assumptions, does not demand a truthful representation of life on the stage. As Brecht indicated, drama is an art that "creates illusions." If the desire for "listening to stories" can be satisfied, the audience "would rather ignore the truthfulness of drama."

On the contrary, the invention of film satisfies the demand for a "perfect re-presentation" of "the image of the whole world, with sound, color and a sense of three dimensions" (Bazin). The capability of film to present reality comes from the technology of the camera and the artistic devices of montage. Thus film not only enlarges the representational space of stage, but also extends or shortens the time of drama. Film is free from the limitations of time and space, and is able to break the constraints of the principles of dramatic conflict that were created to enforce the effects on stage within a limited time and space. The fact that film is not limited by stage time and space means that, fundamentally, film does not have the material condition to create dramatic structure.

Since the basis of film is the recording capability of the camera, performance is no longer the major element in film art. Thus if drama can be called the art of performance, can we not label film the art of the moving cinematograph? As regards the photographic nature of the camera, between the recorded image on film and the object there should be a relationship like that of fingerprint to finger; as to the technical capability to record reality, it requires that the reality on the screen be far removed from its origin in real life. Different from drama, which creates a fantasy of fiction, film is an art that creates a fantasy of reality. "Filmed realism cannot be separated from recorded reality" (Bazin). The aesthetics film provides its audience are based on cinematic documentary reality. The closeness of the imitation in film to reality is the basic value the audience demands of film art. This sense of reality is the aesthetic pleasure the audience wants from the screen (stylization, expressionism, and modernism seek a kind of subjective reality). The story in situational film spoils the beauty of film created on the basis of recorded reality. Thus only if the artistic potentials of imitating reality in film are explored and put into full play with regard to cinematography, narrative style, mise-en-scène, acting, and design can the demands of cinematic aesthetics be met. We call this "recorded reality," an artistic expressive device designed to create a sense of the real on screen, a pseudodocumentary device.

Although the pseudodocumentary device has the external characteristics of documentation, it is not equal to the "redemption of physical reality" (Kracauer). The reality presented by this device is not the same as nonperformed reality. The pseudodocumentary device is nothing but a realistic means of representation characterized by concealing technical methods. Though such a device has existed since the appearance of film, only for the last twenty or thirty years has it been used to construct the plots of feature films and developed into a complete and accepted narrative device.

The fact that the debate between imitation and fantasy has existed since classic aesthetics proves that the two basic artistic spheres — the material world and the spiritual world — and the two basic artistic devices — realistic and expressionistic (concrete and abstract; redemption and expression) — are interrelated. However, the material features of film as a medium constrain its artistic characteristics, its representational sphere — the objective world — and its expressive methods; and the simple mechanical equipment and its limited technology in the early days also hindered its documentary quality from developing into a complete artistic form and style. Nonetheless, the practice of filmmaking has never been held still by technological limitations. Creative artists have done their best to utilize cinematic technology; they have also created new cinematic means, languages, and a variety of styles by overcoming technological limitations. Therefore, while examining the formulation of cinematic narrative devices, we should not only observe the devices of popular structure and genre in a particular period, but also observe, in different periods, all other structures and styles and their influences on the narrative strategies of contemporary film. I believe that documentary film, from silence to sound, has had the most direct and obvious influence on the realistic feature film.

Since its beginning, film divided into two schools. One was the street film, represented by recordings of real life activities made by the Lumiere brothers and the Brighton School; the other was the studio film, represented by the magical films of George Melies. The street film took the objective world as its major representational target, and camera movement as its major strategy; the studio film made subjective fantasy its target and the camera was primarily static. Tan believes that film "formulated its own . . . unique style" only after it "broke the fixed space and time of drama with camera movement," and summarizes the "tendency toward dramaturgy" in Chinese film as a result of the motionless camera, which created "fixed space" and "a definite period of time." I don't think the devices of filmmaking symbolize film as an art. Actually, only films made in the studio adopted the position of someone sitting directly in front of the screen. Strictly speaking, these two methods have existed side by side since film's inception. Films made in the early period — no matter which approach they used — cannot be regarded as art films; we can only label them embryos of art. Film had its own artistic form only after D. W. Griffith used close-ups and parallel cutting, and Sergei Eisenstein turned editing into art and theorized about it. In order to maintain the integrity of reality in time and space, contemporary films often use long takes (static, moving, or in combination) deliberately so as not to break real space and finite time. Such devices were confirmed by the theory of long take represented by André Bazin. As we all know, the most commonly used film language of our time is a combination of montage and long take, a result of the recognition and use of the documentary nature of film. How can we consider it the "tendency toward dramaturgy"?

The two cinematic narrative structures — documentary and dramatic — originated and developed from the embryonic street film and studio film. The contemporary documentarylike feature is a combination of these two narrative strategies. From magic film and farce to dramatic feature, we can see that the dramatic feature has a history of only twenty years or so, about one-fifth of the art's history. Thus we should not regard this strategy as genetic, nor should we consider it the golden principle through which all feature films are constructed.

Nondramatic film is developed along the lines of the street film — the documentary, and the documentarylike feature. Its development parallels that of the dramatic feature. Those who argue that performance is the basis of film art and that cinematography determines the art form of film more often than not only look at the development of the dramatic feature and neglect the other. The fact is that both existed in the silent and early sound periods. For instance, in France there were great comic filmmakers like René Clair and artists like Jean Vigo and Joris Ivens who represented the documentary; in America, Charlie Chaplin coexisted with Robert Flaherty, father of the documentary; in Britain in the 1930s and 1940s, Alfred Hitchcock's films enjoyed the same popularity as the realistic films of the London School. Late in the silent period, documentary films appeared, but soon disappeared with the coming of sound because of the poor quality of the cumbersome recording equipment. Late in the 1940s, after World War II, the large number of battlefield newsreels aroused the interest of those making features. In order to "add some reality to the pure feature" (Archer Winsten), they first introduced to it the narrative device of documentary by cutting battlefield footage in as background. Later those who made newsreels joined feature filmmaking and used documentary techniques directly in their work. The modification of the narrative structure of the feature by the documentary was realized. Many well-known directors of nondramatic films, like Roberto Rossellini, Michelangelo Antonioni, Louis de Rochemont, and Humphrey Jannings, established themselves in this way. Thus the emergence of the newsreel after World War II played a crucial role in stimulating the change of narrative structure in the feature film. The narrative structure of the contemporary realistic feature was thus formulated by discarding theatricality and absorbing documentary devices.

One additional influence on the nondramatic film is the structure of the contemporary (Western) novel, which obviously influenced the stream-of-consciousness films of Federico Fellini, Ingmar Bergman, and Alain Resnais. It is beyond the scope of this chapter to explore in depth this breakthrough past the limitations of drama. I will focus on one kind of nondramatic film: the documentarylike feature. Following are its basic characteristics with regard to narrative structure.

First, the documentarylike feature is not a newsreel documentary. It is also fundamentally different, both in concept and in the use of expressive devices, from the French realist film, the American underground, the kino-eye of Dziga Vertov and the self-reflexive films of Godard. It does not make an objective report of real people and events, nor does it use the interview as its major method. It is a kind of artwork that has plot and is created by the efforts of screenwriter, director, actor/actress, cinematographer, art designer, and composer.

Second, the conflicts in documentarylike features are different from conflicts staged by dramatic performance. They integrate themselves within the plot of the film. Different from dramatic conflicts, which, intensified by the confrontation of moral concepts, reach a climax to reveal their theme, the themes of these films are presented indirectly, by the attitude of characters toward society and the depiction of large numbers of daily events. The ideological tendency in these films is less overt. The very structure of the conflicts rejects direct, obvious, and simple presentation.

Third, the plot of the documentarylike feature is nondramatic. It is not developed through dramatic conflicts, but is a synthesized analysis of major events, with things revealed in the background, and depictions in a documentary style. Thus there is no dramatic climax in such films, but rather a cinematic climax. There are no sets of intensified plots; instead, many travails parallel the major events. Sometimes, in order to weaken the assumption of the main plot and hint at the social experience of the events, these films emphasize a large amount of details and interfere or stop development of the main plot. In this sense, plot is closer to the natural process of newsreels and adds a feeling of reality to film. Consequently, the documentarylike feature is more suitable for dealing with realistic themes in daily life.

Fourth, the narrative strategies of documentarylike features come mostly from newsreels, which use a documentary style as their major means of representation. The structure of analysis and synthesis must harmonize with the realistic technique of the cinematography. This requires that screenwriter, director, performers, cinematographer, designer, and so on, all strive together for realism. If just one aspect goes astray and reveals the artificiality of dramaturgy (like too much makeup, unnatural lighting), it could spoil the artistic effects of the entire film. This is a cinematic strategy based on the aesthetics of respecting reality. It is different from one that emphasizes visual composition. Such films conceal their technical devices.

It is not that documentarylike features do not want to reflect the essence of reality, but rather not "to spoil the origins of reality" while presenting it (Kracauer). However, this does not mean to give an objective and naturalistic depiction of real life. Thus to use documentary techniques in filmmaking is easier than using dramatic devices. These films still select and modify elements from life; it is the method used in so doing that makes the difference.

Fifth, although documentarylike features break with the constraints of dramaturgy with regard to principles of structure, they still maintain the framework of beginning (cause), extension (development), complication (ups and downs), and denouement (ending). Thus plot serves only as the external form of structure; it is not controlled by the internal principles of dramaturgy. As to how weak or strong are the conflicts, how loose or intense the plots, the documentarylike film can be considered a condensed novel or weakened drama.

There are sequences and details of dramaturgy in these films, but they do not serve to intensify conflicts, to create crises, or to stimulate plot development. They are fundamentally different from the dramaturgy required by the principles of dramatic conflict. First of all, such dramaturgy only appears in sequences and details in films and does not intensify conflicts or create crises. It is used only to expose the tragicomic elements of the ordinary so as to make life more interesting and lead the audience into deep thought. This is what happens in *A Corner of the City* when the soft voice of Hu singing Beijing Opera is suddenly "smothered," and in *Sunset Street* when the furious father swings a club to beat his son, only to find the boy fast asleep.

Furthermore, dramaturgy, which in theater is based on performance, in film is presented by cinematic techniques. There is, for example, the brief metaphor cut into the plot (Eisenstein's stone lions in *Potemkin*), or the cross-cutting of comparative shots (simultaneous appointments in the Peng Hu neighborhood and in a luxury hotel in *Backlit Picture*). To distinguish the dramaturgy in these films from that of drama, we would label cinematic dramaturgy "pseudodramaturgy." To Tan, dramaturgy is a "common concept both for literature and for film." I do not agree. The fact is that when people speak about the drama of some sequences (or details) in films or novels, they are not using it as an artistic concept, but rather as an adjective. In the same way we also frequently use "dramatic" to describe the realistic painting *Ivan the Terrible and His Son,* or some Western singing style, or the contrasting movements of a symphony. Nobody would relate this term to the principles of dramatic structure — the laws of dramatic conflict — for it no longer connotes dramaturgy.

For the last fifty years, the advanced development of science and technology and the endless explorations of film artists have enriched the styles, forms, and expressive means of film. With innovations in cinematographic techniques, narrative devices, and editing methods came a revolution in cinematic aesthetics. Today, at a time when world cinema has changed tremendously and the study of cinematic aesthetics has entered into an exploration of the ontology of film, we would not make any contribution to the development of film art if we stubbornly held fast to the concept of drama or to the principles of dramatic structure. Due to interference from various elements, Chinese filmmaking, to a great extent, has neglected the recognition and uses of realism. I believe that to raise the quality of our filmmaking, the present task is not a matter of strengthening the dramaturgy of the narrative, but to increase, through effective training, our basic ability to use the cinematic imitation of reality. I believe that the improvement of the abilities and skills of our filmmakers will help us deepen our study of cinematic characteristics and our command of cinematic principles.

# 7 MY VIEW OF THE CONCEPT OF FILM

Xie Fei

translated by Hou Jianping

Over the last few years, we have gone through discussions of film language, the debate on cinematic literature, and now, of film as a concept. This is encouraging progress for our studies on film art and theory. I believe this research and discussion will unquestionably improve the quality of our film scholars and stimulate even better film art.

## THE REVERSED ORDER OF THREE CONCEPTS

Like "film language," "the concept of film" is a term used as a symbol or slogan in film art and theoretical research; it has no unified, scientific, and strict academic definition. When people use the term, they ascribe to it a variety of meanings. The more recent term to emerge, "the contemporary concept of film," frequently under discussion, has an even greater variety of definitions. But since the concept of film has a practical value in filmmaking and in theoretical research, it is worth a more profound and practical study.

Thus far our discussions about the concept of film and its development (the so-called new concept) have all been made from an artistic perspective. To examine the concept of film from this position, I believe, we must include three topics: the idea of art, the content of art, and the technique of art. All are related, inseparable, and conditioned, and have reasonable positions. Among the three, what has been discussed most is technique, while content and the idea of art have been somewhat neglected. This is the reverse of what should be.

In 1979, when I was shooting *The Guide* in Xinjiang, I watched *Xiao Huar*. The juxtaposition of time and space, the use of color and black and white, the use of fast motion, the flashbacks and still frames shocked me and brought me much freshness. Soon after, many filmmakers tried to imitate this new language. It wiped away the long-standing, obsolete, and dull devices of representation and brought about a formalist tendency in which techniques were overused. At the same time, theoretical journals began the discussions of the "modernization of film language," and of "throwing away the walking stick of drama." Even today, when filmmakers talk about applying the new concept in their filmmaking, more often than not they are talking about devices and techniques such as location shooting, natural lighting, and natural acting. It can be said that the acknowledgment and practice of the new concept of film began for our filmmakers from the technical side. Of course, these techniques are a way of presenting concepts, but they are the most exterior form — their existence and development is determined by content and ideas. The once frequently used compressed slow motion, flashback, and separation of sound and image are the result of abused techniques unilaterally taken as the new concept. Actually, without content and ideas, technique is nothing but a tree without roots, water without a source. It did not take long for people to realize this.

The so-called second position, the content of art, refers to theme, character, plot, structure, and their composition. It contains both ideas and forms. Unlike exterior techniques, these are considered intrinsic cinematic forms. Over the last few years, filmmakers have begun to explore this aspect. It is represented by the appearance of films with a variety of characters and a prose structure, and theoretical positions like chink and plank structure, details over plot, and nondramatization. People realized that it was not enough to pursue the representation of reality only through such exterior techniques as lighting, shadow, color, design, properties, acting, and composition. The contemporary concept of film attempts to present characters, behavior, plot, and intrinsic cinematic forms as the pursuit of truth. People began to discard traditional dramatic strategies, which put emphasis on polishing details, and sought to create a new scheme that could present reality as it is. The flashback and the juxtaposition of time and space were more complicated techniques and more difficult to command. Without a solid background and skills in art, they are impossible to master. *A Personal Life* (Raizman, 1983) is a good example. The film is nothing but the details of the daily life of a retired cadre. No significant events, heated dramatic conflicts, and unusual techniques are used. On the contrary, it vividly depicts a variety of characters, touches profound social problems and philosophies, and is obviously a contemporary product. It reveals the artists' solid command of traditional art and their courage in making innovations.

An important essence of contemporary films is the pursuit of truth. However, it is not clear to everyone what truth is. *The Place of Rehabilitation* is a good film. The theme is new and the content is touching, but because the filmmakers could not utilize cinematic truthfulness and artificiality in proper proportion and thus overused technical devices, the sense of truth in the film is spoiled. One spectator stated that the "coincidences weakened the needed reform." Actually, the filmmakers occasionally realized this and tried to pursue truth and reality through the plot and characters, but since their artistic skills were not solid, these ideas were not carried out thoroughly, and the film was unsuccessful. At our conference, *The Gate of Life* (Bergman, 1958), a film made by the well-known Swedish director Ingmar Bergman, was shown. It was interesting to note that in terms of subject and theme, it is very similar to our *Ward 16,* a film made in the 1980s. The entire story of *The Gate of Life* takes place in a women's ward, centering on the lives of three women and their husbands and parents over a few days. One woman, who desperately wants to have a child, loses her baby at birth; the pregnant but unmarried woman is forgiven by her parents; and the disillusioned woman, who wants no child, regains her confidence in life through meeting her roommates. There is no normal plot, or direct conflicts. It is as simple and ordinary as real life, but it provides the audience with vivid characters and provokes them to think about life. Compared to *Ward 16,* it is more natural and intimate. These ideas and devices, which conceal artificial refinement, are worthy of study.

The most important aspect of the concept of film is the idea of art, an aspect we have studied and, to date, have least commanded. I once wrote that a major characteristic of contemporary film was that it had eventually become a means by which artists could express their own ideas, feelings, and styles. After a few decades of development, film gradually improved its techniques and materials — it went from silence to sound, from black and white to color, and absorbed much from painting, drama, and literature — and eventually provided artists a means by which to freely present their opinions toward society and life. This can be proved by the emergence of various schools in the late 1950s, represented by people such as Ingmar Bergman, Akira Kurosawa, Eugeny Gerasimov, and Michelangelo Antonioni. A film artist, whether screenwriter or director, should have an independent and complete idea of philosophy; a unique and deep understanding of society, time, and life; and a personal style and means of filmmaking. Only with these qualities can one be called a real artist and be capable of producing films that represent the times. Because of this, the idea of art is considered the most basic and important aspect, and the content and techniques of art should be constrained and based on it.

In recent years, our approach to an understanding of these concepts of film has been wrong in terms of priorities. We began with techniques, turned to content, and eventually to idea. This is an inverted process. Furthermore, even today the idea of art has not been given enough attention and emphasis. As we all know, mediocre ideas about film, and a lack of knowledge on the part of our filmmakers of philosophy, sociology, aesthetics, and ideology have created tremendous obstacles that hinder further development of our cinema. Since the fall of the Gang of Four, film has lagged behind literature in terms of in-depth thinking. The few outstanding films such as *The Legend of Tianyun Mountain* (1980), *Love-forsaken Corner* (1982), and *At Middle Age* (1982) were all adapted from literature. The significance of these works to a great extent, lies in their exploration of life. In 1983 a few more good films appeared, but films such as *Country Couple* (1983), which revealed the unique and sparkling ideas of its filmmakers about life, were rare.

In short, we must reverse the order of these three perspectives. Our filmmakers and researchers should start from the solid basis of artistic ideas. With this clearly in mind, they would be able to pursue the truthfulness and stylization of prose in their films and explore technical innovation and modernization. Only through such an all-encompassing concept will they be capable of exploring the broad path of film art.

## THE THREE ASPECTS THAT SHOULD NOT BE IGNORED

It is not enough to study film only from the perspective of art. As a social entity, the concept of film should consist of three other parts, that is to say, film as a tool of commerce and communications, and film as an art. It is sad to see that for the last thirty-five years, we have been unable to treat the relationship among the three dialectically and from all points of view. We either forgot one, or ignored another. When our filmmaking was guided by this one-sided and narrow-minded concept, it was only natural that deviation and mistakes resulted.

Film, a product of modern science and technology, relies on business enterprise and commercial exchange more than any other art. Only if we admit this commerciality, study it — and with it film as entertainment, the psychology of the audience, and the film market — can we guarantee the healthy development of the medium. In the past, the leftist tendency always took marketability as commercialization and accused it of being a pursuit of box office values, a capitalist method. Leftists sometimes unilaterally emphasized the propagandistic and educational functions of film, sometimes considered art as superior — art for art's sake. As a matter of fact, these three divisions, which form the concept of film, should not be separated mechanically. They are interrelated and should merge together in any work.

"Film is in crisis" and "box office values have fallen tremendously" are exclamations frequently heard in recent years. It is said that the film business, which has always earned revenues for our country, will probably be unable to support itself this year. The expansion of television is one reason, but the fundamental cause for this fall is that the quality of our films is now so low they no longer efficiently attract an audience. This is the merciless punishment meted out by our society for our lack of a complete concept of film and our neglect, even violation, of economic law.

One of the important tasks we face today is to adjust our attitude toward the marketability of film. Most of our filmmakers think "art is superior" and the pursuit of art most elegant, whereas the making of commercial and entertainment films is seen as vulgar and without value. The same is true of our teaching methods. In our classes, we show our students art films. We do everything to allow our students to view films of different schools and artists. But we seldom touch upon entertainment films like the musicals, westerns, melodramas, and science fiction, which are so popular. No wonder some older artists worry that our students will all be alike, artistically and philosophically unable to meet the diverse demands of the audience. Thus we might say that our filmmakers all face the problem of stepping out of their ivory towers in thinking and in practice. Currently the entire nation is in the swing of reform, trying to do things according to objective principles, especially economic principles. To apply this to film means we must treat film as both an art and a commodity.

First of all, we must change with respect to the guidelines of filmmaking and overall planning. Based on the current audience, I believe that if we produce a hundred films annually, at least 60 percent should be commercial — made according to audience interest and taste, healthy in content, but with entertainment as their priority. *Shaolin Temple, Gunshot in the Secret Bureau, Behind the Screen,* and the TV series "Huo Yuanjia" and "Blood Suspect" are good examples. Of course, such films should have some educational significance and artistic quality, but their existence should lie in their entertainment and box office values. Propaganda and educational films should make up 30 or 40 percent, meeting the needs of the nation's political and economic situation. These films should spread the policies and principles of the party and government, and educate our youths and children. Films such as *Our Niu Baishui* and *Behind the Accused* have a clearcut content for the times and a popular artistic appeal. Children's films need to put more emphasis on the balance between educational and entertainment functions. The remaining percentage should be allocated to the so-called art film. Artists can make bold ideological and artistic explorations and experiments with these films. As long as their content is serious and their artistic devices innovative, they are worth trying without having a large audience. There is no clearcut leader among the three kinds of films. Films that combine the three principles together exist but rarely.

Second, the concept of film held by our filmmakers, theoreticians, and critics should be changed — an all-encompassing concept should be established. There are about 500 directors in our country. A variety of films should be made according to the unique characteristics and personalities of each one. Among these filmmakers, those who are good at making comedies should be encouraged to pursue this direction, while those good at kung fu and horror films should be granted the opportunity to make them. All of the various genres, especially those that are popular, should have directors specialized in them. The truth is, it takes special talents to make genre films. For instance, Shui Hua has been highly successful with serious social drama. If asked to make a comedy, it is highly unlikely he would make a film as good as Xie Tian. [Both are directors at the Beijing Film Studio — Ed.]

We should respect the principles of art and confront the laws of economics, and our filmmakers should respect and learn from one another. To make commercial films does not mean a filmmaker must be vulgar. Commercial films can be made in a highly artistic style that not only enjoys high box office success, but also provides the audience the pleasure of art. If the so-called art film was only made according to an individual's will, film would eventually have no audience at all. If a director makes three films in two years, two should meet the popular tastes and do well at the box office. For every film to be profound in ideas and great in artistic innovations is not only counter to the law of filmmaking, but also of economics. On this point, theoreticians and critics should take much responsibility. In recent years, film criticism and the evaluation of film awards has focused on the few art films made. Though these films had a limited audience and failed at the box office, our film critics unanimously praised them highly, while refusing to pay attention to films popular among the masses that enjoyed commercial success, simply because their artistic tone was unrefined. Foreign films introduced into China were merely different schools of innovation, or works by artists such as Antonioni and Bergman. Hardly anything was said about successful commercial films. Thus it is necessary that change take place in the circles of film theory and criticism with regard to the concept of film.

Third, currently the most crucial issue is to establish a socialist economic system in its real sense in our process of filmmaking and distribution. A prosperous period will certainly arrive if we carry out as thorough a reform in film as was done with the responsibility system in rural areas. If you want to risk losing money by making art films like *Last Year at Marianbad,* you should have to make some commercial films to earn money. Films such as *Shaolin Temple* and *Mysterious Buddha* can no longer be despised. If you want filmmakers to work hard, you must not pay them the same no matter whether their film is a success or failure. Why can't some in film circles become rich? If the filmmakers, technicians, and managers who run the theatres bring in high revenues, why shouldn't they benefit and get rich first? Today, the wave of reform has come to the cities — factories, institutions, and schools have been swept by it. I believe the film industry will also see a thorough reform of its administrative system. The commercial, communications, and artistic functions of film will eventually be fully and vigorously brought into play.

## STARTING FROM SELF-ANALYSIS

While attending a conference of middle-aged and young directors on how to eliminate the mediocrity of our films, I proposed that we develop our film along the lines of authorship based on the condition that we first make a severe self-analysis and self-criticism. We should examine our own filmmaking teams, establish a clear view of our own merits and faults, and, from the height of contemporary art, decide the direction of our development. We should admit we are about twenty years behind in the development of film form and the concept of film. We certainly cannot catch up in a single day. As demonstrated by *Xiao Huar* and

*Troubled Laughter, My Memories of Old Beijing* and *Country Couple,* our filmmakers have already put a great deal of effort into the exploration of the concept of film and have made significant achievements. Under the guidance of the new concept, our film has made a great leap forward in terms of artistic devices and content, although the ideas of art are still weak. The reason for this should be sought from the filmmakers, especially from the qualities of U.S. directors.

Generally speaking, Chinese film directors can be divided into four generations: the elders, who started their careers in the 1930s and 1940s, including directors like Shen Fu and Tang Xiaodan; the second, including Shui Hua, Xie Tieli, Xie Jin, and Wang Yian, who formed the backbone of Chinese film immediately after Liberation; the third, who made themselves known after the Cultural Revolution, so-called middle-aged and young directors, who for the most part graduated from the Beijing Film Institute; and the youngest, recent graduates or those who just became directors, most still in their twenties and thirties. They include Tian Zhuangzhuang, Xie Xiaojing, Zhang Junzhao, Chen Lizhou, and Chen Kaige among others.

Set the directors of my generation, mostly in our forties, as an example, and our merits and weak points are quite obvious. A systematic education of film theory and filmmaking provided us the skills of cinematography and the basis of art theory; however, our lack of human knowledge and life experience limited the breadth and depth of our thinking. I'd like to say a bit more about this. The study and careers of our generation developed together with the growth of the new China. The twisted road of politics, economics, and ideology in the last thirty-five years also left its imprint on us. The Marxist education and Mao Zedong Thought we had for years laid the foundation for our philosophies of life and society, and our view of aesthetics. However, the obsolete structure of education, together with the influence of the ultraleft, congenitally decided our limitations. The closed-door policy and the passive teaching methods of the time restricted our knowledge. Many subjects required of foreign high school and college students such as humanities, sociology, national and folk customs, world culture, the history of philosophy, and aesthetics were not offered to us. In what was offered, the point of view was biased, the content narrow, and no rich and solid comprehensive foundation of knowledge was laid. To be frank, I dared not make a film dealing with historical topics of the old nationalist period, not to mention ancient China, because my knowledge of history, culture, society, and customs was so limited. In other words, I lacked an artistic sensitivity toward it. Besides, for years we were accustomed to being saturated with ideas. Our knowledge and point of view were not gained through personal experience and independent thinking; these were swept away by the mainstream. It is natural that the only thing gained from this was our lack of a unique and fresh point of view, and the lack of personality in our artistic ideas and styles. In this respect, the younger directors are much better off.

The philosophy of life and social ideas of these young people were formulated during the period of the disastrous Cultural Revolution, the subsequent restoration of order, and the reestablishment of the open-door policy. Because of this, compared to us their thinking is more independent, they are more sensitive toward society and art, and their desire for representation is much stronger. Films such as *One and Eight* and *Yellow Earth* reveal their innovative spirit and their will to break through the mediocre. These films reflect the brilliance of their ideas and art from every perspective. Their efforts should be fully accepted and supported. As we know, more severe than the shortage of entertainment films mentioned earlier is the shortage of unique artistic personalities and deep thought. The younger directors have their weaknesses and mistakes, for which, instead of vigorously opposing them and using authority to force them to change, we should adopt a policy of academic discussion, debate, and guidance. To create a free environment in which artistic ideas and personalities are respected and artists can freely develop their own skills is the condition in which the emergence of talents and the prosperity of film can be ensured.

It is necessary that we critically assimilate and discard our past and present experiences and make an effort to catch up to the level of the authors of our country and the advanced level of the artists of the world with regard to the quality of art and breadth of ideas. To achieve this, first of all, we must learn to ceaselessly absorb new knowledge and information; second, we must become deeply involved with life, enlarge our vision and learn to think about society and life from our own point of view. A good piece of art requires not only deep ideological themes and genuine knowledge, but also a sense of honesty in which the opinions and emotions of the artist are sincerely presented. The study of the concept of film and the future development of film art should not be limited to purely academic and artistic spheres; on the contrary, they should be closely related to the times, to society, and to ourselves. Only by pursuing this line can we have an entirely new concept of film and become capable of making films worthy of our times and our people.

# 8 ONLY SEVEN YEARS: THOUGHTS ON THE EXPLORATIONS OF MIDDLE-AGED AND YOUNG DIRECTORS (1979 to 1986)

Zheng Dongtian
translated by Hou Jianping

The "middle-aged and young" directors refers to those of whom the eldest are almost fifty. Several years ago, when they made their first films, they were about forty. These directors (the younger ones are much more fortunate) are years late in making their achievement, and their films do not have international significance. However, in the rapid development of Chinese film, which has attracted much attention, these directors constitute the most active group and their explorations of filmmaking and film theory to a great extent have determined the new direction of Chinese film. The emergence of this cultural event is a natural result of history and the times; but it is a subject that needs to be carefully studied and discussed.

Recalling the road we have covered in the last few years, as one of these filmmakers, I find myself filled with deep emotion, yet without a distinctly clear opinion. Since we ought to pursue our way, I would like to express my own ideas, based on the love and understanding I have for my colleagues.

## THE EMANCIPATION OF FILM AND THE PEOPLE

It would have been impossible for people to predict what is happening today when they first woke up from the nightmare of the national disaster. The confinement of those ten years, together with the traditional culture of thousands of years in which the unique consensus suppressed humanity and individuality, restrained the prosperity of art represented through individualized feelings and intelligence. At the same time, it resulted in a situation in which the replacement of the old by the young meant nothing more than a natural continuity of generations — hardly any changes or breakthroughs have been made.

Considering that the modes of social life and environment determine the psychological motives for creativity, we can say that these middle-aged and young directors are the most fortunate in Chinese history. Although delayed for years from making their achievements in filmmaking, they at least were able to enter an era in which they had the opportunity to use their talents and skills. These directors, born in the old society [before 1949], spent their childhood during an era in which the new China developed and went through the chaotic years of the country in their youth. The ups and downs they experienced together with the country provided them with a deep but anxious consciousness; and the education most of them got in film provided them with the cultural capability of expressing their thoughts. The accumulation of their ideas took a decade or longer; thus at the end of 1978, when the wave of history brought forth their first films, their emancipated feelings and ideas were enthusiastically represented in the ideology and art they contained.

"The writing and shooting of *Xiao Huar,* including the exploration of its content and form, contains a certain consciousness of 'revolt.'" Huang Jianzhong [director of *Xiao Huar*] frankly spoke his mind, which was quite representative of his generation. The initial outcry at the premieres of films like *Xiao Huar, Troubled Laughter,* and *Reverberations of Life* were precisely the feedback of this "revolt." Later, when people talked about these films, more often than not they only looked at their new and different narrative forms and cinematic languages. The truth is, the direct changes of representations on the screen came primarily from inner and much more profound motivations: changes in the filmmakers' attitudes and ideas toward life and art.

*Xiao Huar* "is not the record of a glorious battle, nor does it shoulder the task of presenting a specific strategic and tactical idea. . . . Only by bravely touching upon the fate and feelings of people involved in war can we make breakthroughs in this film" (Huang Jianzhong, "Thinking — Exploration — Experiment," *Film Art,* January 1980).

*Troubled Laughter* "is not the story of a saint or ghost; it is about an ordinary person. . . . Human beings have a rich spiritual life. Aside from consciously thinking logically with the help of language, many activities of the subconsciousness such as feelings, imagination and fantasies also exist. . . . Since film is a synthesis of various means of depiction, it has the great potential to represent the spiritual life — to visualize and specify it on the screen" (Yang Yianjin, "Study and Research," *The Explorations of Film Directing,* vol. 1 [Beijing: China Film Publishing House, 1982]).

These ideas, though, which had their own limitations and were not fully represented in their films at the time, were the initial and crucial recognition of conscience in the process of the young directors' spiritual emancipation. Under circumstances in which film was severely restricted as a useful tool and we were quite ignorant of the rapid development of world cinema because of the long-term closed-door policy, and in the sphere of the revolutionary war film in which the traditional model had long been accepted — what is more, in the highly forbidden area of representing humanity — these young directors initiated their challenge from every side. From the reconstruction of historical events to the exploration of the contemporary psyche, from the turning of artistic vision to the changes in cinematic language, ideas accumulated by several generations of filmmakers were explored through their films. Various techniques developed over the last thirty years both in the West and the Orient were all attempted. The mixed feeling of spiritual emancipation and historical responsibility made this challenge not only magnificent, but also powerful.

In 1979 films made by directors about forty years old numbered twelve, less than one-fifth of the total production of feature films. Since then, the number has been increasing year by year. By 1982 this group of people had expanded and made about 50 films, 44 percent of the total production of 112. The representative films produced during these three years not only strengthened the tendency to explore everything, but also initiated the appearance of the consciousness of subjectivity.

In 1981, during the process of making *Sha'ou,* Zhang Nuanxin first proposed the idea of a "new concept of film." This new concept, which later was defined in the sphere of film orthodoxy in a number of ways, had a general and broad connotation when Zhang originally used it. In her statement about the use of "modern cinematic language" in making *Sha'ou,* Zhang said that the goal of all these efforts was to make film "a representation of the filmmaker's own personal character and feelings" (Zhang Nuanxin, "How We Made *Sha'ou,*" *The Explorations of Film Directing,* vol. 2 [Beijing: China Film Publishing House, 1982]). That same year, after finishing *Awakening,* Teng Wenji expressed a similar opinion. "When we were making the film, we put emphasis on presenting the filmmaker's 'feeling.' This 'feeling' is a subjective reflection of the objective world. It is a unique opinion of the filmmaker about society and life expressed by means of film so as to influence the audience" (Teng Wenji, "Experiments and Exploration," *Popular Film,* January 1981).

In the character of Sha'ou, a player on the national volleyball team, Zhang Nuanxin involved her own "self-consciousness," her moral view that "a soldier is not a good one if he does not want to be a general," and her own psychological recognition that "the lost time of youth can never be restored." The audience, who were also on the verge of gaining self-consciousness, identified with this. Teng Wenji also put his own ideas about the "contemporary people" newly emerging in China into the images of Tian Dan and Su Xiaomei. He paid for these pioneer yet ambiguous feelings. Due to the different backgrounds in art and specific social circumstances of these filmmakers, the settings and situations in their films are quite different. However, both have an outstanding personal touch and, together with the different trends of exploration revealed in *Narrow Lane* and *Neighbors,* films also produced that same year, demonstrate that the emancipation of filmmakers has reached a higher level on the stage of enthusiasm.

After 1982, when these directors began their second films, film, art, and literary circles, and the entire society provided them with greater freedom and broader directions. Together with the thorough denial of the Cultural Revolution, the overall expansion of reform, the beginning of reflective literature, and the introduction of contemporary culture, a group of films making significant breakthroughs and dealing with current merits and wrongs was established, although not without ups and downs. A most active situation occurred in film theory circles, which provided them with the potential for making sufficient free choices on their way to their second step. In films such as *As You Wish, My Memories of Old Beijing, Backlit Picture, A Corner of the City, Sunset Street, Lawyer on Probation, Country Couple, Our Fields,* and *River Without Buoys* we can easily see the subjectivity of each filmmaker's ideas about life and film.

The tragic love of Jiaoda and Miss Lin in the socialist era is presented with the "beauty of humanity" in Huang Jianzhong's film in which "the composition of the screen reveals a sense of psychological reality." The poetic instinct interacts with rational and philosophical observations of contemporary people. At a time when realistic aesthetics was in full swing, Huang began to touch the sphere of expressionism. He proposed that the director should be "the master of his own cinematic representation. . . . Without a unique feeling and understanding about real life, without the ability to catch the special beauty that touches us, the world represented through our camera will not be able to present the essence of reality and will not have a unique characteristic, nor will it have any aesthetic value" ("People, Aesthetics and Film," *Research of Literature and Art,* March 1983).

In contrast to Huang Jianzhong, Hu Bingliu took another road, in which he "sincerely believes that life has the capability of representing and speaking for itself," but his insistence on expressing subjective ideas was no less than that of Huang. Evaluating his own film, *Country Couple,* he says he intended to seek a "beauty embued in daily life" and a symbol that "leads people into various and deeper thoughts" ("Ideas on *Country Couple," The Explorations of Film Directing,* vol. 4 [Beijing: China Film Publishing House, 1986]). The fact that this film was highly praised for its ambiguity and harmony indicated the sophistication of Hu's artistic skills. However, the lyrical music and visual representation, so filled with the simplicity and quietness of the deep mountain regions, also contained his almost desperate utterance on the closed family structure and cultural psychology that have lasted for thousands of years. When the exploration of the young and middle-aged directors reached this point, its significance was revealed: the personal discovery of art combined with a higher level of historical responsibility was congruent with the whole race's reconsideration of its culture at the time. However, no sooner had they established themselves in film circles and gained the respect of the audience, than the history that had favored them turned its attention to the younger filmmakers. The appearance of the Fifth Generation after 1984 reinforced the emancipation of film.

Although the use of the term "Fifth Generation" and the consequent classification of the filmmakers into different generations still connote contradictions in definition, the classifications have already been accepted by most people. This displacement of generations took place in only five years in film circles, a community known for its stability and reluctance to make changes. This short interval unquestionably symbolized the bright future of film.

> Our generation, which went through many ups and downs in childhood, grew up in a chaotic period for the country. We have seen much suffering and experienced the lowest life. We absorbed much real nutrition from those who endured all the suffering and had the chance to feel and understand our hopes and desires. Because of this experience, we realized that our race is a race without tears — most people never complained. . . . Thus if we do not single out and condemn the stupidity, backwardness, and ignorance of the Chinese people, we will see their internal perseverance. . . . When the

people finally awaken, we hope to make a fresh start and hope the ideas aroused out of the wound will be sufficient to stimulate the spirit of the entire nation" (Chen Kaige, "About *Yellow Earth*," *Film Evening Post*, October 15, 1985).

Chen's statement can be considered an accurate note on the heroic images, profound thoughts, and historical lyrics of the nation, unlimited by time and space, expressed in *One and Eight, Yellow Earth,* and *On the Hunting Ground.* This generation, which only reached maturity during the most difficult times, differentiated their films from all others by forthrightly expressing their subjectivity and by possessing and presenting mixed passions of regret and love for the nation, and thoughts obtained from the experiences of the previous generation. The emancipation of thoughts will consequently stimulate the development of new ideas. The appearance of the Fifth Generation brought with it a new opportunity for competition, diversity, and self-confidence among the young and middle-aged directors. The explorations by this group can no longer be put into one category. Nonetheless, all reflect the further development of social reform, changes in the spiritual construct of society, the wave of seeking for roots and culture and the reconsideration of the nation's inheritance.

The fourth generation is constantly developing and enriching its styles along the line of each individual's personal quest. Films such as *Girl in Red, Childhood Friends, A Woman from a Good Family, Sacrificed Youth, In the Wild Mountains,* and *Sun Zhongshan* represent their pursuit and value, and make people realize that the initiative of their artistic road will last a long time. The Fifth Generation, which is joined by newcomers every year, does not care to fortify its stronghold. Sharing in common the contemporary characteristic of not being easily restricted, it constantly heads toward broader and more diverse possibilities. *Black Cannon Incident, Swansong, Secret Decree,* and *Horse Thief* broke with all the generalizations people have made about them in the last year or two.

If I were to make a general statement about the New Era of Chinese film, I would like to say that it went through a process from unconsciousness to consciousness. This consciousness is indicated by changes in five different aspects of the medium and its reconstruction following the closed-door policy. Film is no longer merely a tool of political propaganda, but a means to express personal experiences and ideas; no longer of only one style (dramatic film) but of diverse aesthetics, forms, and styles; no longer of one genre (political art film), but includes art films, propaganda films, commercial films, experimental films, and films of various combinations. Filmmakers are no longer a dependent collective, but rather a subjective and independent group of individuals. Finally, film theory itself, during its separation from filmmaking in a move toward independence, has also changed. In this entire process, the young and the middle-aged directors have always been the most active force. Their strong awareness of the need to improve the present situation and surpass themselves has brought them into step with the era and related them closely to the nation and the people. The emancipation of artists has eventually brought about the emancipation of film. The time for Chinese film to leap forward after its awakening has finally arrived.

## TURNING TOWARD WORLD CINEMA

In its infancy Chinese film assimilated the Hollywood model and combined it with its own tradition of theatre. Later, during the long period of war and constant political movements, its function as a political tool was increasingly stressed and its own evolution ignored. The tradition of stable and unified, but closed, form was created in film. As a result it resisted the influence of foreign films or borrowed things discriminately. For instance, in the 1950s we only accepted Italian Neorealism film for its political significance, and completely ignored its aesthetics. And without knowing what we were doing, we launched a severe attack on the French New Wave (along with the realist film movement in Western Europe and revolutionary changes in Soviet film), which was in full swing in both East and West during the 1960s. In addition, the doors closed for about fifteen years before and after the Cultural Revolution eventually made our studies of film theory and aesthetics fall increasingly behind the rest of the world. During these years, some cautious artistic experiments and academic research did exist, but because our minds were restricted our topics were ambiguous. The means of filmmaking, the study of aesthetics, and the philosophy of art and literature were generalized into a single concept: the nationalization of film. A study of conventional film was never carried out, to say nothing about changing the domination of the single view of film.

At the beginning of the New Era, when the young and middle-aged directors were suddenly exposed to the achievements of world cinema unknown to them for twenty to thirty years, André Bazin's theory and various other styles and techniques, which were new and exciting to them, had already gone from their initiation and popularization into decline in the rest of the world. However, this backwardness made them shoulder the historical responsibility for breaking through the closed door and joining the mainstream of world development. The filmmaking of the last seven years reveals that by exposing themselves to world cinema, these filmmakers trained themselves in film art. They began to create a new dimension on the Chinese screen, from a completely different perspective than that of the elder generation.

The exploration of film by the young filmmakers had two exceptional characteristics from the start. First, the study of film theory and the practice of filmmaking were carried out simultaneously; second, learning and creating were combined. These characteristics resulted from the constitution of the group itself — among filmmakers, they were the ones who got the highest education. Their delay in replacing the older generation gave them a chance to think more profoundly; consequently, they reflect characteristics of contemporary world culture: the sensibility and ability to absorb other theories and a multidimensional pattern of thought. In 1979 "The Modernization of Film Language" by Zhang Nuanxin and Li Tuo prefaced the exploration. The article, which expressed the eager desire of this generation to learn and absorb new information, proposed that we "create a situation and circumstances in which we can talk openly and rigorously about film art, the expressive techniques of film, film aesthetics, and film language" (*Film Art,* March 1979).

The power and eagerness released after years of suppression filled the first period of this exploration and also left its direction (when we look back today) undefined. As mentioned earlier, after the 1950s, especially after the New Wave, Chinese film began to lag obviously behind world cinema. The modern characteristics then recognized by the young directors, and the new concept of film proposed soon after, revealed that after twenty years of the closed-door policy, we knew nothing about world cinema and didn't know where to begin. The eagerness to catch up and the complexity of the developments and the various schools of film constructed a contradiction. Thus there appeared multidimensions on the Chinese screen. However, the unidentified struggles that appear at the beginning of any movement also contain the power to break through confinement.

This period is now often referred to as one of a formalist exploration or an imitation of technique. But there is no doubt that in films like *Xiao Huar, Troubled Laughter, Reverberations of Life,* and *Ying* there existed not only imitations but also the initiation of the tendency to strive for the independent existence of film itself. "Film should be film," "film is the director's art," "film should throw away the walking stick of drama," "film form is decided by content but also affects the content" — such new sayings joined the experiments with the new dimensions of the screen and the uses of sound. Together with breakthroughs in the sphere of theme and ideology, they created a most active situation for exploration once rid of their restrictions.

The breakthroughs soon focused on the traditional role that theatre, which dominated film for a long time, played in the development of the medium. Because of the historical background, especially because most directors of the previous generations originally worked in theatre, its dominant position as the model for the aesthetics of film and theatre and for the staged film is not only deep rooted, but had never been questioned. But the experience of the new generation in film and their strong tendency toward "nontheatre," which they learned from the evolution of Western film, naturally led them in their explorations. In addition, at that time there was a strong common demand for a change from contrived art (people blamed dramatization for the artificiality that then existed in art), and the emancipation of thought added fire to the topic. The direction of exploration gradually clarified, but the theatrical model was so well established that the changes in structure in the first films by these young directors weren't able to break through it. When the movement needed supportive theory and techniques, it was only natural for Bazin's realist aesthetics to be introduced into China. From 1981 to 1983, the pursuit of realism marked the second phase of this movement.

There has been much literature on these experiments and their limitations. In my opinion, the introduction and practice of realistic aesthetics has a dual task. On the one hand, it must catch up; on the other, it must innovate. Examining the situation of our film today (including films by the young directors), I find their significance quite ambiguous. Bazin's theory, first of all, is a reflection of modernist philosophy. It is a way to acknowledge humanity and social reality via film, essentially based on realism and existentialism. In our country, we lack the circumstances in which to bring such a theory into existence, nor can we fully verify it. It took a process from ambiguity to clarity for the young and middle-aged directors to realize this. Realist aesthetics was introduced at a time when the idea of breaking away from theatre and restoring realism was in full swing. At the beginning, discussion and learning focused on Italian Neorealist films, which existed before realist theory. The medium of introduction was a few second-hand translations. To date there has been no systematic introduction of these theoretical books and films, which is why these experiments remain superficial.

Based on summaries of the long history of the realist concept of film, Bazin proposed a series of ideas on film conventions and aesthetics, and analyzed the limitations of montage and the Hollywood model. It is still a major achievement into the understanding of film and also a necessary stage that film cannot do without. Realist theory brought a fundamental change to world cinema. Though it later evolved further, its effects were left forever on the screen. It was only after montage and realist aesthetics confronted each other that film began a new era of combination and development. In this sense, the catch-up lesson we're making thirty years later is very necessary. The young and middle-aged directors took the first steps, which gave them the opportunity more quickly to make films close to the current level of world cinema.

The catch-up revealed the characteristics of the Chinese take-over from the very beginning. Our area of confrontation is dramatization, which is much broader in content than montage. Thus we took in whatever could replace dramatization. Initially it was technical devices such as the long take, natural lighting, location shooting, and realistic acting (*Sha'ou* and *Neighbors*), then it was documentary styles in lens use and nondramatic structures (*Lawyer on Probation, A Corner of the City, Backlit Picture*), and ultimately films appeared that resembled the works of the realist school in its late period, when it turned to psychoanalysis (*Narrow Lane, As You Wish*). These take-overs each had their own emphasis, yet they also intersected one another. More often than not, they inherited something traditional and formulated a distortion of realism, sometimes consciously, sometimes not. These multifaceted experiments brought about great changes in filmmaking — lens use, cinematography, performance, the structure of sound and music. What's more, they stimulated the study of the conventions of film and the formulation of film aesthetics.

The emergence of the trend of dilution [in contrast to maximizing conflicts — Ed.] initiated in *My Memories of Old Beijing* maximized the exploration of realism. The film was considered the best artistic piece of the New Era, but at the time what people noticed was the harmony of representation, not the fact that desalinization was the only natural ending of realistic aesthetics. Wu Yigong's idea of "invisible directing" and his pursuit of a prose style found its matrix from *Evening Rain* through *My Memories of Old Beijing* to *Sister*. It was an effort to realize "pure" film, in which he absorbed a lot from the philosophy of realist aesthetics and dissolved his narration through the visual and aural outflow. Hu Bingliu's *Country Couple* and Guo Baocang's *Misty Border* followed the experiment, and a few years later *Sacrificed Youth* brought it to maturity.

However, it seemed that it could not be carried further. Such is the result of taking over without a thorough digestion. Once the initial take-over had been achieved, the conventional trend blocked the path to more profound changes in our film. Nevertheless, the wave of innovation could not be stopped.

At the time Bazin's theory was introduced, the first group of the Fifth Generation stepped out of the Beijing Film Institute. Like the directors of the French New Wave, they learned the essence of realistic aesthetics and brought the exploration to a new level. This, the third phase, represented by *Yellow Earth* and *One and Eight,* is universally recognized as the true beginning of the new Chinese film. The Fifth Generation films are difficult to summarize. For instance, some foreigners say *Yellow Earth* resembles Karl Dreyer, some say Sergei Eisenstein, some, John Ford; others say it resembles Steven Spielberg, while the filmmakers themselves say they intended to make a film that had the effects of films by the Lumiere brothers. This indicated the end of makeup lessons and the beginning of self-innovation, an innovation that demands a more independent spirit from the filmmakers since it is based on the accumulation of conventions.

The maturity of cinematic representation is one of the most outstanding characteristics of these films. With the most powerful language and representation on the Chinese screen, they demonstrated their own formal system — the capability of representation. The construction of space that depicts reality and wholeness; the construction of sounds and pictures that are both real and symbolic; the effects of the stylization of color, tone, and rhythm; the use of both single take and montage — all these provide the audience with a new aesthetic experience away from the closed narrative and cinematic stage play. The wave of the Fifth Generation's films aroused criticism, confusion, and concern from all sides. The heat of the discussion far exceeded that of the first two phases, which means it touched deeper levels of cinematic thinking. This rapid progress is a forced experiment that fundamentally changed the state of film as a dependent art. Future development will prove that once film orthodoxy is accepted by more filmmakers and the audience, the sphere of film will be limitless.

The changes in the third phase eventually brought Chinese film closer to contemporary world cinema, something people had been seeking for years. After the shock of the above-mentioned films, both the fourth and fifth generations have been thinking about their next move. Realizing that world cinema has been developing in multiple directions, that there has been no major school to lead the wave, and that no wave has lasted more than a few years since the late 1960s, these directors conscientiously look for subjects and the means by which to express their own ideas on film and art. The emergence of the "multidirection" around 1985 was the mark of the exploration of the fourth phase.

The reconsideration of realist exploration brought about the experiment with the combination of realistic representation and dramatic structure in Yian Xuesu's *In the Wild Mountains* and the success of Zhang Nuanxin's *Sacrificed Youth,* which thoroughly dissolved dramaturgy into a purer "desalinization." What's more, the effects of completeness achieved by documentary devices which had not been experienced by the fourth generation were revealed in Tian Zhuangzhuang's *On the Hunting Ground* and *Horse Thief* and Wu Ziniu's films. At the same time, Huang Jianxin and others continued to explore aesthetic representation. The representational style of *A Woman of a Good Family* and the classic formalism of the presentation of the ancient civilization in *At the Beach* revealed that the directors' artistic personalities were fully expressed. Likewise Huang Jianxin leaped to another level. *Black Cannon Incident* not only touched contemporary contradictions, but also used modern impressionism. On the other hand, while exploring film conventions and the totality of film, they also turned to the psychology of the audience, the position of our nation's aesthetic tastes in filmmaking, and the emphasis to be put on the commercial and entertainment aspects of film. The discrepancy between filmmaking and audience expectations was significantly adjusted in these films as well as in films like *Life* and *Swansong.* Late in 1986 Ding Yinnan's *Sun Zhongshan* took another step toward the huge and fantastic historic past with a strong sense of subjective consciousness.

When the movement toward cinematic innovation took its first step, multiplicity replaced singularity. However, in every direction explored after a few decades of isolation, the imprint of the innovations of others could be found. The passion for making improvements was not enough to shoulder real innovation. But today, the multiplicities that have appeared on the Chinese screen have their own characteristics in world cinema. From each individual director's unique discovery of consciousness, to every film's different representation, all reveal the conscious assimilation by the filmmakers of Chinese culture and world cinema, and their impact on them as well. The movement is also a milestone that indicates the great leap of our film toward a higher level.

[Note: The third section of this essay, "Facing the Second and Third Years," has been omitted from this translation. Ed.]

# IV The Debate on the Nationalization of Film

The debate over the nationalization of film, in contrast to the others, might be considered a theoretical phenomenon with a distinctly Chinese flavor. Strictly speaking, the subject does not belong to the realm of film aesthetics; nonetheless, it did appear and, more importantly, the issue was not only discussed enthusiastically, but the debate has gone on for a decade. The term *film nationalization* was not initiated in the New Era; however, it was during this period that film nationalization has been most seriously discussed.

The cinematic innovation and exploration after 1979 represented by *Troubled Laughter* and *Xiao Huar* invariably evoked differing opinions. In addition, some of the new films reflected formalism, and the abuse of techniques such as the zoom, fast motion, and the flashback was considered by many as an unhealthy bad digestion of foreign devices. Many people in film circles expressed their concern about this. Under such circumstances, the issue of film nationalization was considered a way to guide experimentation in film and thus was resurrected as a form of discipline.

Early in 1980 Chen Lide, a screenwriter, wrote: "*Xiao Huar* reflects a tendency among young directors to imitate foreign devices of representation and to seek formalism at the cost of ignoring film content and distancing themselves from reality."[1] Soon afterward, *Wenhui Daily* hosted a conference on the issue of nationalization, thus initiating the debate. At the conference, young and middle-aged directors such as Han Xiaolei and Yang Yianjin expressed their doubt and dissatisfaction over the importance of nationalization as proposed by elder directors. Han claimed that "there are no specific national expressive forms. . . . To propose the nationalization of film is narrow-minded and against the principles of cinematic art. It can only constrain the development of Chinese film."[2] Yang Yianjin expressed similar reservations, saying that "the proposal of film nationalization will no doubt restrict filmmaking."[3]

In theoretical circles, two schools ran a collision course, but the division was not simply young versus old. The supporters of nationalization believed that "nationalization is the objective principle in the development of the ideology and culture of a nation." Filmmakers must "absorb our nation's heritage of literature and art while learning from foreign devices."[4] "The seventy-five year development of film in China is a process of nationalization; therefore, the need for nationalization should not be questioned because film is international."[5] Xia Yan, chairman of the China Film Association, remarked that the task of film nationalization is "first, to present characters filled with Chinese features through imported foreign forms; second, to make a socialist Chinese film."[6] Others, such as Zhong Dianfei, who were against nationalization, did not hesitate to express their point of view. "Between truthfulness and national form," Zhong argued, "I prefer to put emphasis on the truthfulness of film."[7] "The issue of nationalization is not the major problem in current Chinese film. The overly emphasized discussion is impractical for Chinese film."[8] Zhong's idea was widely accepted and further concerns were expressed over the issue. At a time when our film has just started to take off, "where does the proposal of film nationalization want to lead us?"[9]

This heated discussion was conducted around the issue of inheriting tradition or creating innovation with the help of foreign devices. Strangely enough, neither side made a serious effort to articulate precisely what was meant by the nationalization of film. Luo Yijun, perhaps the only one to persist in dealing with this issue, wrote a number of detailed articles over several years. To him, the crucial point of film nationalization lay in the inheritance and the development of traditional Chinese aesthetics; that is, to "present ideas" rather than to depict reality as is done in Western aesthetics. Luo's contribution and limitations are equally significant with regard to this debate.[10] At the same time, Shao Mujun, a theoretician who holds the opposite viewpoint, also published several essays on the subject.[11] He questioned the rationality and necessity of film nationalization and sharply pointed out that "to propose nationalization on cultural issues will inevitably result in nothing other than following ancient principles and advocating the ancient culture."[12]

The debate did not calm down until the appearance of Rong Weijing's article in 1986. Intending to clarify the confusion, Rong Weijing assessed the ideas of Luo and Shao, finding the concept so confused and inaccurate that the arguments of both men lost their scientific nature and became trapped in metaphysics. This evaluation led him to propose that the core of film nationalization was to make national film an entity that "represents the national spirit and becomes the creator and reformer of nationality."[13] Interest in the issue diminished considerably toward the end of the 1980s, as the environment for its debate weakened. Yet as a theoretical topic, no matter how important it is to film, the subject still has vitality, and people continue to join the debate. Unquestionably it is the one issue that has most intrigued film scholars outside of China. Interest will probably increase in light of the brutal suppression of the demonstrations in Tienanmen Square and its aftermath.

## NOTES

1. Chen Lide, "Exploration and Innovation Must Originate from Life," *Film Art,* January 1980.

2. Han Xiaolei, "Is Film Nationalization Scientific?" *Journal of Literature and Art,* July 1980.

3. Yang Yianjin, "No Nationalization in the Forms of Presentational Techniques," *Journal of Literature and Art,* July 1980.

4. Lin Shan, "From the Structure of Film to See the Learning and Innovation in Filmmaking," *Film Art,* August 1980.

5. Li Shaobai, "Trivial Ideas on Film Nationalization," *Film Culture,* January 1981.

6. Xia Yan, "About Chinese Film," *Research on Literature,* January 1981.

7. Zhong Dianfei, "Issues on Cinematic Aesthetics," *Research on Literature,* June 1980.

8. Zhong Dianfei, "Film Form and Film's National Form," *Film Culture,* January 1981.

9. Ma Xiongqi, "The Saying 'Film Nationalization' Is Also Imported," *Film Culture,* January 1981.

10. Luo Yijun, "Preliminary Research on the National Style of Film," *Film Art,* October and December 1981; idem, "Three Problems of Film Nationalization," *Guangming Daily,* November 2, 1983; idem, "The Style on the Screen in Beijing — the Ancient City," *Film Art,* October 1984; idem, "The National Style in the Films of the 1930s," *Film Aesthetics,* Zhong Dianfei, ed. (Beijing: Culture Association Publishers, 1983); idem, "The Argument over Film Nationalization," *Film Art,* April 1985.

11. Shao Mujun, "About *Love-forsaken Corner,*" *Film Art,* April 1982; idem,

"Summary of Casual Thinking of Film Aesthetics," *Film Art,* November 1984; idem, "The Argument over Similarity and Difference," *Film Art,* November 1985.

12. Shao Mujun, "The Argument over Similarity and Difference."

13. Rong Weijing, "On the Presentation of Nationalism through Film," *Film Art,* October 1986.

# 9      FILM FORM AND FILM'S NATIONAL FORM

Zhong Dianfei

translated by Li Xiaohong

Issues related to film art form can be understood from three perspectives: the unique characteristics of film; the sources of material or the way life is reflected; and its techniques, commonly known as rhetoric. Montage as a feature of film functions far beyond the composition of shots. It is directly related to the method, capacity, and style of film composition. As far as our contemporary practice of film creation is concerned, grasp of the method, capacity, and style of film is especially important. The point that I am going to make in this chapter, that a finished piece is not necessarily a film, is based precisely on this.

The source of material for a film writer is always a brain-racking problem. Of all possible subtleties, its essence lies in the premise of film. In Tolstoy's novel *Three Kinds of Death,* when the tubercular madame blames the chubby, healthy maid, she says, "You hurt me again!" To adapt this paragraph, the director designed five schemes to achieve the literary effects on the screen, but the efforts were to no avail. In fact, such a result is not surprising. The more well known a novel is among the audience, the less satisfied the audience is with the film adapted from it. Even for the author who adapts his own work, the script is never as good as the original novel.

People tend to forget that film and novel belong to two very different categories of art. I even think we should stop having authors adapt their own works. A novel is considered good because the writer makes full use of literary methods. But adapting it to film is like forcing a winning sulky to race on a new road and expecting it to perform the same way. Even though both literature and film are manifested by the same language, they are still two different methods: one is a direct recount of the character's soul; the other is a scheme of the recount of the character's soul provided on the screen. In terms of techniques, there are other principles of rhythm and succinct film language besides the general relationships of montage.

## NATIONAL ART

How are stage plays nationalized? If they are like *Thunderstorm* or *Sunrise,* through realistic depictions of life. As long as pictorial art realistically depicts life, it will be national, well liked by us, and well appreciated by other countries, because such plays have cognitive values for the real world. There is also a question of nationalization in Lao She's *Teahouse,* and in the music of *The Silk Road* by the Gansu Song and Dance Troupe. Because they are abstractions of the life of a nation, or even of a region — abstractions of ideology, emotion, mood, or even personality — the melodies and rhythms form musical beauty. Once musical beauty is formed, it becomes the undercurrent and crystalization of the consciousness and emotions of the people, with a strong local color.

Is there a national form for film? There seems to be. Whether it is Japanese, Pakistani, Indian, British, or American, we don't need to look at the subtitles, we don't need to listen to the sound, we can tell approximately, sometimes quite clearly, their characteristics and differences. But the differences are the results, not the causes, of the way reality is manifested on the screen. Therefore, the differences between music and film in terms of nationalization are due to differences in the media through which the representation of life is achieved. The existing form of a melody is a combination of sounds in time and space, which are then recorded through symbols. The existing form of a film is a combination of images, which reach our visual and audio senses through light-sensitive material.

Thanks to the universal use of audiotapes, music can also record very sophisticated symphonies, just as film can record images. Therefore, the question is also further related to the direct visual perception of film images and the abstraction or cognition of music. A Chinese peasant, lacking knowledge of Western music, even though *Pastoral Symphony* is on the air all day long, still does not understand the language of the music. I may or may not be right on these issues, but what I am really trying to say is that film, with its directly perceived images, does not present problems like those of *Pastoral Symphony*. Film as a means of reflecting objective images can achieve a superhuman visual capacity. Therefore, its main method — the image — does not need translation. As long as life as manifested by film artists is realistic, it — film — is by nature national. How, then, did the issue of film nationalization begin? What is its significance in our contemporary filmmaking and film theory?

## FILM LANGUAGE AND FORM

Once "canned culture" and "canned film," which are natural products of closed-mindedness, are broken open, they naturally make scholars and filmmakers ponder the concept of film, film language, its vocabulary, methods, and techniques. This by itself is a wonderful thing. If we make no moves at all in the face of new things, why do people want us here? Long ago, in *The Communist Manifesto*, Marx and Engels said that once the old tariff barriers were overthrown, literature would become world literature, and that it *had* been world literature for a long time. There is a problem of translation with literary language, but there was no such problem with silent film. Even after the invention of the sound film, it was much less of a problem with the audience than literature and music. In the early days of China's imported films, men were always called "John" and women, "Mary," and the audience was told: "John is kissing Mary!" Therefore, with or without a translation, it made little difference for film. If literature had long become world literature, then film, from the day it was born, should have been world film.

Fellow filmmakers, after seeing the work of others, may not think much of it; some may think it trash, and of no value; some may think it enlightening and useful to them, as with high-speed filming as a means of representation, and so on. I don't think it is enough to call all such things film language. They are after all only a part of film vocabulary, or what are commonly known as film techniques. Some techniques, even before we discovered them, had already become outmoded. Yet we regard them as new, bringing on criticism from the people. We can't blame film artists, nor can we blame the audience. We can only blame the policy of cultural dictatorship in a closed society. Even with the conditional open-door policy now, considering our current standards, we may still have endless complaints, but it does not seem necessary to waste such efforts.

Of course, film art should create a new vocabulary, new structure, and new concepts to push the remolding of aesthetic thinking about film.

We can't answer the question the old way: content determines form. That certain content in art can achieve perfect manifestation and must produce some breakthrough in form is, to some extent, a law. On the issue of form and content, my understanding is that only when disorderly life becomes the content of art can it possess elements of form, although it may not be the most appropriate. The most appropriate form must be able to integrate itself with content.

Film is never an improvisation, at least currently not in our country. Therefore, to encourage film artists to explore form, including style and film language, and the like, is still a necessary and serious matter in the long run. But in our contemporary filmmaking, there still exists the danger of underestimating form as a relatively independent subject. Following a set pattern for any theme — special, close, medium, far, push, pull, shake, follow — can easily strangle the vitality and life of art. Artists have the right to live in this world not just because they have an ability with perception and visual thinking that others do not, but also because of their extraordinary painstaking efforts to explore form.

## FILM AND NONFILM

Under general circumstances, content and form coexist in the mind of the artist. Lu You wrote more than 9,300 poems in his lifetime. If what he wrote first were not poems, but nonpoems, which were then transformed into poems through a subsequent thinking process, how could Lu You have undertaken such enormous labor? Many contemporary film directors, who have produced a dozen or dozens of films, have undertaken the same amount of work as that required of Lu You. Had their conception not been of films, but nonfilms, which were then transformed into films through a processing workshop, or what we often call cinematicization, it simply would be incredible. Marx once said that when studying a foreign language, if you cannot think in the foreign language but rely on your native tongue as a walking stick, and then translate it into the foreign language, you have not really mastered it. Therefore, if Chinese film artists after some thirty years of experience still rely on nonfilms as a walking stick, or see their task as cinematicization, I don't think we can have what we would call film in the near future.

We can produce many pieces, but they may not necessarily qualify as film. Whether a film is considered good or bad in film circles depends on how much literary value it manifests. It may not be good for improving the realities of Chinese film, or it may not be art. In my view, the two tasks of art are: the production of a new art form from related arts and the creation of theoretical support of it. Film is called the seventh art because it benefits from literature, the fine arts, drama, music, dance, and photography. Even to the present day, it is still making use of the other arts. Otherwise, this seventh art would always lag behind its sisters. But this is not the purpose of the study of different art disciplines. The purpose lies in creating a theory that suits its own development after its dependence. D. W. Griffith first combined different shots together; Sergei Eisenstein put them together into montage theory. With the improvement of film culture, montage in the past thirty years has also experienced great changes. As an art, film must study form. Nor is it feasible to separate form and consider it fit for manifesting only certain types of life. Doing so will not only lead to extremes, but will also result in nothing but fantasies.

## RHYTHM AND REALISM

Rhythm as one of the elements of form is determined by content. *The White-Haired Girl* exhibits one type of rhythm. *Today Is My Day Off,* another, and *Hunting 99,* yet another. In *Hunting 99,* in an episode in which workers help fight a house fire by carrying water in basins, the rhythm appears quite slow when compared to that of the whole film, and the firefighting comes across as insufficient. Is it possible for the rhythm of Chinese films to look like those of French films such as *Snake, Silent Man,* and *Z?* Theme itself does not require it. Once there is some requirement, we should fulfill it without reservation. There is no art method that never changes.

Film techniques, like other techniques, are subject to content. But they also assist content. No film that can travel long distances can rest its fame on content alone. The realism of a film will be damaged if the director does not impart a style to the script, if the camera does not impart color to the film, if the actors do not form an ensemble throughout a film, and if artists do not design an appropriate environment for the characters. Therefore, I believe as long as we aim at realism — realism from script to details — we will achieve results that are national, or a national form. Or, if while aiming at realism, we are restricted ideologically, afraid to think in certain ways or do certain things, then we are bound to fall into a can. What we get then will naturally be "canned film." From a long-term perspective of film development, I would rather have films shadowy, fragmentary, or mixed, than fall into a can! What did the eight model dramas contribute to Chinese film? Aren't the lessons shocking enough to us already?

On the twentieth anniversary of the death of Xian Qun, *Popular Film* asked me to write an article in his memory. I then started thinking about national style in some of his films; for example, the treatment of the environment, of Madman Cheng and his wife in *The Dragon's Ravine*. His success lies in the realism of life as presented in the film. Its conclusion is included in the premise. On the other hand, I don't think the so-called Chinese film tradition or national style that *Wave of the Southern Sea* explores is of much value. It uses the pen of the past. It makes people think that they are reading *Oliver Twist* instead of *David Copperfield*. To be more precise, *Legends of the Old West* could not have been made using today's film structure. The success of *Xiao Huar* is an important example. It tells people that the prospects of the nation always lie in the future. Film culture is no exception.

Can we call the portrayal of General Commander Zhu in *Song of the Red Flag,* especially the genre painting of the rural markets on the Hebei Plains shown on the screen, explorations of national form? True, the rhythm of the film does not seek unconventional methods in the treatment of certain shots. Instead, the rhythm is appropriate to the setting of the film and content. This indicated that the result as contained in the premise and the premise is not made to fit the result. It means to seek the realism of life will result in a national form. In *Muslim Team,* there is a shot of a jade bracelet falling on the ground at the death of Ma Benzhai's mother. I don't think of its treatment as related to national form. It is only an implied message. We can say that the director is seeking his own national language in the treatment of details, entrusting a deeper meaning to the acting of the characters, but this does not determine whether the whole film is national or not. Therefore, we must have a clear understanding of film form. There is a Chinese saying that goes like this: "Rather be a shattered vessel of jade than an unbroken piece of pottery." We film artists definitely need such temperament as bestowed by our national culture.

The thirty-year starvation of Chinese film artists has essentially been caused by lack of film culture itself. This is also why Chinese films are sometimes good and sometimes poor, sometimes satisfactory and sometimes unsatisfactory, but unable to maintain a balanced level. If the leading departments of culture could also see this, they would not lay down closed cultural policies for film artists, nor believe that for Chinese filmmakers to achieve a national form, they have to shut their eyes and plug up their ears. Such logic is absurd. To blockade the already limited amount of film research would only make fools of ourselves. If some artists feel threatened by different practices, we can only say that they are not yet qualified to be called Chinese film artists. Generally speaking, many well-known films should not be seen only once or twice, but seven or eight times, and we should learn from them. Therefore, based on the realities of Chinese film, film artists should not only be required to see some films as references, but also ordered to see many of those that may be of important reference value to certain types of film. We should not be restricted by any means from viewing films. Instead, we, the consumers of film culture, should be rewarded.

The reason why we adopt a totally different attitude toward the method on this issue currently in practice is because with more experience you gain the means of representation, and that will naturally result in greater variety in content. In spite of the differences between countries, nations, and classes, any valuable creation in culture is the result of long, hard labor. A lot of early Soviet films not only had a great influence on world revolution, they are still praised by film workers everywhere, even to the present day. On the other hand, Soviet film artists also admit that American films enlightened them greatly. Thus it is not only wrong in theory, but also unintelligent in practice, to impose various wait-and-see, waivering, even hard-shelled methods on film.

## SUMMARY

Quite a few foreign friends hope our films will cross the border. This is undoubtedly necessary. It should be taken for granted even though film is only a creation. We should prepare ourselves from this very moment.

To me, the most important question in film nationalization concerns the 800 million peasants. As long as they can understand the films and like them, it doesn't matter how they are made. The following is a summary of my views on film form.

There has been a tradition in China to neglect the exploration of art forms. During the time of the Red Army, there was no way we could explore them. One tune could be filled with all kinds of content. During the anti-Japanese War period, an anti-art understanding was given to the philosophical proposition "content determines form." Once you have a theme, there is already a form for it. This prevented many people with rich life experiences from producing their own creative works. Another aspect was the Soviet influence. After World War II the Soviets opposed formalism. Under the umbrella of opposing internationalism, they were producing canned culture. It doesn't seem right considering their practices then or the subsequent effects. The former exaggerated Russian culture, but the consequence was that the new generation was psychologically overwhelmed, unable to resist foreign culture.

Strictly speaking, there is no such thing in art as content without form. By this I mean the common normal creative process. But our literature and art, especially film, have long been related to the task of creation. The task of producing a specific number of films certainly includes the task of creating a great deal more work. Therefore, whether subjectively (the production of films), or objectively (the audience), film artists are required not only to explore different themes, but also to integrate different forms with them.

The major problem with contemporary Chinese film is that its realism and acting, not its use of foreign forms or techniques, are not convincing. Therefore, the issue of film nationalization does not constitute a danger to contemporary Chinese film. To talk about this issue glibly is not only inappropriate for the realities of Chinese film, but also, in many respects, objectively hinders Chinese film from making up for its lost lessons, such as the concept of movement in film and the formal inclination of acting. If we don't effectively overcome these, and instead regard nationalization as the most urgent issue, I think it only shows our anxiety. We are afraid that direct imitation will make Chinese film nondescript. This kind of anxiety is groundless. Due to the long-standing ban on themes about intellectuals, the fact that we have more thematic content about intellectuals now is not a problem. But the countryside is a big open market for Chinese film. The peasants are an endless source of material for Chinese filmmaking. On this issue, there remains a great deal of detailed work for Chinese film critics.

That is to say, there is a lot of creative work involved in terms of film aesthetics. The production capacity of Hollywood and Hollywood aesthetics are two totally different things. Hollywood has convinced moviegoers of its aesthetic quality. Its artistic methods are still very useful. But we naturally have our own aesthetic system. For example, we have actors like Zhu Xijuan in *The Red Detachment of Women,* Wang Fuli in *Golden Road,* Li Rentang in *Pioneer* and *Tearstain,* Siqin Gaowa in *Anxious to Return.* Their acting is rooted in our own earth. They have not only established the footnote that realism is naturally national, but also have shown much more than what we know as realism. Simplicity, honesty, profundity, and loyalty, commonly seen in the workers, are manifested into convincing aesthetic beauty.

Therefore, we should boldly study the forms of film art. We are not living up to the expectations of the people if we only engage in ordinary, careless, indifferent, and empty activism in film art. We film artists should have our own audience. We are artists, and our names have extraordinary power among the audience. This is often the landmark of the rise and fall of films in a country.

# 10 SUMMARY OF CASUAL THINKING ON FILM AESTHETICS, PART IV

Shao Mujun

translated by Hou Jianping

Some criticize *Country Couple,* saying that it has "too many foreign things in it." This criticism not only fails to touch the essence of the problem with the film; even its implications are unclear to me. Speaking of "things foreign," film itself is foreign. All film techniques and means of representation are foreign. From editing to the zoom lens, everything is foreign. I think it is meaningless to fuss over what is foreign and what is indigenous in terms of film form. What is important is how to make things foreign serve our national life. This is the major part of film nationalization.

People nowadays like to say that what is more national in nature has more international appeal. It is understandable if they say that nationalization is embodied in the content of national life, because content with national characteristics and local color can indeed arouse more interest in other nations. It is in accordance with the modern mentality to know about life elsewhere. But if they mean that nationalization is embodied in national characteristics in terms of forms and interests, it is incomprehensible. Internationalism means universal understanding. The more international appeal a film has, the more popular it becomes in any country, regardless of nationality. If different nations have different aesthetic forms and interests, and hence develop differences in the way they mold representational methods, narrative structures, and the development of typicality, so that the more national a thing, the more different its aesthetic ideals, how can other nations like it? In other words, if films with more apparent national characteristics in aesthetic forms and interests will be better liked at home, have more international appeal, and be welcome in other nations, then, what about the differences in aesthetic forms and interests among different nations? If larger differences mean more appeal in other nations, then why repeatedly stress that this does not conform to our national tastes, or aesthetic interests?

I very seldom have the opportunity to attend international film events, but based on my limited contact with foreign film scholars, I often find that what they colleagues do not like is exactly what some of our colleagues consider representative of national tastes — narrative structures that have beginnings and endings and go into minute details, provide clear introductions, and give earnest advice — and what they praise are precisely those films with strong local color and unique national features. Quite a few foreign friends criticize our films for using too many zooms, which is mainly an aesthetic perspective, because the rapid change in apparent distance with the zoom does not conform to the viewing perspective of human eyes, and seriously destroys the realism of the shots. While this type of foreign technique is now very rarely used abroad, it is becoming a Chinese specialty.

In my view, we should not emphasize national characteristics in aesthetics. Aesthetic experiences and interests are not conditioned by traditional culture, but change along with developments in material life, while differences among nations in spiritual temperament are matters of heritage. Therefore, we should not cherish the outmoded and preserve the outworn. For example, the Chinese people's ways of expressing themselves are self-restrained, good natured, dignified, and so on. But these are largely the vestiges of such philosophies as "be worldly wise and play it safe," "say one thing and mean another," "think one way and act in another," "pretend benevolence and righteousness," and other hypocritical styles and prudent philosophies that resulted from feudal etiquette and autocratic politics over thousands of years. Here, not much deserves preservation, but much hinders the nation's progress. To be more direct, a few articles prattling about "national characteristics" are in fact trying to protect the vestiges of feudal consciousness. Why is it that in our films romantic scenes are always very awkward? Subtlety and self-restraint are so good-natured and dignified that a pair of lovers talk with a table between them. Is this like real life? In fact, if we are willing to face reality, it is not difficult to understand that Chinese aesthetic tastes are undergoing great changes. We can even say that people of different generations have very different, sometimes even directly opposite, aesthetic interests. The volume and speed of world communications are continuously and rapidly increasing, and the world is becoming smaller and smaller. Consequently, I find no basis for the existence of self-contained national aesthetic standards.

In terms of filmmaking, I do not think it is necessarily bad that there are many foreign things. On the contrary, it would be better if we had fewer Chinese things. To be able to discard the bad parts of the heritage of one's own nation, correctly understand its historical greatness, become adept at absorbing everything in the world that benefits its progress, and restructure all the ancient customs and deep-rooted habits that impede it is not self-degradation, it is a valid prescription for eliminating low esteem for one's nation. In our current study of the development of film aesthetics, besides creatively applying Marxist standards, viewpoints, and methods, we should also pay attention to the realities of Chinese filmmaking. But I do not mean that we must synthesize a film aesthetics with Chinese characteristics or a Chinese school of film study. I have always thought of film as an international modern art. There are no national characteristics to speak of in exploring characteristics of artistic laws. Generally speaking, when we demand Chinese characteristics, it is only out of consideration for a practical proposition that we do so. Therefore, I am for the call for socialist films with Chinese characteristics, but against synthesizing a film theory with Chinese characteristics.

Film circles in every country will unquestionably face different theoretical questions that rise from different creative environments and film practices, but the differences lie only within a particular period of time, not with film theory. In other words, there are only differences of emphasis in theoretical research in different times and places, and under different circumstances. Characteristics of that particular period of time do not constitute national or local characteristics in theoretical issues. Practically speaking, a film theory with so-called national characteristics is totally groundless. Does Sergei Eisenstein's theory have German characteristics or American characteristics? Then how are the Soviet characteristics of his theory manifested? Does André Bazin's theory have any French characteristics? I have never heard that film aesthetics could be categorized into schools according to their nationalities. Bazin and Seigfried Kracauer both belong to the documentary school, but they are not from the same country. Paul Rotha and Alexander Korda are both British, but each holds his own theory of film aesthetics. Is it not true that the Chinese also hold different viewpoints in film aesthetics? Does it mean that someday the Chinese style of film aesthetics will be aimed unanimously at a foreign theory?

In my view, considering the situation of our research into film aesthetics, we should stress the introduction of foreign theories, and pay more attention to foreign countries. The question of what exactly is so-called Chinese national aesthetic thinking can continue, but the purpose should be to eliminate the dross. I do not believe aesthetic experiences and interests established and developed in a feudal society have sufficient value to be preserved. On the question of national cultural tradition, we should not blindly protect everything, nor cherish things of little value simply because they are our own. We must first look outside, and then look to the future. This is the best way to develop film aesthetics in our country.

[Note: Shao Mujun thought this essay too brief for inclusion in this collection and suggested "The Argument Over Similarity and Difference" (*Film Art*, November 1985), which addresses the same issue. Unfortunately, its length precluded its publication. Understanding the problem, the author kindly agreed to let us use the above article and asked that we include this note.]

# 11 A REVIEW OF PART IV OF SHAO MUJUN'S ARTICLE "SUMMARY OF CASUAL THINKING ON FILM AESTHETICS"

Luo Yijun

translated by Hou Jianping

Shao Mujun, in "Summary of Casual Thinking on Film Aesthetics" (*Film Art,* November 1984), formulates arguments over a wide range of film aesthetics that currently interest the entire film circle, and raises enlightening ideas. Part IV, the last part of Shao's article, given entirely to film nationalism, discusses many fundamental issues of film nationalization. These issues are closely related to such questions as on what road and in which direction Chinese film is going, and therefore cannot be treated lightly. Some of the ideas are quite representative of the thought in film circles. Never before has an article been written that discusses these issues in a manner so candid, explicit, and argumentative. This chapter summarizes these ideas into the following categories: characteristics of national aesthetic judgment, Chinese cultural and aesthetic traditions, and film theory characteristic of the Chinese nation.

## CHARACTERISTICS OF NATIONAL AESTHETICS

"Summary of Casual Thinking on Film Aesthetics" draws two principle conclusions on the questions of national aesthetic judgment: "In my view we should not emphasize national characteristics in aesthetics. Aesthetic experiences and interests are not conditioned by traditional culture, but change along with the development of material life." The first question to be discussed here is whether aesthetic judgment differs from nation to nation. If so, is this difference conditioned by traditional culture?

In his book *The Art of Painting Hills,* Zou Yigui of the Qing Dynasty specifically discussed Western painting. Westerners, adept at three-dimensional techniques, paint subtle differences between distant objects and those close to the eye. Characters, houses, and trees are all painted with shadows; colors and sketches are totally different from the Chinese tradition. Based on three-dimensional techniques, their paintings show the changes in perspective. Although this demonstrates skill and craftsmanship, it doesn't belong to the art of painting.

Many Europeans despised Oriental culture at the time when European capitalism was advancing on the world. Hegel, for example, was not complimentary of Chinese aesthetic judgment. "They still cannot present beauty aesthetically, for their paintings do not show differences between close and distant lighting." Although Zou Yigui was a well-known painter in the Qing Dynasty, Hegel's great contributions to aesthetics were historically praised. These two experts were equally matched in their aesthetic judgments. Aesthetic features of Western painting as viewed by Zou and those of Chinese painting as viewed by Hegel are both quite accurate, although subjectivity makes them biased and superficial. Even more interesting is that the elements on which they based their assessments were direct opposites. The aesthetic elements Zou depreciated in Western painting were precisely what Hegel praised. It is on those Western aesthetic elements that Chinese painting lacked that Hegel based his claim that the Chinese could not yet appreciate nature aesthetically. The disparity between Zou and Hegel existed because each was conditioned by thousands of years of traditional culture. Two different aesthetic systems had been cultivated in Oriental and Western civilizations. Their faulty judgments lay in the fact that each did not understand the nature of the other's aesthetic system. Only inaccurate conclusions can be drawn by applying one's own aesthetic standards to artworks completed under a different aesthetic system.

Zong Baihua, in his profound comparison of Oriental aesthetics and Western aesthetics, summarized the artistic features of Western and Chinese painting. His study is of great help to us in analyzing the differences between these aesthetic concepts. "Western painting style, since ancient Egypt and Greece, is based upon a circular object painted in an imaginary three-dimensional space. Zou Yigui depreciated the aesthetic values of Western painting for 'it does not belong to the art of painting . . . although it shows skills and craftmanship.'" Chinese painting has its own origins and aesthetic standards. "Chinese painting considers brushwork as the backbone and structure as the soul." It "uses the traces of brush strokes and qualities of colors to express directly the emotional appeal of life, revealing the core of the object." Chinese aesthetics of painting emphasizes spirit over appearance, and expression over imitation. Knowledgeable as Hegel was, his perspective was basically restricted by the Western aesthetic world; thus he was unable to appreciate the beauty of Oriental art. That a great aesthetician should have such an absurd view clearly proves that there are national aesthetic differences.

The narrow-mindedness of both Zou and Hegel on aesthetic judgment is conditioned by the period in which they lived. In the early eighteenth and nineteenth centuries, contact between Western and Oriental cultures was very limited both in profundity and range. Even the very well educated were not yet familiar with artwork that resulted from other aesthetic ideas.

There are two tendencies in aesthetic judgment that are not mutually exclusive. One is that people start with their own experience, which includes the heritage and conservatism of the psychology of national aesthetic judgment, and become infatuated with it. The other is that people want to develop their own aesthetic experience, broaden their range of aesthetic judgment, and enrich the variety of aesthetic interest, and, therefore, have a desire to appreciate art of foreign origin. The two kinds of aesthetic judgment are not only not mutually exclusive, but also infiltrate each other. Artistic requirements of a nation's tradition develop with the changes of historical aesthetic judgment (including assimilating the experience of foreign art). The remolding of art of foreign origin to suit the psychological state of the national aesthetic judgment is in other words the nationalization of art forms of foreign origin. The increasingly broad and prosperous cultural contact of different cultures has facilitated the merging of national cultures while still preserving the national characteristics of aesthetic judgment. Even in future centuries, the national differences in aesthetic judgment accumulated over thousands of years still will not be eliminated completely.

"What is more national in nature would have more appeal internationally." "Summary of Casual Thinking on Film Aesthetics" affirms this statement on the basis of "the more national features and local color the content, the more appeal indeed it has to other nations. This is in accordance with the modern psychological state of mind of those who want to know about the lives of people in foreign countries." I don't differ with this. But "Summary of Casual Thinking on Film Aesthetics" concludes: "If different nations have different aesthetic forms and interests, . . . so that the more national a thing, the more different its aesthetic ideals, how can other nations like it?" Attempts to solve this complicated phenomenon of aesthetic judgment by simple deductions of formal logic naturally leave national and international aesthetic judgment in opposing positions. Every nation tends to develop gradually, to enrich and change its aesthetic thinking, interests, and experiences. Therefore, national and international appeal are one dialectical unity, including both content and form. They are not in direct opposition.

Just as the Beijing Opera *A Junction of Three Roads* is an embodiment of the Chinese aesthetic thinking, the statue of Venus de Milo is an embodiment of ancient Greek aesthetic thinking. Does the Chinese appreciation of the statue of Venus necessarily exclude her formal beauty? Does the opera *A Junction of Three Roads* enjoy international fame simply because it tells the story of the lives of a few warriors in the Middle Ages in Chinese history? In addition, the same aesthetic object may not produce the same aesthetic experience in different national aesthetic thinking systems. What is familiar in one's own national aesthetic system may become an experience of novelty and surprise for another nation. Both Chinese and Westerners think *Hamlet* and *Dream of the Red Mansion* are aesthetic, but the connotation of beauty is not always identical. This difference between the psychology of aesthetics is often hidden by the two superficial identities, and thus neglected during examination. The dialectical unity of the national and international appeal of aesthetics is established precisely on this basis. Also, not all national features of aesthetic form can have popular appeal in other nations. For example, several famous singers from China have won gold medals at international contests, but at home, few can appreciate the classic Western operas they sing. Such complicated aesthetic phenomena explain the fact that national aesthetic characteristics do exist in the objective world. It is not subjective speculation.

Discussed in the following section is whether or not there is a difference of national aesthetics in the less-than-century-old film art and whether it is isolated from traditional culture. Film is the product of modern scientific technology. The scientific technological function as the basis of film art is endowed with certain aesthetic attributes. From the aesthetic perspective, film best embodies the special quality of imitation theory of Western traditional aesthetics. It is from this point of view that the different kinds of influence of traditional culture on both Chinese and Western film are probed.

In the late 1830s the invention of the camera had a tremendous impact on Western traditional painting. Some Western painters cried out in alarm: "From today on, we will see the end of painting." This is because the aesthetic pursuit of Western traditional painting is very close to photography. Whether imitative painting or photography as an art, both require formal imitation. The introduction of photography into China did not create a crisis for Chinese painting. Neither did it deteriorate the quality of the Chinese style of painting. This is not difficult to understand since the interest and charm of Chinese painting is after all quite different from photography. By way of the continuous visual narrative representation of ideas and emotions, the representation technique of film consists of the composition of lighting, color, and perspective. The similarity between photography and traditional Western painting enables film to borrow visual representation techniques with ease from traditional painting. Shortly after the birth of film, many Western silent movies achieved a high standard. Without the nurture of traditional culture, a newborn art would not have matured so soon. Chinese painting does not emphasize lighting, color, or perspective.

Cinematography of Chinese film cannot borrow easily the representation techniques from painting. Representation in Chinese films, especially in those films of the early period, always lagged behind. Among various reasons, traditional culture is one factor that has always been the cause. On the other hand, Chinese animation enjoys high international prestige in the film forum, which, again, cannot be separated from traditional culture. Unlike narrative film, animations do not require close imitation of the real world, emphasizing fantasy over facts, supposition over verisimilitude. The aesthetic elements of animation are closer to the Chinese tradition. The plain sketches of animations are easily traced to their origins in Chinese paintings. Puppet films and paper cut-out silhouettes are the film version of Chinese folk art. Cartoons based on watercolor paintings are even more peculiar to the Chinese, and are not to be found in any foreign countries. In addition, cartoons that emphasize image representation have more advantages than narrative films in accepting the cultural heritage of the representation of the image, action, background, and music of Chinese theatre and Chinese music.

Compared to Western film audiences, Chinese film audiences, especially those of the early period, pay less attention to the primary elements of film representation. Until the 1930s Chinese film improved remarkably when it self-consciously borrowed techniques from Western film and painting. The national characteristic of the Chinese film in terms of art form lies predominantly in its narrative method. The narrative features of the classic Chinese novel, drama, and talk-song were prominent in early Chinese films. The complexities of plot, dramatization and rich expression of emotion, easily understood narrative, clear beginning-middle-end development of plots, and so on, all conform to the taste of the Chinese popular audience.

The narrative method of Chinese film develops with the changes of time and aesthetic needs of the masses. In the 1980s there has been an increasingly diversified variety of narrative methods such as the criss-crossing of time and space, the prose style, the recording of actual events, and others. From the perspective of film aesthetics, this certainly is progress, which means broader and more modern national aesthetic interests. But this does not mean the end of national narrative characteristics in Chinese film. This national characteristic is not restricted to the narrative method. A lot of good films have tried to create the artistic conception of classic poems by the film method.

A film called *Country Couple* is analyzed in detail in "Summary of Casual Thinking on Film Aesthetics." Is the aesthetics of *Country Couple* really totally unrelated to traditional culture and national aesthetic experience? Hu Bingliu, director of *Country Couple,* gives the following response:

> Chinese traditional culture emphasizes the handling of the relationship between facts and fiction. Fiction contains facts which again contain fiction. Facts and fiction create vitality while empty spaces look like a wonderland. This is, in fact, the consciousness of space in creating an artwork. Chinese paintings and Chinese calligraphy both make use of empty spaces, from which came the saying: "white counts as black." The so-called scene-borrowing in the art of Chinese gardening is another example of the use of facts and fiction in the consciousness of space. The stage effects of the night scene in *A Junction of Three Roads,* the river bank in *Autumn River,* the relationship between water and boat — all are means of representing fiction and emptiness. From the perspective of aesthetics, this way of handling fiction and emptiness has broken through the limitations of consciousness of real space, and this breakthrough is based entirely on the imagination of the spectator. A similar method has been used in constructing some sound films, in order to stimulate the imagination through sound effects, and form a compound representation with screen time and space. In this way, the level of understanding breaks through the capacity of the lens itself. (Hu Bingliu, "Notes on *Country Couple,*" *The Explorations of Film Directing,* Beijing, vol. 5, 1987)

The traditional method used in *Country Couple* is not a direct imitation of Chinese painting, drama, or gardening art. From the aesthetic perspective, it is a breakthrough of the limits of real time and space on the basis of understanding traditional art. Also, through this particular strategy, a compound film representation is created with the combination of sounds and screen time and space, indicating an artistic conception similar to that of traditional art. This is both inheritance and creativity, both borrowing and restructuring. This is the correct way of film nationalism that we advocate. Among the middle-aged directors who made themselves known in the 1980s, Hu Bingliu is the most self-conscious and most prominent in seeking Chinese traditional aesthetics and traditional aesthetic judgment and interest. *Country Couple* and *Country Call,* both directed by him, show rich local color and the Chinese poetic style.

*Life* (Wu Tianming) and *Girl in Red* (Lu Xiaoya) both possess the charm of a national style. Directors and cinematographers of the youngest generation who just started their film careers place emphasis on film representation through backgrounding to embody the national spirit. The representation in *Yellow Earth* and *One and Eight* possesses a distinct emphasis over meaning. Film genres of Western modernism; methods, like location shooting, that seek representation; the avant-garde; the New Wave; and stream-of-consciousness all tried this approach. The efforts of the young generation of Chinese filmmakers in their exploration mainly lie in their efforts to inherit the spirit of the Chinese nation and traditional Chinese culture. The new explorations of film art, and many from the past, have sufficiently proven that the national characteristics of aesthetics universally exist in activities of art appreciation, and that international film language should be nationalized.

## NATIONAL CULTURE AND AESTHETIC TRADITION

"Summary of Casual Thinking on Film Aesthetics" denies that aesthetic judgment possesses national characteristics and that it is conditioned by traditional culture, which, to a great extent, neglects traditional culture itself. This point of view is illustrated by a single sentence: "I do not believe aesthetics experiences and interests established and developed in a feudal society have sufficient value to be preserved." It will be beyond my capability and the scope of this chapter to answer comprehensively what is worth inheriting and carrying on from the aesthetics developed in feudal Chinese society. The following is but an outline related to this topic.

## The Relationship between Aesthetics and Material Production and Material Life

Based on the logic of "Summary of Casual Thinking on Film Aesthetics," the unimportance of the Chinese aesthetic tradition is related to its derivation from a feudal society. That is to say, the value of the human aesthetic experience is dependent on the economic structure from which it is produced. Shao also said that "The human aesthetic experience changes with the development of material life."

Marxists would not deny that material production (and the material life related to it) is a decisive factor that ultimately influences the view of aesthetics. That Greek art, which is centered on mythology and the earth will inevitably disappear has been scientifically demonstrated by Marx. Relying on imagination and illusion to conquer nature, mythology will lose its basis for existence once governed by nature. But this refers only to the entire macrodevelopment of human history. We cannot make a simple and direct connection between material production and the special spiritual production of art. Accordingly, Marx made his famous statement about material production and the imbalance of art production: "Certain prosperous periods of art (including aesthetic thinking contained in the form of the highest aesthetic judgment) are not in direct proportion to normal social development." Marxist laws of the development of art are universally applicable, whether in the West or in China.

The relationship between the development of Chinese and Western film history and material life is not just a body and shadow relationship. In the 1920s martial arts, fairy tales, and family moralities were popular in China. The 1930s saw a large number of progressive realistic films that dealt with the contradictions in a socialist society, which represents a great shift in the concept of film aesthetics. However, material life in China saw no qualitative change in the 1920s and 1930s. In the 1940s, early 1950s, and late 1970s, Chinese film experienced distinct changes in the concept of aesthetics, none of which can be explained by the changes in material life only.

I think the prescriptive nature of consciousness of aesthetic judgment lies in where horizontal time and vertical history overlap. Considering time horizontally, besides the influence of material production and material life on aesthetic judgment, different ideologies, philosophical, political, ethical, or spiritual, have great and more direct influence on aesthetic judgment. Vertical history refers mainly to national cultural and aesthetic tradition. When affirming the ultimate governing function of economics on higher abstract ideological spheres such as philosophy,

Engels points out that "Philosophy develops on the basis of what its forerunner passed on and its development is pre-conditioned by specific ideological resources. Therefore, economically underdeveloped countries are still playing the first violin in terms of philosophy." Aesthetics as a branch of philosophy is also preconditioned by the ideological resources passed on by its forerunner. When we make an aesthetic judgment of art, we cannot directly relate it to material life. Otherwise, many complicated phenomena in art history cannot be explained.

We wonder if Shao Mujun's proposition that aesthetic judgment is determined by material life was put forth solely to disparage the Chinese aesthetic tradition. "Summary of Casual Thinking on Film Aesthetics" highly praised Aristotle's *Poetics,* which Shao believes to be "the first work that scientifically explained the concept of aesthetics in Western aesthetic history." Shao also quoted aesthetic principles of *Art and Society* by Horace. I am not against admiring Aristotle or quoting Horace. But what is difficult to understand is why Western aesthetic thinking, born and developed in slave societies, is still worth inheriting and carrying forth, while aesthetic thinking born and developed in Chinese feudal societies is not.

## The Oriental and Western Cultural Tradition

On the issue of national culture, Lenin put forth a theory that every nation has two cultures, namely, the culture of the exploiting class and the culture of the exploited. The culture of the exploiting class not only possesses the resources of material production, but also holds dominant positions in the spiritual domain. From the perspective of world history, world culture is mainly made up of Western culture, centered in Europe, and Oriental culture, centered in Asia. The two cultural systems are exchanged in many domains, which is a by-product of the rise of European capitalism and its expansion to other parts of the world. Western nations in dominant positions internationally are, in fact, also dominant culturally. Some of the exploited Oriental cultures of colonial and semicolonial nations are submerged, some are despised, and some are neglected.

That Western nations are dominant in the world indicates that contemporary Western culture in many domains such as social systems, science, and technology is more developed than in the East. Since the mid-nineteenth century, Chinese intellectuals have sought truths that would save the people and the country. Marx's birthplace is also in the West, but the traditional culture of a nation cannot be deduced on the basis of that rationale. This would make Oriental culture seem always behind Western culture. Joseph Lee, a British scholar, after he thoroughly examined the history of science and technology, concluded that "Between 300 B.C. and the 13th century, the standard of science and knowledge in China left the West far behind." But on the question of traditional culture over a hundred years, European centralism has been popular. Human civilization seems to have come down in one continuous line from Egypt, to Greece, to Rome and Western Europe, and the East only represents the dark side beneath that illumination. It was Westerners who brought light to the East.

With the awakening of Oriental nations, traditional culture should also return to its true historical nature. There is a lot of hard work to do if remnants of European centralism are to be cleared away. For example, on the question of art tradition and aesthetic tradition, we first of all have not sifted scientifically and studied systematically the art tradition and aesthetics thinking that are rich in local colors. Film is an art of foreign origin, but the fundamental characteristics of film aesthetics are closer to Western traditional aesthetics. This can easily lead to a misunderstanding that the lacking of traditional aesthetic understanding is considered as the lacking of traditional aesthetics itself, and that Chinese filmmaking and film theory are considered as art practice and theory generalization isolated from Chinese tradition.

Shao Mujun, in his *Survey of Western Film History,* believes that "Art, from its earliest period, whether in the East or the West, depended on the imitation of reality. Ancient representational art and narrative art were both roughly representations of reality." It is possible to make such a generalization of Western traditional aesthetics, but it would not be appropriate to make such a generalization on Chinese traditional aesthetics. Chinese art has always emphasized the representation of human nature, ideology, and emotion. Painting emphasizes formal expression (Gu Qizhi) and vivid temperament, not the imitation of reality. Narrative art and oral art do not depend on imitating nature either. The difference between emphasis on expression and emphasis on representation is exactly where the boundary line is drawn between Chinese and Western traditional aesthetics. To mention the aesthetics of two different systems in a single breath and to use imitation theory to evaluate Chinese traditional aesthetics would easily lead to the incorrect conclusion that the Chinese traditional aesthetic experience does not leave much to inherit and carry further.

## How to Treat the Vestiges of Feudalist Ideology

"Summary of Casual Thinking on Film Aesthetics" denies the characteristics of national aesthetic judgment and despises the national aesthetics as "in fact only trying to define the vestiges of feudalist ideology."

Vestiges of feudalist ideology are undoubtedly a heavy psychological burden of the national heritage. The complete system of feudalist ideology formed in society over 2,000 years ago is deep-rooted. China's democratic revolution overthrew the feudalist political system, destroyed the feudalist economic foundation, and also fiercely attacked feudal ideology. However, we are still far from fully understanding the embeddedness of the vestiges of feudal ideology. The successive political movements after Liberation never aimed at them. What is more, historical remnants came to life again under the umbrella of revolution. The Cultural Revolution is just one such example that revived the historical remnants in the name of revolution. During the current drive toward the four modernizations, obstacles to economic reform and the establishment of the legal system of socialist democracy are still those ideological biases closely related to feudalism such as small-scale peasant economics, the bureaucracy, the patriarchal clan thinking and behavior, and so on. It was also inevitable that these would be reflected in film. The taboo of dealing with love is just one such example, although love is not the only one. In opposing the feudalist vestiges, I do not differ with Shao, but I can't readily subscribe to some of his illustrations.

Different topics are forcibly drawn together and deduced with transformed concepts. For example, the simplicity of the Chinese in expressing emotion is directly linked to vestiges of the feudalist ethical code such as the philosophy to "be worldly wise and play safe," and the ethical positions to "say one thing and mean another," "think one way and behave in another," "pretend benevolence and righteousness," and so on. This on the one hand lacks theoretical evidence; on the other, it does not generalize the vitality of the practice of life and art. As to simplicity, which is an aesthetic term, if it is not aesthetic, then is it direct exposure? Of course, there is much to be discarded from our national temperament. Rapid changes of contemporary life and understanding of aesthetic judgment facilitate changes in national temperament, including the means of expressing our ideas, and the understanding of aesthetic judgment. It can be said with certainty that these changes cannot separate from their contemporary basis, nor should they be the same as those of other nations.

Chinese art is known for its brevity. It becomes clear if you compare Chinese classic poems and novels with those of the West. As to preaching and pouring exhortations into the ear, they are products of leftist thinking of politics in place of art, in the past dozen years. What do they have to do with national tradition? Emphasis on emotion, and emphasis on the dynamic role of the system of aesthetic judgment in appreciation, are other features of Chinese traditional aesthetics. Advocating inheriting and furthering the national aesthetic tradition, to a large extent, is directed against those who have forgotten or deviated from it. "Summary of Casual Thinking on Film Aesthetics" considers the overuse of zoom lenses that destroys realism in our films as a problem of national aesthetic judgment. Abuse of the zoom could be a result of the many years the door was closed to cultural exchanges. Thus, when borrowing from foreign film, superficiality is attained while details are lost. Chinese audiences do not appreciate this chipping away at techniques. The Chinese always use nature for artistic decoration, thus even the use of foreign techniques cannot be nationalized, which is exactly what Shao opposes strongly.

When criticizing the vestiges of feudal ideology, we should honestly and scientifically analyze the culture of feudal times. We must distinguish essence from the dross, and must not use national nihilism in opposing feudalism.

What we borrow or carry on, as accepted through common practice, is mainly the democratic essence. It goes without saying that we must not learn the decaying ideology of the Western bourgeois, nor should we carry the mantle of Chinese feudalism. In general, age-old Chinese art is often static, as was appropriate to the relatively static life of ancient societies, but not to dynamic modern life. Chinese traditional poetry, painting, drama, and architecture have all faced or are facing various reforms in the twentieth century. Lost in this formal aesthetics instead of reform, we are only cherishing the outmoded and preserving the outworn. But those ancient arts rich with thought and thoroughly tempered aesthetic forms are exactly what is nurturing contemporary art.

In China, Lu Xun, more than anyone else, fiercely criticized the weaknesses of our national character and the heavy psychological burden of feudalist traditional culture on our nation. But Lu Xun never denied our national traditional culture, as can be seen in his creations and art theory. National nihilism is not effective in eliminating the remains of feudal ideology. Using prejudice to oppose another will inevitably bring repetition to itself. Advocating the direct-copy approach is to enrich and develop ourselves, but not to deny ourselves completely, including our past and our present.

## CHARACTERISTICS OF CHINESE FILM THEORY

Shao believes that all film techniques and means of representation come from abroad. From the old techniques, such as editing, to the new, like zoom lenses, everything is from abroad. Merely to distinguish foreign from native in film is meaningless. What is important is how to use foreign techniques to serve the native country. Film is an international modern art. When we explore its artistic laws and features, there are no national features to speak of. In general, the suggestion to seek Chinese characteristics was raised as a practical proposition. Thus Shao advocates "making socialist films characteristic of the Chinese nation" and opposes "formulating film theories characteristic of the Chinese nation."

If these points are to be evaluated, it is necessary to clarify the meaning of two key concepts: (1) components of film form; and (2) whether aesthetic judgment is restricted only to art forms.

It is indisputable that editing and zoom lenses are imported, but are the techniques that comprise the whole of film art and representation also totally imported? Such a conclusion is difficult to accept. Film, as a comprehensive art, besides editing and zoom lenses, which are peculiar to it, also borrows generously from its sister arts such things as structure, representation, acting, music, sound, and so on. The sum of all these artistic elements makes up the complete form of the art. When these traditional elements are used in film, they must be combined and restructured in accordance with the unique features of film. Discussing film form without mentioning its component parts would undoubtedly lead to the error of replacing truth with prejudice. The relationship between film art and traditional culture is obvious when it comes to film categorization. Shao avoids mentioning the component parts of film in an attempt to erase the traces of its national characteristics.

On the category of aesthetics, though Shao admits that the content of film should manifest national life and filmmaking should have Chinese characteristics, he denies national characteristics of aesthetic judgment. This implies that the features of national life in film content will be eliminated once aesthetic concerns are involved. That is to say, aesthetics applies only to film form. Aware of it or not, Shao thus falls into the trap of formalism. Based on a Marxist point of view, in art creation and appreciation, content and form are integrated in the aesthetic understanding. Neither form without rich content, nor content without form can evoke a strong sense of aesthetics. A narrative art like film, which places most emphasis on representation, does not restrict aesthetic activities to form only. In film history, attempts have been made to seek form while neglecting art content, yet, in his *Survey of Western Film History,* Shao does not consider them as examples to be followed.

The long-standing leftist ideology led to a lack and imbalance in Chinese film theory. We tend to approach film form from political and sociological points of view, and neglect, even suppress, studies of film form itself. Thus to be interested in film form would mean separation from politics. That studies of political and sociological aspects of film are seldom integrated with the special laws of film often results in abstract popular discussions of politics and sociology. Since the late 1970s, this bias in film theory has been somewhat corrected, but Shao may be going to the other extreme. According to Shao, studies of film theory have to do with form only. Film elements with Chinese characteristics and socialism are closely related to content in the production of artworks, but Shao seems to have thrown them out of the domain of film theory. Film theory becomes an ideology unrelated to class and nation. The catchphrase to "make socialist films characteristic of the Chinese nation" is in fact itself a summary of film theories with a clear ideological bias and Chinese characteristics.

Any imported philosophy, social science, or theories of literature and art, once applied correctly to social practice in China, will leave an ethnic stamp. Fundamental principles of the Marxist theory of scientific socialism, an international theory of modern revolution, are universally applicable, but when Marxism is used to guide the Chinese revolution, it should also be nationalized and manifest Chinese features. The harmfulness that dogmatism has brought to the Chinese revolution is well known. Only nationalized Marxism, that is, the birth of Mao Zedong Thought, can lead the Chinese revolution to victory. This is also applicable when we strive for the new prosperity of socialism. Political and economic theories such as the conception of "one country, two systems," and "open policies abroad and flexible economic policies at home" are all scientific summaries of the most recent practices of Chinese socialism, which are Marxist theories with Chinese features. I do not think we can directly borrow foreign film theories to guide Chinese filmmaking. Of course, we should not refuse to translate and introduce useful theories from abroad. Chinese film theory should be a generalization of the experiences of Chinese filmmaking, including the assimilation of experiences from foreign films. Based on this presupposition, why should Chinese characteristics only be a practical proposition rather than a theoretical proposition?

There is no need for reticence because Chinese film theory is still quite poor, and indeed we haven't yet formulated a systematic socialist film theory with Chinese characteristics. This is by no means the same as the conclusion by some that China has film criticism but no film theory, nor is it the same as the conclusion by Shao that there are no Chinese characteristics to speak of in film theory. I believe, if a theory could explain the art of Chinese film, and explore characteristics of the aesthetic judgment of Chinese films and the inheritance of traditional culture, to some extent this theory would become one possessing Chinese characteristics.

We do not know why Shao recommends "look abroad and look ahead" as the "correct road" for the studies of Chinese film aesthetics, while disapproving a review of the traditional culture of our nation from which film has greatly benefited. Many worry that theories of film nationalization, the national characteristics of aesthetic judgment, and the like, would block the long-closed channel of international exchange. We cannot say there is no evidence for such apprehension. A great nation is always good at assimilating imported culture to substantiate and develop its own. In this modern world, where the volume and speed of communications are increasing rapidly, and intellectual production is at a saturation point, no nation can be culturally self-sufficient. The exchange of culture is becoming increasingly broader, more frequent, and more profound. If foreign culture were to be denied, which would include films from outside the nation, there would be no need to talk about the nationalization of film. A nation becomes a great nation for the creative spirit by which it contributes to the development of the world and human culture. Art with high aesthetic value exists in human culture, which is always built on the criticism and heritage of a national culture. This is exactly where the significance of the nationalization of film lies.

# 12 ON THE PRESENTATION OF NATIONALISM THROUGH FILM

Rong Weijing

translated by Li Xiaohong

## THE NUCLEUS OF FILM NATIONALIZATION

During the more than six-year exploration of film nationalization, many invaluable and important views have been voiced although they have been quite diverse. Though both sides in the debate are quite adept at dialectics, the tremendous excitement of the debate itself often traps them into the metaphysical arguments that have long been awaiting them. While neglecting the major issues, they hang onto and argue over a few digressive topics. This leads to a vicious circle, wherein the debate becomes more and more one-sided, and more and more extreme, leading nowhere.

Though the late 1970s are generally considered the beginning of the debate over nationalization, Luo Yijun's "Preliminary Research on the National Style of Film" (*Film Art*, October and December 1981) can be said to be the first comprehensive essay on the subject. There is no doubt about its impact, including some serious problems. In his long essay, Luo ambiguously uses a series of related yet not synonymous phrases such as national characteristics, national style, Chinese flavor, Chinese style, nationalization, and others. On the one hand, Luo points out their differences; on the other, he uses them together, as though they were synonymous and could be substituted for one another. For example, he says: "The meaning of nationalization is not the same as that of nationalism, national characteristics or national style. Assimilation ('-ization') is based on the presupposition of absorbing what is foreign. Without importation and assimilation, what is there to be 'assimilated'? To 'assimilate' means precisely 'to absorb'" (Luo 1981, 10). "Having originated in the West, film is an article of 'importation.' An imported art, when transplanted in the national soil, has to go through a process of importing, digesting, and absorbing. Only then can it become true art of one's own nation" (Luo 1984, 8). "The modification of an imported art to fit in with the psychology of national aesthetic judgment is the nationalization of an imported art form" (Luo 1985, 4). "Foreign art is imported to represent the Chinese soul, whose unique qualities and spirit are to be assimilated with the style of art. This requires tailoring and improving the imported art so that it possesses national character- istics. . . . This is the ongoing debate over film nationalization" (Luo Yijun, *Research on Literature and Art,* February 1988).

What is the cause of his confusion? Though this has to do with Luo's theoretical logic, a more direct cause lies in the misunderstanding of the concept of film nationalization. What is more, the impact of this incorrect explanation is so extensive that an opposition has already formed, with both parties starting off from this very unreliable point of logic. Even those who believe that those papers that "talk glibly about 'national characteristics' are in fact defending the remnants of feudalist consciousness" (Shao Mujun, "Summary of Casual Thinking on Film Aesthetics," *Film Art,* November 1988) are not aware that their target is but a shadow, which is in effect still directing their way of thinking. "'Nationalization' is a catchword aimed at foreign cultures. It requires positioning the impact of foreign cultures under the domination of the national cultural tradition, assimilating foreign cultures into one conforming to characteristics of the national tradition" (Shao 1985, 11). This definition is essentially the same as the one postulated by Luo Yijun, with differences only in areas of emphasis. Until we begin to reanalyze and clarify the concept of film nationalization we cannot avoid this confused battle, and resolve the relationship between nationalism and national style. Film nationalization is a proposition of art that manifests and creates nationalism through the medium of film. With this manifestation and creation of nationalism as a presupposition, the nation's psyche constitutes the nucleus of film nationalization.

Linguistically speaking, -ization is the suffix of the stem *nation*. The meaning of words made up of a stem and a suffix is determined by the stem, though its meaning is more abstract and general. Therefore, our interpretation of the phrase should focus on the stem *nation* rather than on the suffix *ization*. Whether it be *militarization, collectivization,* or any other words ending in *ization,* the essential and primary meaning derives from the stem, not the suffix. Therefore, I believe film nationalization is a process of manifesting and creating nationalism by means of film; it is not "importing, digesting, and absorbing," and the like, for the meaning of nationalization lies in the stem of the word rather than in the suffix. The reason why I used *nationalism* instead of *nation* is simple: the former is an abstract and generalized form of the latter, and therefore more common and universal.

What we call *nationalism* includes the unique characteristics of a nation. Its principle component is a common psychological attraction and the unique mode of a national psyche. If we break up the broad meaning of culture into three layers — material, material-consciousness, and psychological — then what this mode precisely represents is the innermost layer of a nation's culture, wherein lies its soul.

Though the globalization of world culture is increasingly evident, the differences among the nations, especially those between the East and the West, remain distinct. Therefore, national differences exist objectively in films. Otherwise, why would there be different schools of filmmaking in the USSR, France, Italy, the United States, and other countries?

The shaping of nationalism has undergone a long, hard journey parallel to the evolution of history. It has to do with genetic inheritance, natural environment, and climatic conditions, but it is even more closely related to the productivity of the society. Different levels of productivity and different life-styles provide different cultural structures and psychological composition. The productivity level of ancient Greece determined that people could control and conquer nature only by creating God. Out of necessity, the Mongolians made shoddy pottery, the Eskimos made iron forks, and the Bushmen, poisonous arrows. But there was no concept of religion among these peoples besides their shallow belief in ghosts and devils. Such beliefs could not have become a steady, systematic format for worship. The higher the level of productivity, the more civilized the culture. The genetic factors and characteristics of a race affect the evolution of a nation far more than does the nurturing of a cultural form. Language, the initial and primary content of culture, is the first step to civilization after the millions of years of barbarity human beings have been trying to escape. Engels said, from apes to humans, from the evolution of the ape's brain to that of the human, language and labor simultaneously "became two principle motivating forces" (*Natural Dialectics*). From this perspective, nationalism is in fact the same as cultural difference between nations.

The whole purpose of this deduction is to show that the meaning of film nationalization is not confined to national aesthetic consciousness or aesthetic ideals. In other words, studying these wouldn't resolve film nationalization. The meaning of film nationalization is far more extensive. It includes social, political, religious, moral, natural, and self consciousness. The significance of film nationalization is broad and profound, as nationalism extends from an awareness of aesthetic judgment to cultural psychology. Therefore, whether it emphasizes the "differences in characteristics of aesthetic judgment" (Luo) or the "similarity among differences, with similarity as the essence in characteristics of aesthetic judgment" (Shao), both are biased because both neglect to a great extent the tremendous influence of the psychological affinities of a nation, which determine its characteristics of aesthetic judgment and film nationalization. "In every nation, there is a central spirit emanating to the outside" (Rene Welleck, *Theory of Literature*). This "central spirit" is what we mean by nationalism dominated by the national psyche. Only when Chinese cinema grasps the central spirit of the nation, manifests it through the visual language of film, and becomes creator and transformer of the national spirit and nationalism, can it become a true national cinema and possibly a school of film. This I consider the nucleus of film nationalization.

Indeed, if art is to become substantive and meaningful, it should serve the interests of the people so that they can experience the essence of the soul and emotional pleasure. The proposition of the nationalization of film aims at realizing the manifestation and creation of nationalism via an integration of national content and form, and achieving the purpose of representing the national soul through that integration.

## FORM, CONTENT, AND THE NATIONALIZATION OF FILM

Content and form are philosophical categories commonly used in the discipline of art. There is no doubt that they are also categories that the discussion of film nationalization often involves. But many are confused as to whether film nationalization refers to content or form. For example, Luo Yijun believes that film nationalization is to be understood through an integration of content and form; however, he neglects their absolute integration with each as a presupposition, focusing on the relativity of their independence, which leads him to believe content is the dominant factor, and form only a necessary measure. "The art form must be the focal point and generalized with 'national style'" (Luo 1981, 10). Just as

Luo's understanding of content and form is metaphysical to some extent, it is natural that he includes national style in his argument, and uses it often to replace the concept of nationalization in order to make up for what would be disjointed in logical alignment. Shao Mujun distinguishes the two even more clearly. He says that he welcomes film nationalization as far as it refers to content, but if form is also to be nationalized, it is utterly "incomprehensible," because film form in nature is "international." In my view, content and form are inseparable and dialectically integrated. The nationalization of film aims at neither content nor form; its objective is the organic whole of art.

Philosophically, we are aware that content and form are relatively independent, yet when we apply this concept to the domain of a specific art, we tend to neglect its philosophical and dialectical significance. In that domain, the categorization of this into content and that into form leads to a ruthless division of the whole and an impractical explanation. The mechanical and ruthless division of the whole of film as an art not only fails to explain one's own experiences, feelings, and the components of the art object, but also brings harm to the life of art.

If we want to represent the national life of a certain society through art, a specific form must be used. When the two merge into a unity, national content is integrated with the unique form it requires, and this unique form will become a national form with nationalistic content. This is a process through which a potential artistic representation becomes a practical one. That is, it is a process through which an unnatural artistic domain is created by a form with one type of content, or another type of content is created with another form. There is no abstract form, nor is there content without form.

An art form is not the same as an artistic method of representation. They do not form a causal relationship on a one-to-one basis. The same method can result in more than one art form. A method is a technique. A technical method can be learned, whereas an art form cannot. *Yellow Earth* uses the method of symbolism in achieving Chen Kaige's conception of history. This is because symbolism can gratify the expectations of Chen to represent reality and his wishes to go beyond the limits of real life, so that a specific instance can serve as an abstraction. The common method of realism cannot achieve this. Although the method of symbolism is often practiced in film, the way it is used in *Yellow Earth* is unique. Although I am not saying it is unattainable, any artistic repetition or duplication would be of no value. As long as the conception of *Yellow Earth* is not repeated, there will not be a form identical to that of this film.

In fact, the separation of content and form is often very subjective. Only if we can conceptualize a rational understanding of the internal factors of artistic life would there be slight shadows of form distinguished from content, subject matter, theme, and so on. It is difficult to generalize a form (external factors) with a concept. The most we can do is to give an ambiguous description with clumsy, strong perceptual language, which is often done by way of prescribed content. (This phenomenon is often found in our film studies and criticism.) This, in fact, has already denied the feasibility of this analytical method. Therefore, the social cognition and artistic ideals of film artists determine how they manifest the content of interest, which in turn determines the means and method used for the unique form required and is integrated with it. The overemphasis on whether the nationalization of film should be subject to form or content is of no significance. It is even more absurd for film nationalization to be confused with traditional artistic styles and features, and for concepts such as "between truth and falsehood," "white as black," "artistic land," "beginning and end," and others, to be treated as its objectives.

I have my reservations on the proposal that the phrase *nationalization* be replaced by *nationalism* (Xiao Xiao 1986). First of all, the meaning of nationalization is richer, broader, more profound, and more characteristic of a theory. Secondly, national characteristics and national styles are more inclined to superficiality, and their usage is rather loose. Finally, the term *nationalization* is already in wide use. What is of top priority now is not the substitution of a different name, but rather a qualitative grasp of concept.

## FILM NATIONALIZATION AS A DIALECTICAL UNITY OF HISTORY AND TIME

In the studies of film nationalization, Luo Yijun, from the very beginning, has been aware of the integration of history and time. He states that the "aesthetic characteristics of Chinese film should have the qualities of progressive aesthetic judgment that are still developing, and carry forward critically the fine Chinese aesthetic tradition" (Luo 1986). Though this view is a keen insight, it is confined to the issue of aesthetic judgment. Luo has thus far not furthered his study on the issue.

I think film nationalization is the manifestation and creation of nationalism with a dialectical unity of history and time. Since nationalism falls into a category of history, nationalization is naturally not a constant in historical movements. If we analyze nationalism longitudinally, we will discover an invisible power that has been internally governing the thinking, behavior, beliefs, speech, and style of every member of the nation — this is the flow of the national psyche over thousands of years from the Qin Dynasty until today. This is the historical aspect of nationalism. This histrrical accumulation looks like a spirit that gradually moves and grows a priori in the soul of the people, subconsciously influencing one generation after another. This phenomenon of cultural assimilation is precisely the psychological affinity of the masses and the origin of cohesive force. It is also the origin of the relative durability and stability of nationalism and the national psyche.

In China this can be traced back to Confucianism in the early Qin Dynasty. Benevolence is the nucleus of Confucian thinking. Apart from blood origin, psychological principles, humanism, and individualism, the general characteristic of this way of thinking and mode of the national psyche is practical reason. It is a rational spirit and attitude, but is related to practical and utilitarian purposes. Practical reason infiltrates every cell of our organic body, and works in everyday life, politics, and morality, and requires us to be governed by reason, to adopt a positive attitude toward life, to emphasize utilitarian over analytical reasoning, to put people before gods, moral education over religious beliefs, and to become adept at adjusting to community life. In real life, reason is preferred over emotion, and fanaticism is opposed.

The national psyche mode of practical reason, after the ups and downs of thousands of years of evolution, eventually became an invisible norm that guides people in their thinking and behavior. For example, *Sacrificed Youth, On the Hunting Ground,* and *At the Beach* all praise harmony, tranquility, friendship, peace, and a self-sufficient attitude toward life and living style. *In the Wild Mountains* attacks to some extent the traditional values of marriage and family carried over from feudal society, but the film ends with a they-lived-happily-ever-after message, a transition from disruption to harmony. It still tries to prove that a peaceful and stable family is evidence of a successful marriage. Even though the creative work of *Yellow Earth* contrasts with several decades of traditional Chinese filmmaking and is strongly and totally against the artistically simplified and politicized view, the rational mood and the ambiguous, yet explosive, mind the film seeks is still more or less related to the traditional Chinese national psyche. As long as a person belongs to a specific society and time he must be influenced by them. Instead of evaluating the advantages and disadvantages of the national psyche of practical reason, I will try to explain the powerful self-control of nationalism in film practice.

Even a rational and progressive central spirit will be stamped with characteristics of the times. Development would mean negation. Without negation, breakthroughs and criticism would not develop, continue, and renew. This, at the same time, is the objective law for the development of a national psyche. The duration and stability of a national psyche is relative and temporary. It needs to be developed. There would be no life without development. It needs constant revision, self-adaptation, and integration of the breakdown of thoughts and behavior. Each period adds to the mode new colors and new features. Under new historical conditions, the mode manifests a new outlook and regulatory qualities. This is the importance of the manifestation and creation of film nationalism in relation to time.

Our analysis of the underdeveloped, unstable factors in the organic whole of the Chinese nation is a product of the contact between Chinese and Western culture. Of course, a more direct cause is our introspection during the Cultural Revolution. At first, people only saw the visible disasters of the decade, then, second, the inherent relationship between blind worship (at the expense of reason, and with the vicious inflation of belief) and the feudal rule of 2,000 years. Third, they saw a shift from the recovery from external scars to macrophilosophical thinking about history, and finally the search for the origins of the national psyche. This questioning and revolt against the traditional cultural system is also reflected in filmmaking from the standpoint of our times.

The introspection in *Life, At the Beach,* and *A Woman from a Good Family* is macroscopic and ideologically profound, because they all focus on the inertia of traditional culture that had been distorting liberal humanism. It is regretful that artistically they fail to represent the deep introspection, severe criticism, and heavy sense of historical responsibility. While the creators devote their enthusiasm and sympathy to the unfortunate people, even though they criticize and negate rationality, they perceptually are inseparable from ceaseless emotion. With their rational and emotional attitudes in conflict, their emotional criticism fails to support rational criticism. No matter how sophisticated it is, art always appeals to people through emotions rather than reason. The underlying function of reason is always realized through superficial emotion. Therefore, *Life* and other films fail to reach the expected philosophical degree of macroretrospection. For example, Wu Tianming's positive portrayal of Gao Jialin and sympathy for Liu Qiaozhen constitute an antithesis: Qiaozhen is "pure gold" — the traditional benevolence (kindness, virtue, diligence) of Chinese women that is embodied in her conceals what is backward and conservative from our vantage point. What is more important is that the glory of the gold constitutes a contrast with Gao Jialin, who, while seeking personal goals and a new life, becomes a mere child. Though Wu's positive depiction of Gao Jialin is deep, his sympathetic love and deep sorrow for Qiaozhen has more appeal. Tears that fall on the red scarf are more convincing and more appealing than the imaginary planes, high-rise buildings, and the United Nations.

The fishing village in *At the Beach* is more likable than the satellite city because the former is full of life, even though the latter represents the industrial civilization of a more developed society. The fishing village is weak and has to struggle to keep life going. The satellite city is powerful, though its power is unbalanced, and makes the city cruel and inhumane. The embrace between Xu Yan and Xiao Mei, which symbolizes the victory of civilization over the old society, makes the prayers of the old fishermen seem impotent.

There is a similar contradiction in *A Woman from a Good Family*. The emotional appeal of the film is the intimacy and harmony between older wife and younger husband, and the background that looks like a pastoral poem. Though we sense the film condemns the fate of Chinese women bound by "the three obediences and four virtues" of thousands of years, it is subtle and not strong enough to shake our hearts. We can certainly use external harmony to set off internal disharmony, conflict, and humanistic ferment, but Huang Jianxin's overemphasis on external harmony exposes naturally the internal disharmony. The love relationship between Xing Xian and Kai Bing is ambiguous, and hardly treated directly, nor is the rich and energetic inner world of Xing Xian explored either. The wakening and betrayal of depressed, restricted, and distorted human nature should have been the theme and main frame of the film. The use of appealing harmony cannot accomplish a criticism of the feudal aspects of traditional culture, but we can see the duality of rational thinking and perceptual representation in conflict in the image. Perhaps the differences between criticism through art and criticism through science lie at exactly that point between rational doubt and ambiguity where emotion thaws. Can we say that a historical criticism of film is achieved through this state of doubt and ambiguity?

The introspection of *Yellow Earth* is calm and serious. Characters in the film possess elements of semiotic and abstract thinking, the significance of which is less than the symbolic signification of the whole. From the vantage point of our contemporary civilization and consciousness, the artist traces the stories, which may be unimportant, but which have a clear relationship to history. The subjectivity of the film is embodied in Cui Qiao looking for Du Dage, Han Han shouting in the running crowd. Tendenciousness, criticism, and discussion are integrated with the visual system to represent direct honesty, simplicity, kindness, and naïve ignorance directly so that people can experience and see more in their imagination, association, and reflection. This observation is a type of comparison, a rational deduction in an atmosphere of emotion. What is positively presented is honesty and kindness, but what we experience strongly is something else — backwardness and ignorance. Reason here is the emotional drain, the main body of the visual system. The great power of subtle symbolism is that it provides food for thought, yet this is also why it fails to appeal to more audiences.

To sum up, in the development of Chinese film to this day, one thing is unquestionable: the natural manifestation of nationalism nurtured by national culture. It provides a "common psychological basis transcending individuality that universally exists in every person. . . . No writer, even though he is an international citizen, can escape his own national ideology and way of thinking" (Rong Ge, *Collective Unconsciousness and Stereotypes*). Poet and aesthetician Schiller's description is more specific and emotional. "Language itself is enough to limit oneself to certain forms and give his work a kind of nationalism" (Hans Mayer, *Schiller and Germany*). I think this principle applies equally to film. French director René Clair regards the "international" films elaborately produced by Americans as "meaningless products" from a "typical commercial point of view." Those that conform with our film ideals all possess genuine national characteristics, which in no way hinders foreigners from understanding them. What is the difference between the two versions of *War and Peace* produced by Bandarchuk and King Vidor? Why is it that *Doctor Zhivago,* by British director David Lean, and *In the Name of Revolution,* by Li Enjie and Shi Daqian, are different from Soviet films of the October Revolution? This is an interesting and thought-provoking question.

Our film artists are currently in the historical/philosophical grasp and aesthetic concerns of nationalism. This shows the urgent need to reestablish the new mode and principles of the psychological state, life-style, and habits that conform with our contemporary times. Indeed, this criticism and affirmation of nationalism, from a new perspective, is not only defending traditional culture, but also bravely creating a new ideology consistent with productivity. Here the restrictions of old values and the sacred responsibility of the present reality are dialectically integrated. When more and more issues of globalization are faced by different nations, and when modern industrialization and the rapid means of communication merge different national life-styles together, people will become increasingly conscious of those qualities that make up the unique characteristics of a nation. The conscious criticism and dialectical negation of nationalism therefore become the internal factors in the revolution of national culture, and in the advancement of culture promoted by the development of productivity.

## THE PRACTICAL SIGNIFICANCE OF FILM NATIONALISM

The nationalization of film is very important in that it is an integration of history and time, a longitudinal development and transverse transformation, through which qualities of our time become more positive, innovative, and lively. History is subjective to time. Therefore, the practical significance of the nationalization of film is even more pronounced. Since the meaning of film nationalization is broad and changes constantly, we need to develop a broader understanding of it. We should not automatically think, as we did in the past, that nationalization refers simply to rural themes, as if other domains were not national in nature. I think *Happiness at the Door* is national. *Black Cannon Incident* is national. *Tan Sitong* is national, and so is *Under the Bridge*.

Increases in material wealth first of all produce artists, who are the center and main body of art. Therefore, as long as our camera aims at national life, the films produced will be national. We must use the film eye, film thinking, and film method to seek and explore the great soul and eternal beauty of our nation, to represent the people who have worked on the rich, beautiful land generation after generation, and to describe their lives, feelings, and desires. Thousands of years of history and thousands of miles of land make up the endless life source for filmmaking. As long as our films truly represent our history, reality, spirit, psyche, and images through specific historic conditions, they will be national, and they will have accomplished, or partially accomplished, the manifestation and creation of nationalism.

There is no history, character, or emotion that cannot be represented, remolded, or expressed in art. However, there is a question of whether it is realistic or not. As Zhong Dianfei put it: "As long as imitative art truthfully depicts life, it will be our national art" (Zhong Dianfei 1981, 1). Realism is undoubtedly an important criterion for film nationalization, but I have reservations about Zhong's proposal to replace nationalization with realism. His reasoning is that nationalization "not only does not fit the reality of Chinese film, it objectively hinders China from making up for the missed lessons of the past" (Zhong 1981). Realism is indeed a problem to be solved in Chinese film. Since realism is a general law and basic requirement followed by all arts, it naturally establishes a direct and indirect relationship with other problems. Be it montage, long take, theatrical or natural lighting effects, natural or personality acting, synchronized or postsynchronized sound — all are related to realism. Can we then replace them all with realism? The answer is obviously not, for they are of a different kind of issue. Nationalization would not hinder realism; on the contrary, it would become a specific requirement for realism.

Since a natural logic exists between truthful representation and things national, then, is it also true that it exists between things national in art and truthful representation? It is not scientific to find nationalization and "making up for the missed lessons" contradictory. The problem here lies in misunderstanding of the word *hua* (-ization). Thus the significance of film nationalization lies in the intersection of the traditional national psyche in which Chinese film should be consciously established and the contemporary international consciousness, and in the development of a direction of practice that is good for the healthy growth of a national film close to the hearts of the people. Therefore, this proposition (of film nationalization) is not a narrow-minded localism. Instead, it is an extensive and open-ended nationalism in which internationalism is included. At least I hope this is so.

It is not right to believe that the key to the nationalization of film is to "carry forward and develop traditional Chinese aesthetics and its vision of art," or, from a futurist attitude based on the phenomenon of globalization, that "we should do our best to extend our vision to world art, rather than to the quintessence of Chinese culture alone" (Shao, "Summary of Casual Thinking on Film Aesthetics").

In fact,

> Every nation has its own pride, which is claimed to constitute the national characteristics that are distinct from other nations. Every city or district also has something it is proud of; every citizen also feels proud of what every other common person feels proud of. An individual feels the same way, and so does the nation that is made up of these individuals. Every national has a patriotic pride that is believed to be superior to others, and an anxious heart for victory that will never die (R. Loliee, *Short History of Comparative Literature*).

The proposal of film nationalization may have to do with this pride, but there is no doubt that it is related to the something that a nation is always proud of, and the superior patriotic pride, and the never-dying anxious heart for victory. One always calls the country one is brought up in the motherland. The motherland is a collective body of emotion, which is beyond the interests of classes, politics, and country. It is the solidarity of the national interests. This supreme emotion forms the emotional basis for the proposition of the nationalization of film.

# V     The Debate on Tradition and Innovation in Film

Broadly speaking, all the debates presented thus far are related to tradition and innovation in film, for this issue has long been both beginning and end for virtually all of them. Ironically, unlike these other subjects, however, the discussion of the relationship between innovation and tradition has no clear beginning. During the New Era, the reaffirmation of the policy to "let a hundred flowers blossom, let a hundred points of view contend" encouraged innovation. In addition, the open-door policy let Chinese filmmakers see at last the work of foreign colleagues denied them during the years of chaos. Inspired by what they saw, they began to pursue new directions for the medium. In 1984 the first works of the Fifth Generation directors reached the screen. Explorations such as *One and Eight, Yellow Earth,* and *On the Hunting Ground,* markedly different from traditional Chinese film, electrified film circles and sparked intense debate.

The heated discussions provoked by the innovations of the Fifth Generation ranged from newspaper articles to scholarly seminars. "The Debate on *Horse Thief*" by Xia Hong,[1] which made an in-depth assessment of this typical exploratory film, evoked a sharp response from his colleagues; a series of articles in Shanghai's *Wenhui Daily* between July and August 1986[2] severely criticized Xie Jin's model as a Chinese reproduction of Hollywood. This debate spread to Beijing, where the *Journal of Literature and Art* and many critics and filmgoers actively participated; however, despite its significant impact on film circles, it was somehow interrupted and suppressed by official will.[3] Shao Mujun in "The Road of Innovation in Chinese Cinema" claimed that Chinese film had always lacked innovation. His condemnation of most Chinese films, including the highly praised works of the 1930s and almost everything produced in the thirty years following Liberation in 1949, angered many filmmakers active during those periods.[4] Zhang Junxiang was the first to question and oppose him.[5] Later, at a symposium attended by elder artists in Shanghai, Shao's argument was severely criticized and rejected.[6] The editors of *Film Art* also held a symposium in Beijing and published a number of articles discussing the issue.[7] Overall, these discussions broadened the debate from that of exploratory film, Xie Jin's films, and the tradition of Chinese film to the sphere of world cinema and Chinese culture.

During the process of discussion, a number of disharmonic tones were heard, primarily from the filmmakers. Two are most representative. The first, which claimed that theory was misguiding filmmaking, blamed the confusion of ideas among young directors and the dissatisfaction of the audience with explorative films on the discussions about the new concept of film and the encouragement given to the Fifth Generation by theoretical circles. Theory, they complained, was muddled and prescriptive rather than descriptive.[8] The other argued that the issue of whether film was cinematic or theatrical was of little significance. According to these filmmakers, Wu Yigong among them, film was a popular art, an entertainment for the public; Chinese filmmakers "should be faithful to the people."[9]

These claims hurt the people in theory circles, who believed that every director had the right to choose his own style and themes, and had no obligation to follow any kind of theory. On the one hand, they criticized filmmakers who lacked the sense of subjectivity in an environment in which many opinions and schools existed; on the other, they began to reexamine the development of film theory in the New Era, and to discuss the features and values of film theory proper.[10] It was impossible to make a clear division between supporters and opponents. Based on the individual positions, cultural backgrounds, observations, and methods of the participants, a wide variety of personal ideas were expressed. Because of this, the debate does not appear as intense as the others given here, but it had greater significance, for it pointed to the continued deepening and development of theoretical discussions since 1979.

## NOTES

1. Xia Hong, "The Debate on *Horse Thief*," *Film Art*, July 1987.

2. Zhu Dake, "The Drawback of Xie Jin's Model," *Wenhui Daily*, July 18, 1986; Li Jie, "Xie Jin's Era Should End," *Wenhui Daily*, August 1, 1986.

3. See Xie Jin's "Speech at the Board Meeting of the China Film Association," *Film Art*, October 1986.

4. Shao Mujun, "The Road of Innovation in Chinese Cinema," *Film Art*, September 1986.

5. Zhang Junxiang, "A Letter to Comrade Xia Yan," *People's Daily*, November 3, 1986.

6. See "Also on the Road of Chinese Film Innovation," *New Filmscripts*, March 1987.

7. Li Shaobai, "My Understanding of Film Innovation," *Film Art*, December 1986; Dai Jinhua, "A Discussion with Shao Mujun," *Film Art*, December 1986; Zhong Dafeng, "Also on the Tradition and Innovation of Film," *Film Art*, December 1986; Yuan Wenshu, "Film Tradition and Innovation," *Film Art*, June 1987.

8. "Speeches at the Meeting of the Presidents of the Nation's Film Studios," *Film Reference*, March 1987.

9. Wu Yigong, "To Be a Loyal Artist to the People," *Film Reference*, May 1987.

10. Li Shaobai, Rong Weijing, and Li Shun, "Issues on Film Theory and Criticism," *Film Art*, February 1988; Shao Mujun, "Pure and Impure — An Analysis of the Direction of Contemporary Film Theory," *Film Art*, March 1988; Li Jisheng, "Theory, Reality, and Styles of Study," *Film Art*, August 1988.

# 13 THE DRAWBACK OF XIE JIN'S MODEL

Zhu Dake

translated by Hou Jianping

From the moment the shrew turned into a good mother in *Ah, Cradle* through the repeated efforts in *The Legend of Tianyun Mountain, The Herdsman,* and *Garlands at the Foot of the Mountain,* a style I call "Xie Jin's model" came into existence in Chinese film history and became one of the most noticeable cultural phenomena.

Xie Jin's model consists of a variety of both superficial and profound cultural codes. All follow some kind of common structure, function, and characteristics. An outstanding example is the magnification of emotions: the moral enthusiasm tactically centered around the protagonist and ingeniously extended to others evokes profuse tears from performers and audience alike, manipulating the audience to accept the conventional morality of the artist. Anyone with a bit of common sense will quickly discover that these obsolete aesthetic ethics designed to manipulate emotions have much in common with the dissemination of religion in the Middle Ages. This is a negation of the currently heated discussion of issues such as the independent consciousness and subjectivity, the contemporary characteristics of reform, and the rationalism of science. However, it is this manipulative technique that has made his films so immensely successful at the box office.

As in any models of popular culture, the moral code of Xie Jin is always arranged in a regular pattern. "The good wronged," "the discovery of values," "morality changed by persuasion," and "the ultimate triumph of good over evil" are the four principal topics. In *The Legend of Tianyun Mountain, The Herdsman,* and *Garlands at the Foot of the Mountain,* good people such as Luo Qun, Xu Lingjun, and Jin Kailai are unfortunately wronged and deprived of their human dignity. Inevitably following this, angelic women such as Feng Qingfeng and Li Xiuzhi arrive and comfort the lonely, suffering souls, eventually moving the selfish such as Zhao Mengshen and his mother, the weak such as Song Wei, and those who betrayed their friends, all the while tearing at the heartstrings of the audience. The power of the aforementioned morality always guarantees a happy ending in which good triumphs over evil. Luo Qun is rehabilitated, while Wu Yao is sent to study at the Party's institute, Xu Lingjun becomes a teacher and suddenly confronts a huge fortune brought by his father from America. Though Jing Kailai's case offers some deviation, Lei Zhen's angry words that "this is definitely wrong" lead to the inevitable happy ending. Xie Jin provides his audience with a magnificent moral fairy tale in which all social contradictions are resolved.

It doesn't take much to discover that Xie Jin's moral tales bear a close relationship to Hollywood films. Stories like *Cinderella* are among the major models of Hollywood films. They follow the pattern in which good is wronged (Cinderella is ill-treated by her stepmother); value is discovered (the prince falls in love with her at first sight); morality changes through persuasion (stepmother realizes her fault); and good conquers evil (Cinderella marries the prince). Many Hollywood classics such as *Waterloo Bridge* and *The Sound of Music* came out of such structures. No doubt these Hollywood films heavily influenced Chinese filmmaking, especially that of the Shanghai Film Studio. These films functioned as cultural colonialism and trained Chinese filmmakers to follow Hollywood aesthetics and conventions. However, only through Xie Jin's outstanding talent is the Hollywood model fully represented on the Chinese screen. This is why Xie Jin's works bear the identical imprint of popular film.

The point is not that Xie Jin's films have good commercial values. What bothers us more is that the morality Xie Jin favors has nothing at all to do with contemporary consciousness. His ethic belongs to a kind of traditional culture we call the Chinese national characteristic. This ethic becomes the racial foundation of Xie Jin's model. When it was extended without limitation and became the firm nucleus of his model, a kind of remodeled cinematic Ru school appeared on the screen.

The symbol of Xie Jin's Ru principle is his representation of women. They are amiable, kind, industrious, and intolerable. They follow "the three obediences and the four virtues" and are fully self-sacrificing. Their characteristics, the accumulation of standard images of women from the old days, are nothing other than the products of a patriarchal culture. Women, entirely dependent upon men, are used to discover and approve male values and to make men happy. Those small houses and yards filled with local color silently reveal the willful longing for the agrarian life in which men plough the fields and women sew the clothes. The comfortable family of the Middle Ages is the highest stage of human happiness. Consequently, the destruction of the family is the ultimate tragedy. By the same token, the most serious punishment given to people like Wu Yao is to allow Song Wei to leave home out of anger and make him lose his family. The aforementioned cohesive family can be presented under the code of patriotism: the fact that Xu Lingjun refuses to go abroad to inherit a large fortune not only deprives the nation of the opportunity to gain a large sum of foreign currency, but also reveals a kind of psychology that protects and adheres to the traditional way of life, a kind of peasants' dependency on family and land.

If we examine Xie Jin's films merely from a cinematic point of view, we will see that these films fit perfectly with the conventional laws of film: they have good commercial value, and meanwhile, they are able to satisfy the lack of morality and the wishes of their audience. They are both refined and popular, and are able to please everyone. However, if we go beyond the framework of film and look at his films within a broader cultural context, we will see that they deviate far from the evolutionary processes of Chinese culture and are a major retreat from the spirit of the May Fourth Movement. Thus to decipher the codes of Xie Jin's model and to reevaluate and surpass them critically becomes an urgent historical necessity.

# 14

# XIE JIN'S ERA SHOULD END

Li Jie

translated by Hou Jianping

Xie Jin's era should end. Although the cinematic aesthetics represented by Xie Jin's films is not, and for a while, will not be, on the passing record of history, I still want to raise this issue.

It is not because Xie Jin's films are inferior or mediocre that we challenge them. On the contrary, it is because Xie Jin's model, so intelligently used, has brought him a series of successes. Xie Jin is a rare and talented director. We are sorry to see that for various reasons, both subjective and objective, his talent has been brought lopsidedly into play, and a kind of psychological structure we call Xie Jin's model has been formulated. This model, unfortunately, cannot be characterized as a specific artistic style, but rather a model that panders to all kinds of tastes. Whenever we view Xie Jin's films, we feel uneasy, for we realize that this talented director nods from behind his screen in whatever direction will gain enthusiastic albeit blind cheers and applause. Such pandering tells us that Xie Jin's filmmaking is more a process in which he caters to audience desires than one in which he makes artistic explorations. He tries through various means to assess the audience's psychological expectations, then finds the prescription to combine perfectly the three major aspects of Chinese film — politics, entertainment, and art — the best way he can in his work. Patriotism is united with contentedness; concern for country is tied to personal suffering. A dramatic transformation will take place at the same time someone is wrongly condemned. His images of masculinity are sorrowful, but not sentimental, angry but not resentful, while his feminine figures are kind, amiable, and refined. Although tragedies do occur, the films always end happily so his audience can leave the theatre smiling after shedding a few tears.

I don't deny that such a model succeeds greatly with the support of conventional aesthetic tastes, but I'm sorry to see such an accomplished director as Xie Jin gain his success this way. Once the conventional cultural tastes of the nation, which emphasize mediocrity and close-mindedness, end, the market value of such a model will cease to exist. In an era in which national traditions are being challenged and replaced, such a film model, whether out of artistic conception or cultural perspective, will become an obstacle that hinders the development of film art and the replacement of cultural psychology by the new, and will eventually be discarded. If we say Xie Jin's model is a closed model of stability, then the next development of film art is to break through and surpass this stability. That is to say, we need to reinforce the politics, entertainment, and arts so smoothly combined in Xie Jin's model. On the one hand, we should make political or social reform films such as "New Star" comedies, movies, and thrillers, which serve primarily as entertainment; and on the other, we should also make artistic films such as *Yellow Earth* and *Black Cannon Incident*. Once the separation of the three functions is achieved in our films, the conventional shackles put on contemporary film will be cast off. Although Xie Jin is accepted as a successful filmmaker, his model unquestionably, in truth, is a tragic phenomenon in Chinese film. To put an end to Xie Jin's model and to stop his practice of filmmaking are different matters. It is based on the idea that this obsolete film model should be discarded that we propose: Xie Jin's era should end.

# 15 THE ROAD OF INNOVATION IN CHINESE CINEMA

Shao Mujun
translated by Hou Jianping

## INTRODUCTION

The problem of innovation has long been a crucial issue in film circles. *The Monologue of Innovation,* published in 1962, evoked a mighty uproar. Ju Baiyin, the author, was subjected to persecution because of it. By the time he was rehabilitated, he was seriously ill, and died soon afterward, never realizing his desire for innovation. Under the limitation of historical circumstances at the time, *The Monologue of Innovation* had to be written in a very difficult style — applying the sayings of the ancients to express the idea of eliminating clichés. Some basic issues such as the demand that film serve politics, and that only realism could be applied to filmmaking, which hindered innovation, were not questioned (it was out of the question) at all; on the contrary, they had to be repeatedly emphasized as the basis of his argument. However, *The Monologue of Innovation* definitely holds an important position in Chinese film history. As the first stepping stone to success on the road to innovation for Chinese socialist cinema, it is unquestionably an intelligent and courageous work. Its significant contribution cannot be ignored.

In 1979 "The Modernization of Film Language" rekindled the fires of innovation. Zhang Nuanxin and Li Tuo got their initial inspiration from Bai Jingsheng's proposal to "throw away the walking stick of drama," but in their article developed the argument further. In 1979 the political situation in China changed greatly, and the discussion of innovation appealed to everyone. Though the call for modernizing cinematiclanguage started an immediate debate, the key issue was not whether to eliminate clichés and open a new route, but how to go forward along the innovative path of socialist Chinese cinema. After a difficult spell of nine-teen years, the issue of cinematic innovation was finally raised from "muttering to itself" of necessity, to the open debate of the innovative road for Chinese cinema. A red line of theoretical ideas was constructed, initiated by "The Modernization of Film Language," and followed by issues concerning cinematic concepts, theatricality, literariness, nationalization, dramaturgy, and the like, which to a certain extent both stimulated the development of Chinese filmmaking in the New Era and put a limitation on it.

This debate reminds me of the historical debate in the West during the 1960s and 1970s between the aesthetics of montage and that of the long take. Until recently, we knew very little about the details of this debate, for during this period, we were trapped in the catastrophe of the Cultural Revolution. The primary resources of the time were impossible to get, so we could only get a survey from materials obtained after 1979. Generally speaking, our debate actually belongs to that between two aesthetic systems. Early in 1979, when the debate first began, the theories of André Bazin and Seigfried Kracauer had not circulated widely in China except for some introductory excerpts published in the reference journal, *Translations of Film Art,* in the 1960s. As for the criticism of realist aesthetics among Western film circles for the last decade or so, we know almost nothing. However, we may say that our thoughtful and explosive middle-aged generation caught the opposing points of the two systems intuitively. Although for a while it appeared that there was lack of a solid theoretical basis, and judgment of the drift of world cinema was quite subjective and arbitrary because the country had been closed for so long, yet the line for sailing forward was finally opened and the crucial problem of innovation for socialist Chinese cinema was raised.

## THE LIMITATIONS OF INNOVATION IN FILM

Chinese film is one part of world cinema. It is, on the one hand, independent, and has its own system; on the other, it has grown with the development of world cinema so as to contain and enhance its vitality. Thus a study of the innovative road of Chinese film cannot be done without relating to the experiences and current situation of world cinema, with special attention paid to Western film.

Why emphasize Western film? Because all the new trends, new phenomena, or new devices, no matter on forms or content, originatefrom Western countries that dominate world cinema. There are three major reasons for this. First, in the advanced capitalist countries of the West, the severe competitive environment dictates that to create something new is the major strategy for survival in this cruel world. Such an environment makes it necessary for people to pass each day with some sort of innovation. Second, legislation and legal administration are emphasized and executed. Everything under the protection of law can be done without interference. Third, their science and technology are highly advanced. The innovation of film form and representational devices relies, to a great extent, on the development of science and technology. The detailed analyses and significant discoveries of contemporary Western science and technology on the intelligence and psychological structures of human beings, and on the organization of society, are without doubt very helpful in presenting in art human life in depth. Of course, we should be critical when we learn from the West.

To examine Western film from the perspective of innovation, we should pay attention to one of their experiences: the limitations of innovation in film. To face its limitations is very important for those determined to innovate in film, for they can save their energies, avoid unnecessary waste, and reduce their useless worries and make them more realistic. The limitations of film innovation refer to the reasonable boundaries that are beyond innovation to surpass, compared with those of other art forms.

First of all is the collectivity of filmmaking and its audience. Looking at the film history of the West, we find that there has been a continuous testing of these reasonable limitations, reflected in the confrontations of commercial films with art films, genre films with directors' films. Commercial films and genre films are actually identical concepts, and directors' film is an accurate definition for art film. So-called commercial films refer to those released in theatres and on television by way of commercial distribution. The term is not degrading. Only in the eyes of the narrow-minded who look down upon commerciality is the term unacceptable. These people insist on an eloquent term that has nothing to do with trade so as to maintain their psychological balance. Commercial film as a general term certainly also contains films low in quality and vulgar in content. But this is nothing — the existence of low-quality products does not mean all the products must be poor. As to the nature of the genre film, it is a film that aims for a large audience and is formed and controlled by market information. In the 1950s an experiment was made with nongenre films — assorted genres — in America. Musicals contained criminal cases, comedies contained philosophical ideas, and science fictions criticized politics. Since the audience didn't buy them, they proved to be failures and were treated as a lesson. The making of art film is an effort to turn filmmaking into an individual activity, as is the case with most other arts. The art film does not go through commercial distribution and appears removed from commerciality. However, it is a pity that art theatres also have ticket-selling windows and people cannot go inside without paying money.

In Western film circles, the art film has always been in an inferior position since its intent is to go against the collectivity of filmmaking and the film audience. It is impossible to imagine that a film that is successful both in form and content can be made without the cooperation of a screenwriter, director, cinematographer, art designer, makeup man, costume designer, soundmen, and grips. The director may be in charge of the team, but unlike a composer or painter, he cannot simply do as he pleases. Thus, if filmmaking were individualized, it is most unlikely the practice would lead down a common path. Terms such as *nonplot* and *independent* become inseparable from the art film. In the West, people involved in making art films are mostly well-educated professional photographers, art designers, or painters, with a small number of young and talented people not fortunate enough to enter the film industry. Consequently, the nonnarrative philosophy of space and time, and formal interests dominate the Western art film. However, these films are unpopular even among the highly educated in advanced Western countries.

Except for the functioning of the deep-rooted idea that to watch a film is to seek entertainment, another reason for this situation is the special element of the psychology of the audience. The difference between film and any other pictorial art is that film only exists when its images are projected on the screen, whereas the other forms are static and can be read repeatedly. When people enjoy nonnarrative pictorial arts, their pleasure comes mostly from the imagination stimulated by repeated viewing of the artwork, something that film, with its images constantly changing, cannot provide. Thus individualized filmmaking is against not only the collectivity of filmmaking, but also that of film enjoyment. This dictates that the art film will always be in an inferior position with regard to commercial film. That is to say, commercially, the art film will never become a dominant force in Western film; meanwhile, it often enhances the attractiveness of commercial film by losing its artists to that side. This can be seen in all the artistic movements of the West — the leading artists end up making commercial films. This has happened so often in Western film history, I will not list any examples here.

Why mention all these clichés while addressing innovation? The point is to tell those filmmakers who are determined to get involved in innovation not to act without constraints and not to forget the characteristics of cause and effect when it is related to the collectivity of filmmaking and film appreciation. It is also wrong to think that only directors can carry out innovation. Some of our filmmakers gave up their own professions so as to become directors. To do this actually exploits their weak points while it avoids using their expertise. It is not good for them or anyone else.

Filmmaking needs a large amount of money and labor. This is another reasonable limitation of film innovation. However, when the film studio is controlled by capitalists, the economic elements sometimes become shackles to the filmmakers and may not be fair. Every new film movement in the West began by opposing these commercial shackles. When young people are determined to commit themselves to filmmaking, and yet cannot find enough economic support to realize their ideas, they often initiate their struggle by using strategies that are not expensive. It is not accidental that all Western film movements started with documentaries. In the West it is impossible to expect a film producer to put up large sums of money so unestablished youngsters can realize their dreams. In most other arts, the unestablished can prove themselves and gain trust through their work; only in film must such trust be gained before the making of a film. In order to show their filmmaking talents, these young people make short documentary films, which are much less expensive, since they need not pay for script, actors, and locations. Once their talents are recognized, the doors of filmmaking are open to them and, at the same time, their sense of filmmaking is immediately filled with the profit-making principle.

On the other hand, in the West profits come from the box office; thus whatever an audience might enjoy can be made without limitation. There is no doubt that vulgar and low films are one result of this; nonetheless, some new and original work may also be produced. In other words, economic shackles certainly kill many good ideas, but for those obsessed with presenting themselves or mysterious philosophical ideas or playing with forms, these constraints may be reasonable. Because of this, I never wholly endorse new film movements in the West and give a critical analysis to protest economic limitations.

## FILMMAKING BEFORE AND AFTER LIBERATION

Cinema was imported to China from abroad. Thus Chinese cinema had to go through a considerably long period of imitation. Two aspects of Chinese film history before 1949 deserve attention. First, Chinese film had no independent development at all, but on the contrary, was closely related to the traditions of theatre; second, it never went through an aesthetic movement — all practice was carried out around the issue of politics. The former confined Chinese cinema within the tradition, and the latter overwhelmed it with the utilitarian concepts of politics. Obviously, neither was good for filmmaking.

In *The Monologue of Innovation*, Ju Baiyin writes that the 1930s was an "era of vigorous innovation" for Chinese cinema. It is true that many people think highly of films of the 1930s. The attack on "the black line of 1930s' films" during the Cultural Revolution also functioned as a counterforce that raised their position. Some foreign scholars not only agree with this, but also believe that Chinese cinema of the 1930s formed a realistic style that surpassed in artistic achievement the films of Italian Neorealism that flourished in the late 1940s. I remain skeptical. Research into Chinese film history cannot be isolated from the general historical background of the development of world cinema. As we know, in the early 1930s film as a newly developed art was violently shaken by the coming of sound. The sudden emergence of sound pushed aside the few artistic experiences accumulated since film's birth. Many well-known film artists protested loudly, and regarded the coming of sound as a destroyer of film art. They regretfully believed that at a time when silent film had not yet reached maturity, the interference from sound would end the potential of silent film forever. The confusion lasted nearly ten years. Thus observing the development of world cinema, no matter in the West or in the USSR, no significant works appeared before the 1930s, to say nothing about a climate for art.

It was not until the late 1930s that considerably mature films gradually began to make their appearance. Sound film was introduced to China in the early 1930s. It, too, went through two stages: technically, sound on disk and on film; artistically, dialogue in part and in whole. Of course, Chinese film of the time had little artistic experience, and suddenly to apply sound required a period of experimentation. Under such general circumstances, it is hard for me to imagine that the 1930s in China would be a glorious time for film art. On the other hand, as we all know, when people from left wing literature stepped into film circles, they had no filmmaking experience at all. Those works highly praised as progressive films of the 1930s, to a great extent, were maiden works. I don't mean to say that maiden works cannot be significant, but it is abnormal that "an era of flourishing innovation" that holds an outstanding position in film history is marked by a group of maiden works.

Another aspect we should note is that when people spoke highly of these films, they didn't consider their artistic value; instead, they thought of the screenplay. If we examine the situation at the time, we readily discover that many scripts by left wing writers were directed by unknowns. Obviously it would be inaccurate to make judgments of film history based merely on the plots of scripts. We are still able to see such highly praised films of the 1930s as *Plunder of Plums and Peaches, Crossroads, Street Angel, Song of the Fisherman, The Big Road,* and *New Women.* It's not difficult to see that they were full of dramatic coincidences and misunderstandings, full of overwhelmingly staged performances, idealized characters, and frank preaching. As works of art, the progressive films of the 1930s lagged far behind those of the 1940s, not to mention the Italian Neorealist films.

The reason why the progressive films hold such an important role in Chinese film history is that the Communist leadership began to function early in the 1930s. This allowed Chinese films gradually to obtain a critical view of the society and eliminated the foul atmosphere from film circles. However, the history of film is not merely that of political struggle. It couldn't be considered innovation if those with new ideas lacked the ability to present them as strong images on the screen. Consequently, it seems to me, to put the progressive films of the 1930s in such a high position is not a measure of their artistic values. "Politics first" or even "politics alone makes things happen this way" are the wrong criteria for judgment. Thus I think that the true flourishing of Chinese film before Liberation came in the late 1940s. Considering the situation of world cinema and the experiences of Chinese filmmakers at that time, it was only natural that, after World War II, the Chinese contributed a group of considerably mature films that effectively combined ideas and art into a whole. Actually, films such as *Along the Shonghua River, Eight Thousand Li of Moon and Cloud, Spring in a Small Town, Spring River Flows East, Myriad of Lights,* and *Crows and Sparrows* are far superior to those that preceded them in terms of critical ideas and artistic techniques. This is really amazing.

After Liberation, the objective circumstances for filmmaking changed radically. Theoretically, the fact that workers, peasants, and soldiers became the protagonists in films should be considered a thorough and timely innovation. But what I understand as innovation is not that the protagonists represented new social status and spoke new ideas. Such innovation seems oversimplified, for the images of workers, soldiers, and peasants could be depicted on screen and revolutionary words could be expressed through them, but not as a result of the artists' efforts — it was a gift presented by the power controlled by the working people. From early Liberation to the late 1970s, Chinese film was in a stagnant, even suffocating period in terms of innovation. Aside from the chaotic era of the Cultural Revolution, the main reasons for this stagnation are the following:

First, it was a result of disrespect for the law of art, which, simply defined, is that everything should revolve around the subjects of art. Feudal monarchies never respected this law, for they ordered their subjects to write poems regardless of their true feelings, which is why so few were good enough to be handed down through generations. To create a work of art is to import, contrast, filter, arrange, and export the perceptions of the artist. If the artist doesn't have enough knowledge stored in his mind, even if some immediate message could be forced into it, it could only be brought out as an imitation of the original, the so-called formulistic work. Soon after Liberation, film as the most influential mass medium received a great deal of attention from the Party and the government. Filmmakers of the time partly came from the "liberated" areas where they had experienced work in the countryside and a life full of battles but no filmmaking, and partly from areas under Kuomintang control where they had filmmaking experience but knew nothing about the life of the workers, peasants, and soldiers. But under the slogan that art must serve politics and the working people, these experiences were not only put aside, but were regarded as unorthodox and constantly criticized. Those just starting to work in film didn't care much to learn. They seemed to believe that they could create artistic images naturally by drawing upon the life experiences they already had. The result was that useful experiences were ignored and the good-for-nothing were put into effect. This ideology of utilitarianism, which ignored the law of art, formed gradually during the first eight years after Liberation, developed further during the antirightist and antileftist movements, and reached its climax during the Cultural Revolution. How could the idea of innovation be considered under such circumstances?

Second, Chinese film was under the pertinacious influence of the Soviet model of literature and art in the late 1940s. Soviet literature and art were deeply entrenched in the ditch of dogmatism after World War II. The principle of nonconflicting, political models made Soviet films dull and artificial, and artistic images were replaced by sociological formulas.

In the surge of learning from the USSR, these extremely wrong models of literature and art were mechanically taken over and looked up to as the standard. Even worse was that when the Soviets began to correct the dogmatism during the mid-1950s, China, under the guidance of antirevisionism, still persistently carried out and further developed the theory that regarded art as the servant of politics. The severe damage and strong effects of this, I'm afraid, have not been completely eliminated even to the present day.

The third reason does not need much articulation. In the first thirty years after Liberation, China closed its door and restricted its way of thinking. The constant movements of antibourgeois and antirevisionist thought not only didn't provide people with more knowledge of Marxism, but on the contrary, extended the concept of feudal ideas under the cover of revolution. All the passive aspects of traditional Chinese culture and ways of thinking such as restraint, unity, and similarity became sufficient weapons to limit minds. Under such circumstances, innovation is the most dangerous act.

To say that the thirty years after Liberation was a stagnant period for film innovation doesn't mean there were no innovative works at all. In those thirty years, there were some peaceful situations in which the leftist wind held still, or some faked openings whose purpose was to "lure the snake out of the hole in order to kill it." Some innovative and artistic works appeared during such gaps. Though their creators were punished more severely afterward, at least they wrote a glorious page in Chinese film history. What is noticeable is that the themes of such admittedly innovative works as *New Year's Sacrifice, The Lin Family Store, The Song of Youth, Early Spring, Stage Sisters, Lin Tse-Hsu,* and *The Opium War* are almost all about history or life in the Kuomintang regions. The workers, soldiers, and peasants, who should have left a permanent image of the heroic characters of the time, disappeared soon after their appearance. Of course, there were exceptions like *The Battle of Shanggan Ling* and *Li Shuangshuang,* but they were rare.

Obviously, the law of art was functioning. These films had innovative qualities, for they not only expressed new ideas, but also created vivid and lively images that were reflections of the times. Certainly the new ideas we require of an artist are mainly those that have not been expressed before. Today when human thought has reached an advanced stage, it is overly critical to ask that artists say something unique. Lu Xun's saying is very reasonable: "The words of artists are actually those of society, except that the artists are very sensitive and express their feelings ahead of others." To explain humanity and the universe, to explain the essence of society — these things belong to the sphere of logic, and in such matters, philosophers and social scientists are much wiser than artists. Great artists are not necessarily great thinkers. Balzac and Tolstoy as thinkers are far from great. To call Griffith and Chaplin great thinkers would probably result in laughter, but we have to admit the tremendous innovative abilities of these film artists. There are people who are both artists and thinkers, but they are few. So we can't regard unique ideas as a general prerequisite for artistic innovation. To speak of it too abstrusely, people would stay away from it in awe; lacking self-confidence, they would first of all lose their courage to innovate. The advantages of artists are their abilities of perceptual thinking; that is to say, they are good at putting thoughts expressed by others, ideas that already exist, and the works of society into real images of life full of the artists' personal feelings and style.

## THE FIVE GENERATIONS

The success of innovation in art rests on the artists themselves. Filmmaking has many restrictions from external conditions and is under even greater pressure from economic and political situations, as well as from social conventions. The passive position of working artists often forces them to follow the mainstream, distort their personalities, and change their styles. The road of filmmaking is full of twists. It is the same in China and abroad. But the success or failure of innovation for filmmaking depends crucially on the artists themselves. Grim circumstances can certainly stifle the urge to innovate, but a favorable situation can't automatically fill artists with innovative ideas.

There had never been a favorable situation for filmmaking until the late 1970s when the move to liberate thought began and the open-door policy was established. Film circles then were just like any other intellectual circles. Most people were still full of doubts even while they were visibly pleased. It was only possible for the middle-aged and old generations who had rich experiences with political movements to treat the apparently new situation with the attitude of observers, and they seldom took any reckless actions. Thus the task of rekindling the fires of innovation in film circles historically and naturally rested on the shoulders of the youngest generation, who were barely in their thirties. Most of these young people, who already had children, had worked in film circles for more than ten years, with their lofty aspirations unrealized, and thus had fires of indignation burning inside — they were waiting anxiously for the chance to stretch their muscles and joints and display their talents.

They had heard about the horrors of the antirightist movement, and observed the cruelty of the overthrow, but they didn't have personal experiences, so they didn't have as much lingering fear as their elders. It was they who opened a new road for Chinese film. However, they had their own shortcoming: they didn't have enough education in art, especially in film art. Of course, this was not their fault; they grew up in a closed culture. The generation that preceded them only knew a little about Hollywood films of the 1930s and 1940s; what could be expected of them?

These young people have been called the fourth generation over the last few years. By the way, I don't know who originally created the division of the so-called five generations of Chinese film directors. It is said the five generations are directors of silent films, directors of sound films of the 1930s and 1940s, directors between the period of post-Liberation and the end of the Cultural Revolution, directors after the Cultural Revolution, and recent graduates of the Beijing Film Institute (the first after the Cultural Revolution) in 1982. This division has a truly Chinese character, but it is not scientific. To regard the year a director began to make films independently as the basis of division cannot explain his characteristics. Within a given period of time, directors may form some common characteristics due to features of the era, but artists, especially talented ones, change with the passing of time. As time goes by, their characteristics may disappear, to be replaced by new ones that are the same as those of the next generation. For instance, some people concluded that the fourth generation was especially good at thinking and especially interested in learning from others and abroad. Doesn't the third generation in the New Era have the same traits? Maybe their way of thinking is different and their emphasis on using others' experiences is not the same, but this would probably be true even within the same generation.

The judgment on the Fifth Generation is even more excessive. Almost all the features (such as explosive spirit, a keen sense of time, a serious attitude toward history, and a new vision of film) that an outstanding artist possesses are attributed to them. That is really outrageous. If we examine the films made in the last decade, we will see that films with the above-mentioned characteristics were not all made by the Fifth Generation, and all works of the Fifth Generation didn't have these characteristics. Generally speaking, from a global view, a more reasonable division is the old generation and the young one, or old directors and the new. Here, first of all, old and new doesn't only refer to age. Werner Fassbinder died at age thirty-eight, but had long been an old director; Frank Schaffner (director of *Patton*) didn't start filmmaking until he was forty-three, and he could only be regarded as a new director at the time. Cesare Zavattini, an old screenwriter of forty-four, and Vittorio De Sica, an old director of forty-five, created Neorealism. We cannot say they were not full of an exploring spirit. Second, the old and young keep changing. The old today were young some years ago, and the young today will be old some years later, and another generation will appear. Thus there are no definite and common characteristics of a generation, but only those of a certain school or individual. The division of five generations is not scientific, and what is more, it is easy to create separations and sects in film circles, and extremely harmful.

A group of new directors made its appearance in the late 1970s. The first steps they took in innovation basically belonged to the sphere of techniques. There were two inevitable phenomena: one was that the ideology of the time and their own insights couldn't allow them to penetrate deeper into real life; the other was that after a long period of isolation, the sudden opportunity to glimpse world cinema naturally led them to be attracted first of all by new (to them) techniques. As luck would have it, the films they saw first were those of the 1960s, when technical innovation was in its most flourishing period. The 1960s was an era in which the position of realistic aesthetics was rising and the wave of modernism in film was in its second vogue. In order to adjust to irrational, plotless, and impersonal content, the conventional structure and time of theatre were shattered. Devices such as flashbacks, optical distortions, jump cuts, slow motion, and the split screen were all used to alter time and space, and to depict the inconsistent stream of consciousness; and the strategies of the long shot, and simple editing techniques, were used to imitate the stream of real life. All these techniques were extremely popular for a while. However, they had already declined by the end of the 1970s, when Western film saw the rejuvenation of montage and the restoration of plot. Yet in China, these devices were not only new and amazing, but had a strong attraction.

The attraction came from the possibilities of those new techniques that could create fantasy and imitate the stream of consciousness, and the ideological basis for these forms was temporarily ignored. Ever since its first appearance, Chinese film has been tied indissolvably with artificiality. Their insistence upon political propaganda, and their symptoms of theatricality, make Chinese film go further down into the ditch of the artificial. Filmmakers can do nothing about the policies concerning literature and art; they can only turn to art itself to find a way out. Thus it was very natural and reasonable that Chinese filmmakers launched their first attack on film form, moving closer to realistic aesthetics and trying to cure the disease of falsehood.

In 1979 a group of films including *Xiao Huar, Troubled Laughter,* and *Reverberations of Life* appeared on the Chinese screen. Many new technical devices were used and some forbidden themes, such as the dual nature of contemporary Chinese intellectuals and the pressures on governance on human nature, were preliminarily touched upon. Under the circumstances of the time, these films were unquestionably fresh and new, but their rigid accumulation of techniques created a sense of superficiality. At this time, the debate initiated by "The Modernization of Film Language" performed a crucial function in filmmaking. As I mentioned at the beginning of this chapter, the key issue of the debate was how Chinese cinema could travel the road of innovation. As the debate went deeper, the filmmakers were constantly adjusting their steps and searching for the best road to take to make Chinese film a combination of high and popular art, and an entertainment both inside and outside of China.

## FILMMAKING IN THE 1980s

The first adjustment was to surpass the level of technical devices and to explore new themes and philosophical ideas. Cinematic technique is an amazing field. Film is a visual and aural medium, and control of the relationship between the two provides film with a territory of technical innovation that no other art form can achieve. Because of advanced scientific technology, film not only has the ability to depict the redemption of reality, but also has the ability to distort reality. Compared to other arts, the technical devices of film are the easiest to master. The techniques of language, painting, music, sculpture, and dance all take a long time to learn, for they are not technological processes. They require the artist to obtain the skill personally. Film techniques are different — they are a pure process of technology and can be carried out completely by machines. The skill of the artist rests on whether he can handle them properly or not. Thus for filmmakers, to make good use of the technological devices, especially to play games of pure form, is the least difficult.

In the history of Chinese film, all technical devices were imported from abroad due to the backwardness of science and technology in China. The rejuvenation of Chinese film in the late 1970s was another climax of the importation of technology. The reason for this I have already mentioned. Fortunately, its vogue soon declined. Both the old directors, who had always had a clear view of technology, and the new directors, who had been driven to this road by an unconquerable urge to innovate, soon turned to the exploration of new themes, profound studies of humanity, and deeper thought about the real life of our nation. Maybe because formalism had always had a bad reputation in China, this change came quickly and naturally. When Chinese film entered the 1980s, it was enjoyable to see the appearance of *The Legend of Tianyun Mountain* and *Sha'ou,* two milestones of the New Era. Both surpassed the level of merely using technological devices for their own sake, touched the forbidden field of theme, and explored the essence of life with a different concept of film.

The second adjustment was to surpass the level of the concept of film and explore the sphere of culture. *The Legend of Tianyun Mountain,* which started the vogue of innovation in the late 1970s, provided us with an important message: the potentials of conventional form are far from exhausted. During the sixty years before and after Liberation, Chinese film was coerced by politics, and didn't have the chance to develop the traditional principles of classical films such as pattern, speed, harmony, imitation, hidden techniques, and calm control over the audience to perfection, so that a new way needed to be found. *The Legend of Tianyun Mountain* is highly dramatic, and its use of the law of conflict is natural and obvious. Because it bravely touched the contradictions that exist in real life, its dramaturgy not only didn't seem false; on the contrary, it reinforced the sense of reality. Meanwhile, the appearance of *Sha'ou* represented the start of another style: it was no longer visual images of ready-made plots, but the revealing of the director's senses, imagination, observations, and perceptions. The way to catch the audience's attention and feelings is not to excite their enthusiasm, but to play upon their thoughts. *Sha'ou* experimented with the long shot, but its use surpassed the level of pure technique — its purpose was to depict the psychology of the protagonist in the continuity of time and space.

The practice of filmmaking in 1980 revealed that the innovation of Chinese film in the New Era was developing on two different levels, which were running parallel and more often than not were helping one another. In the first few years of the 1980s, some outstanding films paid more attention to the real depiction of details and used many location shots, though their story structures were still highly dramatic, and those films that put more emphasis on a realistic style didn't neglect the artistic ability of expressionistic devices such as montage and subjective music. As a matter of fact, this is a common phenomenon in world cinema. In recent years, the introduction and research of foreign films was done not without being subjective and biased; as a result, the misunderstanding arose that the so-called modernist concept of film (or new concept) had already replaced the traditional concept of film. This initiated a series of unnecessary debates.

It turned out to be wrong to take the concept of film as the standard for criticizing the art. The concept of film is the cognition of its characteristics and of the relationship between film and the other arts. The cognition can be different with different people: some put more emphasis on theatre, some on literature, or on painting, or deny the relationship with other arts. But since film is the subject, there is no way to depart from the combination of sight and sound. I have always advocated that the concept of film be diverse, emphasizing that though the concept of film is a key issue of film aesthetics, for it is useful in exploring the function of other arts depicted in film, it is not the basic principle in filmmaking. Filmmakers should use the forms they think are most applicable in expressing what they are most familiar with and what they want to say, ignoring the interference of others' concept of film.

The practice of filmmaking in the 1980s indicates that the controversies about concept of film have not hindered the flourishing of filmmaking. Theoretically, the new concept of film (that is, the concept of film form based on the realistic aesthetics of Bazin and Kracauer) is prevailing, but filmmaking is not restricted by it. Not all films have shown the intention to weaken or eliminate plot; the depiction of characters is still the main device for portraying the image. When we see more and more foreign films, we find without difficulty that dramaturgy is not at all a forbidden phenomenon, and the restoration of montage and plot is not someone's imagining. As Christian Metz already pointed out in 1978: "the contribution of new film lies in its enrichment of the content of cinematic narration" ("Modern Film and Its Narration," *World Cinema*, 1986, p. 62). In the few years following 1980, a group of innovative films (including *Love-forsaken Corner, Rickshaw Boy, My Memories of Old Beijing, As You Wish, Garlands at the Foot of the Mountain, Yellow Earth, Black Cannon Incident, Spring in Autumn*, etc.) were not fettered by considering whether the concept of film was old or new; they were the vanguard of the time, the great achievement of a thorough and detailed analysis of Chinese culture (including the way of life, thinking, and responding). They greatly enriched the content of cinematic narration and represented the character of contemporary Chinese film.

The third adjustment was to go beyond the level of redemption and touch the level of expression. To go beyond redemption is an important turning point on the road of innovation in the New Era.

Redemption as a concept of film aesthetics contains a special meaning that the whole source is real, which is not completely the same as that of the other arts. Bazin has a well-known saying: "Between reality and its redemption, there is only the mechanism of things functioning." The idea evoked much criticism. The argument of its opponents is that the eye of the camera is also both objective and subjective. This is an oversimplification. The important fact is that the "mechanism" Bazin pointed out is the only possibility in cinematography. Ten artists cannot paint exactly the same portraits of one person under the same condition, but ten photographers can take the same photos of one person under the same conditions. This possibility is the basic principle of realistic aesthetics, for it doesn't reject the selection before taking the picture, it only objects to "artificial creative interference" during photographing and processing.

The political initiation of realistic aesthetics that developed after World War II was the orientation of ideology in Western film, which actually was progressive. After the overthrow of the Gang of Four, the new generation of filmmakers in China found the positive function in this theory to fight the artificial realism of Chinese film, and meanwhile they also noticed that in its emphasis on objectivity, there were certain points that were non-Marxist. Therefore, the reconstructed theory of redemption performed a useful function in their filmmaking. Many films (including films made according to the traditional concept) appeared to contain some sequences that accurately depicted reality. This was no doubt a great moment in Chinese film, for before that, Chinese film had basically been on the level of the diagram — it could neither seek for the reality of the whole resource, nor could it seek for the necessary personal feelings on the level of expression.

However, if Chinese film remained on the level of redemption, it would be tragic. The crucial fault of the theory of redemption is its exclusion of imagination in depiction. Real is better than false, but real is not equivalent to beautiful. To say that the life of art lies in reality is not accurate. Aristotle believed that the image of a painting should be more beautiful than the real person. Hegel stressed that the beauty of art should be superior to the natural, for the beauty of art is the beauty created out of a person's heart. Tolstoy believed that to overemphasize the real would destroy the main condition of beauty — fantasy. These are some well-known opinions with which we are familiar, but they were rejected as the "traditional concept of art" in the 1960s. To separate film from the traditional concept of art was wrong, and it was also criticized in the West. If an artwork contained only the real, it would be just like a body without blood, flesh, and soul; thus the life of art unquestionably lies in the rich imagination based on reality.

Before the invention of film, Western literature and art had already begun to change from redemption, which was based on the theory of imitation, to expression, which emphasized the creator's personal feelings. The fact that Western literature and art turned to expressionism had its profound source in cultural pessimism; it was not merely a fear of the imitative ability of film. Because of this, expressionism soon penetrated into film. However, when film was still a flowering industry entertaining the public, expressionism could not prevail. Film had its own way of development; it could not leap from childhood to adulthood. The accumulation of expressionism didn't appear until the late 1950s, especially in the films of Ingmar Bergman, Jean-Luc Godard, Michelangelo Antonioni, Federico Fellini, and Alain Resnais. They put emphasis on expressing, directly and indirectly, their personal views of life, creating a new model for the modern Western film — "expressionism based on redemption." Their films (or the written record of their films) of the 1950s and 1960s were the main works that the new Chinese directors in the early 1980s used as examples to follow. In them it is possible that, while these filmmakers favored realistic aesthetics, they also noticed issues of expressionism.

The latest adjustment in innovation for Chinese filmmakers was to experiment with expression based on redemption. It was not so evident before 1984 when a group of younger directors made their first films. Obviously, many of these were determined to break through the limitation of mere redemption, creating sequences that were not intended to depict the real, but were full of personal feelings and imagination.

## THE FUTURE

It has been only ten years since the overthrow of the Gang of Four. It is less than eight years since Chinese film set foot on the road of innovation. It is difficult to predict the future. With the acceleration of social evolution, the circulation of messages will speed up accordingly. Foreigners have already started to discuss the prospect that in the contemporary society of fast communications, the tools of communication will be non-mass media, and the audience will be decentralized. To what extent can these changes influence the features and direction of filmmaking? There have been no concrete symbols to seek out, thus far, even in the West. The popularization of VCRs and cable TV, at least, won't eliminate the similar taste for pleasure of most people in a given period of time. Based on its standard of material production now, China seems far away from the time of an instantly changing culture. Of course, it is good to have a farsighted vision, but to be divorced so completely from reality may create the impression of parading a fashionable vocabulary. Observing the current encouraging situation for innovation in film, I think the following two aspects are worth mentioning.

First, innovation in Chinese film should regard the emphasis on modernity as its principal line. What is the modernity of film? The development of technology may bring new possibilities for technical devices, which can certainly add a modern tone to film, but it can't automatically enhance the modernity of the medium. The new technologies can only transmit information more thoroughly and more diversely, but they themselves are not messages. The modernity is that of the message the film communicates.

China is, and will be for quite a while, in evolution from the old to the new. The main content of reform is the renewal of ideology. Our nation has an ancient history. It has never gone through the advanced period of a commodity economy and has always carried the feudal concepts of a patriarchical clan system and the heavy burden of an agrarian culture whose main ideology is that of small producers. In our contemporary daily life, our structures of concepts, ideas about values, social psychology, models of thinking, moral principles, aesthetic tastes, behavioral principles, or way of living, all are more or less combined with a layer of feudal filth. The loud attack on bourgeois thought in the last few decades didn't touch this layer at all. On the contrary, it had the side effect of reinforcing it to a certain degree, which made the urgent project of elimination even more difficult now. Our film should participate actively in this tough project.

As we all know, there has been a vogue for culture over the last few years in China. People realize more and more clearly that we must put traditional Chinese culture against the vast background of world culture and reexamine it there. Frequently using a conceited manner such as saying "the Chinese have their own . . ." to treat new concepts of thinking is not only ridiculous but also harmful.

Second, Chinese film must break through the state of a uniform style and absorb and use every available device in every possible way to further the flourishing of Chinese socialist film.

In 1979 I was worried that the new generation's interest in the new concept, such as the structure of nondramatic films, might lead them astray toward modernism. However, it is ironic that what I worried about didn't happen. On the contrary, the problem now is that their imaginations are restricted by realism. It is not that the development of realism is frightening, but the uniform concept of realism hinders the development of a variety of artistic styles. Of course, we should not cast away realism, but neither should we allow it to become a strong conventional force that dominates everything. After suffering enough from the narrow concept of realism, the USSR has already turned to the open system of socialist realism, and greatly enlarged the realm of socialist filmmaking. We should be enlightened by this.

Many of us regret that within Chinese socialist film, different styles or schools have never appeared. This is a consequence of the long-term uniformity of filmmaking methods. Recently, new names such as "Western film" or "city film" appeared, intending to create some unique style or school, but I'm afraid it is only a concept of type, that is to say, a kind of genre formulated according to certain themes and locations, like the American Western, which can only be a genre, never a school. To let a hundred flowers blossom instead of one flower in a hundred colors, our vision of art has to become wider and wider.

It takes courage to be innovative — this call began in the Middle Ages. Today innovation needs intelligence, but for the time being, it also needs tenacity and will power. The old generation of directors will treasure the coming future. With their superiority of rich experience and accomplishment, and their willingness to absorb the new nutrition of art, they will make a new contribution to Chinese socialist film. The young generation of film directors, with their diligence in thinking and bravery in exploration, will forever be the main force of innovation.

I place great hopes on Chinese socialist film.

# 16 FILM TRADITION AND INNOVATION

Yuan Wenshu

translated by Li Xiaohong

Chinese film developed in a unique situation. Art was despised in semifeudal and semicolonial China. Film even more so. Those who worked in film circles were ideologically backward, led a dissolute life, and were isolated from the new cultural circles. As recorded in *The History of Chinese Film,* (Cheng Jihua, ed.) film was imported from abroad in 1896, which is why even now some still call it an import. The Chinese began to make their own films in 1906. As soon as such an import came into China, it went into the hands of merchants and capitalists whose sole purpose was making a profit. In order to make money, they made many films that propagated feudalism, superstitions, gods and spirits, and heroes of the martial arts, like *Hongfen Kulou, Heiyi Nuxia, The Burning of Hongliansi,* and other traditional operas.

Under these circumstances, the Chinese Communist Party in 1932 set up a film delegation, headed by Xia Yan, to work with the medium. Other members included Ah Ying, Zheng Boqi, Situ Huimin, and Shi Linghe. Working as consultants, they helped write scripts whose content focused on fighting feudal suppression, exposing the dark side of the old society, and relating stories about the sufferings of the lower class. By doing this, not only were they able to unite with some directors who understood film, they were also well received by their audience. At the same time, they brought economic benefits to the leaders of the film companies. Thus old Chinese films took on a new look, and were redirected onto the road for the people and for the progress of the society.

In those hard times, they made such films as *Wild Torrent, Spring Silkworm, Three Modern Girls, Street Angel, Crossroads, Jiemeihua, The Big Road,* and others. The films they made later include *Myriad of Lights, Eight Thousand Li of Moon and Cloud, The Spring River Flows East, A Beautiful Woman, Crows and Sparrows,* and others. These well-received films told of the bitter life inflicted on the Chinese by the invasion of the Japanese imperialists. This was the immortal contribution made to Chinese film by the cultural movement of the leftists. However, the real foundation of Chinese film was established after the founding of the People's Republic of China in 1949 when two film groups, one from the Kuomintang-controlled area and the other from the liberated area, met. In 1951 the first "film month" of new China showed twenty-six new films. This was the first wave of Chinese film.

During the seventeen years after 1949, themes of Chinese films became more diversified, and the films more artistically mature, as in *Bridge, Chinese Sons and Daughters, The White-Haired Girl, Metal Soldiers, My Sixty Years, Red Flag of Cuigang, The Dragon's Ravine, Battle on Many Fronts, Guerrillas on the Plain, Dong Cunrui, The Battle of Shanggan Ling, Sacrifice, Li Shizhen, Ever-Present Electric Wave, Young People in Our Village, Five Girls, Lin Tse-Hsu, The Lin Family Store, The Song of Youth, Nie Er, The Red Detachment of Women, Warclouds at Jiawu, Red Flower on Tianshan, For Peace, Early Spring, Little Soldier Zhangga, Storm, Li Shuangshuang, Doctor Bethune, Serfs, Scholartree Village, Song of the Red Flag,* and others. Historical and contemporary images of the Chinese people came to life on the screen. One of the most prominent features was that the workers, peasants, and soldiers became masters on the screen. These films were closely related to our social life and the pulse of our times. This could be said to be the second wave of Chinese film.

The Marxist theory that art reflects society is the guiding principle of our aesthetics, while revolutionary realism is the best approach for filmmaking (thought not the only one). During the seventeen years after 1949, the mainstream of our filmmaking was good. Our policy for filmmaking, that education should be integrated into entertainment, was correct, which is why the films were well received. At one time the audience numbered more than 29 billion in one month. However, there are always two sides to a story. Under the influence of leftist dogmatism, the relationship between politics and art was seen as one in which art was subordinate to politics. Thus in practice, politics became art. Some films were full of preaching, without any artistic appeal.

Realistic power was already weak among our film teams. After May 16, 1966, with the wild torrent of the so-called Cultural Revolution, film was the first to be affected. More than 600 films made before that time were labeled "black," and locked away. This was an unheard-of calamity in world film history. That a billion people watched only eight model dramas became a joke at home and abroad. All intellectuals were sent to the countryside or factories to be reeducated by the workers, peasants, and soldiers through physical labor. Some were thrown into prison, to experience life behind bars. The way a culture and intellectual talents were strangled was unprecedented. The result was a void in Chinese film history.

In July 1977 the Third Plenary Session of the Eleventh Party Congress called on the people to emancipate the mind, seek truth from facts, unite as one, and look to the future. The policy to "let a hundred flowers blossom, let a hundred schools of thought contend" (Mao Zedong) was rereleased, correcting the unscientific guiding ideology that had impeded our filmmaking. Under the appeal of a new era, writers and artists of the old generation regained their youthful spirit. Young and middle-aged film workers showed even more vigor and vitality, putting all their hearts into their work. It wasn't long before they made such fine films as *The Legend of Tianyun Mountain, Evening Rain, At Middle Age, Scar, Xi'an Incident, Storm at Zhongshan, Neighbors, Blood is Always Hot, Rickshaw Boy, Sha'ou, Happiness at the Door, Yamaha Fish Stall, Under the Bridge, My Memories of Old Beijing, The Herdsman, Anxious to Return, Garlands at the Foot of the Mountain, Girl in Red, Ward 16, The Girl from Huangshan, In the Wild Mountains, Our Discharged Soldiers,* and others. More diverse themes and more complete artistic depictions were achieved. This can be called the third wave of Chinese film.

Meanwhile, in film theory, discussions were initiated into the characteristics of film art and aesthetics. Valuable reference books and articles were translated. Publication of film theories and plays from home and abroad added to the wealth of the development of Chinese film. Some actively introduced foreign theories, trying to distribute them in China; some made their own films, following the methods of foreign, especially Western, films. Suddenly, going to foreign films became the fashion. Of course it is not wrong to consult foreign films, but we must do so selectively. We should also analyze them according to our specific needs. Once selection is made, we can make use of what is good and discard what is bad. Some, however, want to copy everything, and do away with our own tradition entirely. They say that modernization is the goal for the country and that modernism is the goal for film.

Along with the wave of experimentation with new ideas, the trend of a new concept surged in film circles. There were two reasons for this. One was the mentality of adversity. There was a strong repugnance among the middle-aged and the young creators for the "three prominences" (loftiness, greatness, and completeness), which were the guiding ideology of leftist dogmatism when the Gang of Four was in power, and the subordination of art to politics. The other was the bandwagon mentality that began after the fall of the Gang of Four and was coincidentally similar to the distorted mentality of Western artists after World War I and World War II as reflected on the screen. They thought this the new international trend, and took it as the ideological basis for their worship of the West, but they forgot what kind of country they were in.

Proponents of the new concept propose to copy everything from Western modernism, but this concept of the West isn't new at all. It was derived from the concept at the turn of the century that began in Germany and spread to France, wherein a small group of people, to entertain themselves or to relieve themselves of boredom, proposed to make "pure" films. They opposed mass appeal as well as commercialism. They were only interested in "manifesting the good." They advocated not only nonplot, nondramatization, noncharacterization, but also irrationality and ambiguity. They should not be blamed if their nondramatization did away with stage performance or the three prominences, for this was not what they had in mind. The qualities of drama were what they opposed. Alienation or ambiguity was what they sought. They wanted to dilute plot, representation, reality, politics, and so on. Thus we see the true nature of the new concept. Their so-called dilution of reality is nothing more than a divorce of film from real life. The more distant a film is from life, the better they think it is. Following are some of the views expressed by proponents of the new concept to which I cannot readily subscribe.

## NATIONALIZATION AND TRADITION

Proponents of the new concept deny nationalization. Since film is an import, there is no nationalization or national tradition to speak of. The dramatic structures and linear conflicts in films of the past can only be obstacles for innovation. Nonetheless, some also think that as long as films reflect life, they are national; hence no need to talk about nationalization. I think that every nation has its own tradition of aesthetic habits and thought. In the decades since film was introduced into China, it has already become an essential part of entertainment. Generations of film workers not only have had a basic grasp of the art, but also understood the tastes of the audience. In short, a blood relationship has been formed between Chinese film and the Chinese audience. It is true that times are changing, society advancing, and aesthetic standards improving; therefore, our films should experiment with new ideas. Otherwise we would lag behind, and be isolated from the masses. Representation in our films should make a clear arrangement of ideas, exercise sound judgments, be fair and reasonable, and explain things clearly and implicitly. This common law is one manifestation of nationalization.

However, proponents of the new concept say that to allow for new ideas, we must "eliminate the walking stick of drama." I already mentioned earlier that if the walking stick of drama refers to the three prominences and stage performance on the screen, they make perfect sense. This is exactly the scar we have been trying to get rid of all these years and still haven't been able to do. Yet if we also want to eliminate plot and dramatic quality, we will have to follow the same road as the modernists, but this would lead to a dead end. Later, others put forth the idea that "film should be divorced from drama," and advocated "pure film," saying that "film is film." Taken literally, they are absolutely correct, film is film. Film is not literature, nor music, nor dance. Film is a synthetic art. However, if the so-called pure film refers to total isolation from the other arts, it can only become what some Westerners call a "dreamland." A few are more specific: "Film is an art because it possesses aesthetic functions, and its mission is to give aesthetic pleasure. We cannot eliminate aesthetic functions, nor can we go backward" (*Chinese Film Daily,* January 15, 1987). Their goal is to have "pure art," with no other purpose. I don't approve of the eagerness for quick success and instant profits, nor do I agree that film shouldn't uplift the people.

In terms of creative methods, proponents of the new concept have not only become national nihilists, they have fallen completely into the quagmire of modernism. On this issue, I quite agree with Pang Pu: "When we see tradition as belonging to history, we should also see that tradition is reality. . . . I propose that, while we fully understand the negative side of tradition, we also analyze its positive side. Only then can our criticism of tradition become profound. . . . We are used to making comparisons with the West, because of 'Western European egocentralism.'" Even Westerners no longer take pride in western European egocentralism. Westerners themselves were the first to oppose it. It is lamentable that we still haven't realized this.

## FILM AND THE FILM AUDIENCE

Film is an art that belongs to the masses. Without the masses, there wouldn't be film. Therefore, I think film workers must fully understand the relationship. The masses are the most influential critics. Our films can accomplish their mission only if they are liked by the masses, welcomed by them, and exert a positive influence over them. But proponents of the new concept ask, "Who does the audience think it is? They are our enemies." This is an extreme example. There is another view that opposes film as a popular art under the umbrella of opposing art for both refined and popular tastes. They think audiences are multilayered. Since China has a population of one billion, many of them illiterate, film should have specialized audiences, such as the more cultured and the less cultured, with no integration between the two. It is lamentable that people still advocate art for both refined and popular tastes in a country with thousands of years of glorious cultural history.

Of course, high-brow art and popular art are two different matters. There are differences between high and low, between the more cultured and the less cultured. Their objects of appreciation are indeed quite different. We can't simply ignore that here. As responsible film artists, we should help them improve their aesthetic standards instead of condemning them. Now is a time when high-brow and popular art are integrated. Our proposal of art for both refined and popular tastes also considers improving the quality of film. Otherwise, if your film is high-brow but the majority of the people do not understand it and therefore call it a dream film, it will have to be left for your own appreciation alone. Are we going back into the Western "ivory pagoda" of the 1920s and 1930s? With the increasing development of science and technology, more and more varied methods of representation are available, but we can't turn them into dream factories. Lenin said film is the most popular art. Only when we make films beneficial to the masses can we rest easy.

Confusion over some of the theories and criticisms has resulted in confusion in filmmaking. In recent years, some proponents of the new concept have imitated films of the modernist school in the West in order to break away from traditional filmmaking. The so-called exploration films, also called experimental films, do not have plots, characters, or realism, and replace innovation with subjectivity. Of course the audience cannot accept them. Although these films stimulate much excitement in small seminars, or in newspapers and magazines, they only attract a small audience in theatres. This has to be the response they deserve as the result of their dilution of life, plot, and reality. According to some statistics, *Yellow Earth,* once highly praised, sold only thirty prints, with an audience of 29,160,000, and a profit of ¥308,000. *One and Eight* also sold only thirty, with an audience of 41,780,000 and a profit of ¥447,000. *Sacrificed Youth* sold thirty-nine, with an audience of 42,260,000, and a profit of ¥422,000. *On the Hunting Ground* sold only two prints, and we needn't mention the rest. Say one print sells for a few thousand Yuan. A film must sell at least sixty to eighty prints to earn back its production costs, because money must also be paid in taxes. We film workers have to take this into consideration.

Exploration and experimentation are not at fault; they should be encouraged. It is wrong to oppose exploration and innovation, but it should be understood that reality must be taken into account. We must not repeat what has already proven hopeless in the West. For example, we cannot say the avant-garde, the modernists, and the New Wave were insignificant in the West, but evidence proved that they were unable to win the support of the broad masses, and were short-lived. Why then should we waste our youth and the nation's health? Some of the films may have an audience in the West, but in our country we are uncertain that they will be appreciated. We cannot blame the audience for its low level of appreciation; instead, we should blame ourselves for having broken away from reality. The essence here again is the issue of national aesthetic thought mentioned earlier. Therefore, whether it is exploring, borrowing, or innovating, they must all take into account the national aesthetic judgment, and real life. We cannot go too far. If we ignore the realities of the masses, their aesthetic interests, we are sure to be discarded by them. What happened to the experimental films mentioned earlier proves this. There is no way out for worshipping and having blind faith in things foreign.

If we think the foreign moon rounder, we will be called elitist (because we despise the feelings of the Chinese audience), or accused of having a slavish mentality toward all things foreign. We have always maintained that Chinese film should consider our realities, use advanced methods from foreign countries selectively, and improve our representational ability. We must not forget our own origins and follow others blindly, nor can we forget that capitalism and socialism are two different systems, and that there can be no reconciliation between the two ideologies, though in film the differences may sometimes be hidden and very subtle. Chaplin, a progressive comedian, from 1917 to 1952 made seventy-eight films of varied length, and won the love of the broad masses, yet eventually he was rejected by the government, and not allowed to return to the United States, only because he had exposed the ugly acts of capitalist monopolies. Maybe we all still remember the "Hollywood Ten" fabricated by the American Congress in 1947. The cause of that incident was that they had offended the interests of the American ruling class. This requires no further explanation. Is this a manifestation of legislation and law in contemporary capitalist societies where nobody can interfere as long as it is legal? Is this a free environment that to some extent guarantees individual creativity? The reason I mention this is that I do not want our comrades to think of the United States (and other Western film countries) as heaven.

## REALISM

Marxism says that all art and literature reflect society. We believe in this. We believe that art and literature must reflect social life. Life is the one and only source of creativity. Any artwork, once divorced from life, without a solid foundation, will come to no avail, nor will it have any positive influence. This is why we adhere to realism. But it must be made clear here the reason our earlier discussion involved only realism was because our concern was with the trend of modernism. In truth, romanticism is also important, because it plays an important role in expressing the warm feelings people have for their careers and their supreme ideals. Although realism itself also possesses such capacity, it is after all different. This is where our contemporary films are weak. By the way, we do not absolutely refuse to learn about modernism and modernists, but we are against promoting them and we subscribe to those who ignore their national dignity while devoting their energies to retrieving what is backward, superstitious, ignorant, and unhealthy among the people in exchange for the praise of a few foreigners. Of course, as we repeated earlier, we say realism is the best approach, but by no means is it the only one. There is no doubt that people can choose at will what is best for them in their creativity.

Proponents of the new concept think that realism is already going downhill, because, first, the premise of realism lies in admitting that art can realistically reflect reality, but cannot account for the gap between art and life; second, representations of realism also show its internal shortcoming; one image cannot stand for many images; third, the catastrophe in literary circles also began by upholding the legitimate position of realism. The first two reasons are common sense, but the third involves the Cultural Revolution, which proponents of the new concept insist "began by upholding the legitimate position of realism." We must clarify some of the facts here. *Lin Family Store,* although later discredited like many other fine films, was not what they targeted first. History professor Wu Han wrote a historical play called *The Dismissal of Hairui from Office,* which was accused of redressing justice for Peng Dehuai, because Peng Dehuai was "dismissed from office" at the Lushan Meeting. Therefore, the key line of *The Dismissal of Hairui from Office* lay in the dismissal. Another example relates to a national conference on scientific and educational films presided over by Peng Zhen. When Lu Dingyi gave his speech, Kang Sheng suddenly broke into a fit of hysteria, criticizing *Beiguojiangnan,* claiming that it was for blind Communist party members. The accusations of a series of films were nothing but exaggerations based on the same incident. In no way were they "upholding the legitimate position of realism." The reason proponents of the new concept fabricated the story was that they wanted to oppose realism and promote modernism. To treat a political conspiracy to usurp power as legitimate in academia is a serious matter. Whether contemporary or classic, whether Chinese or foreign, whether in film or in literature, realism has been the dominant trend.

To deny art as a reflection of society is in essence to deny Marxism. It is unimaginable to discuss making Chinese-style socialist films without Marxism as the guiding ideology. Filmmaking as an ideology has to be conditioned by the creator's world view. For example, *8 1/2,* by the Italian director Fellini, and *Last Year at Marianbad,* by the French director Resnais, are worshipped by some and thought to give artistic pleasure. This is all right. We needn't worry. As private experiences, there is no problem, but if they are to be promoted, we have to treat them differently.

## CONTENT AND FORM

Proponents of the new concept are thoroughly exposed by their vivid descriptions when denying the content of art. They say "a well-known metaphor is that a work of art is like an onion. If you want to get rid of its skin (form) to get to the core (content), you will find that even the last layer is still a layer of skin" (*Film Art,* December 1986, p. 12). This example is fine indeed; unfortunately, an onion is just a plant. As long as there is soil, water, and sun, a layer of skin will grow wherever you plant it. But film is an ideology. It is created by thinking based on objective reality. It belongs not only to a society, but also to a class and a nation.

They are two entirely different things. But proponents of the new concept quite definitely conclude that form is art and art is form, and that their experimentation is with form. People appreciate film to appreciate form as though no content existed in their minds. Therefore, they believe that as long as *8 1/2* or *Last Year at Marianbad* have a unique form and possess the effect of alienation, they are good. This reminds me of a kind of "emphasis" on the "essential elements of art itself" that Sima Yuchang quoted. Sima says, "when people appreciate modern painting, they will distinguish images if they can. If they cannot, the surface of the painting becomes everything." It takes a new concept to be able to experience "the surface of painting . . . as everything," because "the subtle blend of color," "the tension of moving lines," and "the textures of special materials" can be interpreted as one wishes, for example, as "the vault of heaven, great rivers, snowy mountains, a sea of clouds, a swamp, or a pit." Though a film is made of a different form, both film and painting are of the same master — modernism. Take the films mentioned earlier, for example; if someone says they are strange, that's blasphemy, and they will immediately protect them. In fact, when they claim there is only form and no content, they are after all opposing the progressive and revolutionary content of film. They think what contaminates our people and humiliates our nation should be represented, and will be appreciated by a few foreigners. This, they think, is the historical responsibility of artists.

Since the open-door policy, our film circle has benefited a lot. First of all, people are more creative, and the themes are broadened for filmmaking. Theories of various foreign film schools, art and literature, and trends of various periods have been introduced, which help us understand many things. However, there has been a singling out of both the good and the bad. Suddenly diverse films have been on the screen, and various repercussions have resulted among the masses. There is no denying this, but from the broader perspective of film overall, this is nothing to worry about although critics cannot neglect it.

From an optimistic point of view, the present situation can be said to be lively, because it pushed research in the academy into the characteristics of film, film aesthetics, the use of sound, acting, and the like, despite the unavoidable divorce between theory and practice. From a pessimistic point of view, it is also confusing, because in the past two years much that is unsuitable for our socialist filmmaking has been disseminated in the print media and film. This has had a highly negative effect. We need to broaden our positive aspects and reduce the negative (because it is impossible to look at only one side of the issue). We firmly believe realism and positive romanticism will surely survive, because they are scientific approaches that will develop with human history. Of course, other approaches also will have their markets, but they are only tributaries. As long as we adhere to socialism in China and aim at reform and innovation, our cause will undoubtedly develop, and our future will be prosperous.

# 17

# TO BE A LOYAL ARTIST TO THE PEOPLE

Wu Yigong

translated by Hou Jianping

What I want to talk about today has been lingering in my mind for a long time. For the past few years, I have been thinking about it and discussing it with other filmmakers; some of my ideas have actually accumulated through these discussions. I can say that all that I will address has gone through a lot of consideration. Of course, since I am a director, my opinions are unlikely to be all correct. I hope that they will be treated as the result of a director's thinking.

There have been a variety of unfair complaints made about Xie Jin's model since late last year. I feel that such a tendency is actually going to lead Chinese film astray. I am not just saying this after what has already happened. My mind was relatively clear even at that time. I have always believed that it is useless to talk about the creative road of artists, their characteristics and styles, or their models, without relating them to the people and to things that are mostly concerned with the people. No matter how rigorously these styles or models are praised, in the end they won't be accepted anyway. On the contrary, if an artist closely relates himself to his time, to the happiness and misfortunes of the people, and arduously pursues his goal with his skills, his works will eventually be accepted and appreciated, and their power to survive will eventually be revealed no matter what complaints they may get from a small number of people. His time will never end and his work will never become obsolete. "If reality is ignored and to 'proceed ahead of one's time' is insistently pursued, there would be no difference between this and self-evident idealism."

Objectively, convention and innovation are closely interrelated. An artist cannot come into existence out of nowhere like the Monkey King. The development of ideas and feelings, the formulation of personality, and the accumulation of skills require a curing process. How can one completely throw away convention? Actually, convention would stagnate and stiffen without innovation and development.

A hot issue being discussed nowadays is the awareness of proceeding ahead of one's time. To me, the concept itself is ridiculous. The significance of an artist lies in his sensitive discovery of the present and his deep understanding of the past. Those who choose to ignore present reality and insist on proceeding ahead of their time are people who, as Lu Xun noted, want to leave the world by pulling on their own hair — they only create an illusion. Is there any difference between this and self-evident idealism? Though it is impossible for artists to create without generating a self-consciousness in their work, if self is put ahead of everything else — putting on the airs of a lecturer — neither his time nor the people will accept his work.

Someone suggested it might not be a good thing for a film to have a large audience. I find this baffling. To be frank, every filmmaker has a certain audience in mind. To say my film is only made for myself is an utter lie. What is the real motive for filmmaking?

Of course, the desire to make films for a certain audience cannot be forced upon the filmmaker. But history is fair. If an artist does not aim to serve the whole nation and the people who raised him, his work will never survive even though it might enjoy temporary success or praise among a limited number of critics. Looking at the great works of literature and art handed down from ancient times, isn't it true that every single one has stood the test of time and the people?

Let me now turn to Xie Jin. I feel that the most wonderful thing about him is that he always bases his work on reality. He brings his entire honesty, passion, and artistic skills into play and enthusiastically portrays a number of characters who are representative of their time. He has imprinted his feelings and opinions about the real on the screen. Such films probably will be of some historical value to future generations.

In the discussion of Xie Jin's model, some proposed that the combination of popularity and elegance be thrown away, and the quality of art, the function of entertainment and education be separated. Well said. Why don't these people try to make an example? The ancient Chinese highly appreciated a work of art that suited both refined and popular tastes; however, it is very difficult to reach this level. It is not easy to make films that have a limited audience and high aesthetic quality, and it is even more difficult to make films that have both a large audience and a high level of art. Most of our filmmakers cannot make either kind of film. Thus our theoreticians and critics should not isolate themselves and further narrow their circles. Some people constantly talk about making explorations. It seems their level and status would be highly raised by addressing this topic. However, the truth is that not every director can make films that are the same as or close to Xie Jin's.

One significant contribution Lu Xun made to literature is the portrait of Ah Q. I dare not make groundless guesses about some critics' motivations, but at least I can say that there exists a consciousness similar to that of naughty kids — who break your window to let you know they exist. Actually, if we take a close look at their essays, it is not difficult to find that they do not have a solid theoretical basis.

Although I have been indignant about the discussion of Xie Jin's model, knowing that its direction is wrong and ours is right, I never fully expressed my ideas for fear of my lack of study and theory, of strong devices with which to talk back. I realize only in retrospect that our directors in the Shanghai Film Studios should have had more self-confidence.

**Saying there is a Shanghai film clique reveals that Shanghai film has been regarded as a conservative and ossified model. It not only denies Xie Jin himself, but the whole group of middle-aged and young directors in the Shanghai Film Studio.**

The Shanghai Film Studio was in a very difficult situation last year. To begin with, it was pounded by the discussion of Xie Jin's model followed by talk of a Shanghai film clique, labeling Shanghai films canned products, conservative and ossified models, and calling the studio a base for vulgar productions. Thus such talk condemns not only Xie Jin, a director of high achievements, the backbone of the Shanghai Film Studio, and well accepted by the audience, but also the middle-aged and young directors who constitute its most active part. What's more, a third wave was pounding the studio. Three recent graduates who belong to the Fifth Generation were also accused of being "assimilated" and "degenerated," because they made films that were close to real life and enthusiastically praised real life. All of a sudden, Shanghai Film was fully under attack. Someone even cried out that "it's time the Shanghai Film Studio closed!"

What was the actual situation of filmmaking at the Shanghai Film Studio last year? In terms of artistic practice, there was a great improvement in the variety of theme and style, in the exploration of new subjects, and in showcasing the personalities of directors. For instance, the studio permitted three young directors to make films on their own. Among the films made were *The Last Sun, My Classmates and I, Death Line of the Iced River, Scripture for Women, Kids' Restaurant, The Missing Girl Student, 84 and 85 in T. Province, Special President,* and *Hibiscus Town.* During the process of making these films, the old, middle-aged, and young directors used all their skills and played their roles well. In terms of the film market, the average number of prints sold for distribution in 1986 was 157. This was above the average for the industry and ranked number one among film studios. It was during this prosperous and active period of production that the Shanghai Film Studio was attacked three times and most of its directors condemned. Was this just a coincidence?

After 1982, I felt that some tendencies in film theory were not right, but I didn't have as clear a notion about them as I do now. At that time there were people claiming that the Shanghai Film Studio "lacked theoretical guidelines." It was true that Shanghai emphasized filmmaking and the construction of theory was a weakness. Because of this, more often than not, we put up with whatever was being thrown at us and didn't argue about it. Now we have established a Section of Art and Theoretical Research and we are determined to catch up on this point. We admit people who are willing to make a commitment to this section. It does not matter that we are starting low. We will gradually improve ourselves.

## Some theoretical research has landed at a dead end in the last few years — taking the concept of film as a priority, making film art abstract and mysterious, and moving film further away from its basis in mass communications.

The study of perception in theoretical circles had a very good start — the discussion about the "divorce between film and drama." However, later on, the study gradually came to a dead end — the concept of film was given priority and film art was made abstract and mysterious. Film deviated further from its basis in mass communications. Nowadays, theoretical circles are probably committing a serious error; that is, they are reversing the order of the values of the concepts. Which value should be ranked first, the act of making a film or the kind of film being made? If a director should make a film without considering his audience at all, what does he think about perception as a mass communications medium? It seems now that the act of making a film is more important than the kind of film being made. I believe this is a reversal of values — the activity of filmmaking is put on an inappropriately high level. I am not denying the role of the activity, but if too much emphasis is put on it, the function will be counterproductive.

I do not think I am a dogmatist. In France, Italy, and other countries, experimental films that focus on the exploration of narrative means and strategies do exist. But differences exist between experiments and practice. It is wrong to take foreign experimental film language as the doctrine of our filmmaking. The quotient of the activity is not high, the crucial matter lies in the perceptual value of the film. In 1983 I wrote in my summary on directing *My Memories of Old Beijing*: "The key is what you are presenting, not how you present it." But now, some in theory circles have reversed the relationship, taking "how to present" as the key and leaving "what to present" far behind. I think this is against the principles of art.

Because of this theoretical error, many filmmakers have a misconception. It seems that to them, films that put emphasis on the activity are high-level and those that stress the kind of film being made are low. I'd like to make a remark about this idea: taking activity as most important, if you piss off the roof of the International Club, you may be immediately known internationally, but is there any value in your action? I believe that the purpose of film studies is to improve our film, not to play with cinematic strategies. Pure play has no significance at all.

Someone may ask, "In your opinion, where do the brilliant achievements of Griffith and Eisenstein lie?" It is true that they created the close-up and montage theory — precious fruits of film theory. However, these achievements were made under conditions in which they grew along with the principles of art. What was more, it was only when these devices merged with the intention of the artists to express their ideas that the theory was born and its power revealed.

I have always thought that film theory and filmmaking should be separated and basic theory and film criticism likewise. I read an article about *My Memories of Old Beijing* in which the author used many lines and dots to illustrate his ideas, and pointed out, at one point, that the power of shot 270 was originally created by shot 47. Such a study means nothing to me. Of course, people may pursue their studies as they wish, but I will never apply them in my filmmaking! It is undeniable that theory plays an important role in guarding practice. But theory, after all, is formulated according to practice and not vice versa. The relation between the two should not be reversed. It would be a miracle if a director made a good film when he, instead of having enthusiasm about life and sensitive feelings about art, was only filled with concepts and symbols. There would be no art if artists were dominated entirely by concepts and lost their honesty.

## Great artists in the past all sincerely loved life and the people. However, some of our filmmakers are now obsessed with salon art and only aim to serve a minority.

This is a matter of the attitudes of artists toward life and their sense of responsibility toward society. It sounds like an obsolete legitimist preaching, but it is an irrefutable truth. Great artists in the past all sincerely loved life and the people. However, some of our filmmakers are now obsessed with salon art and aim only to serve the few with their work. Actually, they put their hats on the roof while they themselves are standing on the ground. There is nothing terrific about them. Film is after all a medium of mass communication. It is not philosophy, nor is it atomic physics. It is an ordinary medium. Our responsibility is to produce films carefully. Some people say that I made some progress from *My Memories of Old Beijing* to *Sister,* but fell back when I made *College in Exile* and completely degenerated when I made *The Misfortune of the Young Master.* I personally do not agree at all.

It was with a conscientious, positive, and clear mind that I decided to make *The Misfortune of the Young Master.* I want to express my own opinions about life and film in my work, not to appeal to a certain taste. From *Our Kitten, Evening Rain, My Memories of Old Beijing,* and *Sister,* to *The Misfortune of the Young Master,* what I intended to express is the same theme: the discovery in people of their own values. I had another idea in mind when I made *The Misfortune of the Young Master,* which was to prove by making a comedy that the pursuit of box office success and entertainment was not vulgar or low.

Many young people nowadays look down upon Chinese film. Aside from the fact that Chinese films have their weak points, another reason is that our critics have not given particular films appropriate comments and honors. Some may call me conventional; I don't care. I just want to be a Chinese artist, not a foreign artist or a slavish artist. Without a Chinese nationality, there would be no internationality. If a film cannot be accepted by the Chinese audience, how could it be welcomed internationally? The major reason foreigners praised *My Memories of Old Beijing* was that they thought it a beautiful Chinese film.

It seems to me that there are two ways for Chinese film to enter into international cinema. One is to make films such as *Yellow Earth* and *My Memories of Old Beijing* to hold a place in foreign academic circles. But that is not enough. We must have another way, which is to gain an international film market. Some of us feel quite pleased with the success in the salon. I feel it is quite shortsighted.

I readily agree with the idea of Shi Fangyu. He said that since mediocre work would exist in any period of time, the idea of "eliminating the mediocre" is ridiculous. To be frank, in the realm of literature and art, only a few great artists have existed. Mediocre artists naturally produce mediocre art. It is the same in any era of time; the only difference is in content. Thus it is impossible to overcome mediocrity unless you can eliminate all mediocre artists. In a given historical period, if all filmmakers became great artists, new mediocre people would make their appearance, and they would be better artists. I believe that art has its own natural way of development. Excessive enthusiasm can only spoil things.

## Many people are talking about the new concept of film. The so-called new concept is nothing but one among the variety of concepts. The essential for art is to take in everything.

Many people are talking about the new concept of film. The new concept is nothing but one among a variety of concepts. I have always stressed that it is essential for art to assimilate everything. Some have severely criticized Zhao Huanzhang. Does this mean you are better and more intelligent than he? Zhao's audience numbers 6 billion. Do you have so many? Do not so vigorously degrade a director who is so popular among the masses. In the latest film awards sponsored by *Wen Hui Daily* and *China Film Post,* he was still elected best director. A major mistake film theory circles are committing is that they are trying to make everyone a member of the Fifth Generation. Xie Jin is Xie Jin, Zhao Huanzhang is Zhao Huanzhang. Do not try to turn them into Chen Kaige. Every director has his own social and cultural background, and his own intrinsic personality. All these are formulated through a long historical process. It is impossible and ridiculous for a theorist to try to change them. Unfortunately, some filmmakers were confused by these theorists and blindly wanted to change themselves. It is all right to respect a good point made by others, but there is no need to change yourself. If you do, you will not be yourself anymore. If I were asked to imitate Tian Zhuangzhuang and Wu Tianming, I would never make it. One can only hold his position by maintaining and efficiently using his strong points. I believe that a person who lacks self-confidence can never become an artist. The point is not what others say about your film, but how good it actually is. Many filmmakers have been confused by all the theories. Maybe this is a natural phenomenon before the artists eventually mature. Once they mature, they will have their own ideas and will be incapable of being influenced by these theories. They will be like Xie Jin, who persistently pursues his own road in the middle of these discussions and reproaches.

### Once we have set our mind on the goal, we should resist any interference and go through with our task.

I met American director Steven Spielberg several times, had a few long talks with him, and viewed a videotape of him at work. I admire him a lot. His films are very successful at the box office in America and each has a high artistic quality and a great deal of freshness. He is extraordinary because he can devote himself to filmmaking and not care at all about what the critics say about his work. His success cannot be suppressed by any kind of criticism. American critics all admit that it is very interesting to watch his films, but they are reluctant to accept them. It is a kind of jealousy. I am afraid it is a common attitude in the world. He has never received an Academy Award, which only indicates that the Academy Awards represent the power of select groups. I hope our Golden Rooster Awards do not become dominated by select groups on such a grand and spectacular scale. Spielberg is a very honest artist. He is as pure and innocent as a child. He devotes himself to filmmaking and cares little about common customs, including honors. All that he thinks about is his next film, and the next. He does not waste his time and talent. By comparison, we can see how some of our directors are occupied with meetings, interviews, and writing about a film as soon as it is finished. Sometimes they go on like this for half a year or even a year. Another film might as well have been finished during this time. If our filmmakers could be as open-minded and easy as Spielberg, we could gain a real spiritual freedom.

I have always tried to defend the unity of film circles in the past, hoping people in the same boat would help each other and together create a prosperous situation for film. Since the filmmaking conference held in Beijing in May, I found myself a person of goodwill. China is a big country. The existence of different opinions by different schools and regions is inevitable. Since ancient times, scholars have tended to judge each other. Unfortunately that is still true today. I tried to get over this, only to realize that it is impossible. People cannot live in a vacuum. Living in a specific culture, one is inevitably influenced by it. China is a large culture. The world is even larger, while Shanghai and Beijing are smaller. Thus I believe that when the casting out of Xie Jin's model was proposed, there probably existed another model that would have replaced it. However, the action was not taken justly and honorably through art. Although the "Shanghai clique" was blamed, there must have been another. By the same token, while one concept was criticized, another had to exist. Thus the intent to avoid a confrontation of the South and the North and a confrontation of the East and the West is very naïve. Everyone can go along his own road. There is no need to force everyone to act in unison. I suggest we heighten our self-confidence. Once we have set our mind on our goal, we should resist any interference and go through with our task. If, in the future, history proves that I am good for nothing, I will be willing to accept that judgment.

# VI — Chinese Film Theory in the New Era: A Conclusion

The New Era, which began in 1979, survived for a decade. Though it is premature to assess its historical significance, clearly the spirit of the times brought new life to Chinese film, both its theory and its practice. However, for us, with the first gunshot of the bloody massacre of the students demonstrating for democracy in Tiananmen Square on June 4, 1989, the era was put to its end.

In the difficult processes of any theoretical retrospective such as this, more often than not we find that what was once thought crucially important is no longer sacred, that debates once exciting to all no longer arouse enthusiasm. What was once seen as serious and intellectually stimulating turns out, in retrospect, to be naïve and, at times, ridiculous. Nonetheless, whatever happened has a historical existence that bridges past and present; thus when in the future we reexamine the issues of these debates, we will not fail to see that they represent discussions that were, at the time, the largest and most extensive in Chinese film theory.

The year 1979 marked a significant turning point for film study in China. In the decade that followed, the study of film shifted from the external to the internal, from the superficial to the profound, from the uniform to the pluralistic, from the naïve to the mature, and from the barren to the prosperous. We will subsequently come to understand that the basic characteristic of Chinese film theory in the New Era was the close interrelationship it developed with filmmaking, which led to an improvement in the look of Chinese film. Nobody can ignore the great achievements in film theory and filmmaking in the country during this period. However, theoretical discussions never focused selectively enough on a few concrete problems, probably because of the loosely defined content of the issues. The discussions were extensive, but not profound; filled with enthusiasm, but short of scientific and systematic methods. Thus, in the end, they reveal the limited vision and knowledge of Chinese film theoreticians.

The advances and limitations of the debates presented here define the path of Chinese film during a decade filled with the difficulties, excitement, and restlessness of every significant intellectual or aesthetic movement. It will do no good to celebrate these debates with simple optimism any more than to reject them with blind pessimism. It is still too early to reach a conclusion about them; that must be left for the future. Clearly, however, Chinese theory continues to be developed, and needs to go much further. Since the basic question of "what is film?" which seemed to be resolved, in turn, by D. W. Griffith, Sergei Eisenstein, André Bazin, Jean Mitry, Christian Metz, and J. Dudley Andrew, among others, remains unclarified, the Chinese are beginning to confront it. Zhong Dafeng, in a published dialogue with Li Tuo and other film scholars, summarizes the current situation of Chinese film theory and indicates the start of further research:

> The trend toward specificity in film research is a result of ongoing detailed studies of film culture. People nowadays can read every audiovisual image with reasonable accuracy. Accordingly we now want theory to use scientific methods in studying and regularizing every reaction/response between us and the image. The birth of scientific approaches seems to have itemized art, but in fact, it is a trend toward an enlarged wholeness based on a deep understanding of film culture and a sensitivity toward the medium. If film is seen as a system, there should be a theoretical system to generalize, explain, and analyze it. This is very natural, not a question of adaptation. It is also a demand of historical development, and is not subject to human manipulation.[1]

In Chinese filmmaking, two phenomena emerged by the end of the decade: one was the growing separation of filmmaking from theory. Filmmakers began to pay less and less attention to theoretical issues; the other was the division within filmmaking itself. With the wave of economic reform sweeping the country, the commercial value of film was given unprecedented emphasis. Thus, except for a small number of directors (with the Fifth Generation at its core) who still make efforts at cinematic explorations, the majority have turned to films expressly designed to earn money. Between 1987 and 1988, as many as 80 percent of the films produced were of poor quality, although there were, to be sure, a few that were outstanding: *Old Well,* which won the Tokyo International Film Award, *Red Sorghum,* and *Evening Bell,* which won the West Berlin International Film Award in 1988 and 1989 respectively. Though few in number, these films represent the rising level of Chinese film. To gain recognition at international film festivals or to succeed at the box office have become distinctly separate goals among filmmakers. At the same time, film theory has lost its vitality and the pioneer spirit it once had. Praise for outstanding films and criticism of commercial films have become the major concerns of Chinese film theory and criticism.

The final chapter in this book, written by the young scholar Chen Xihe, is an appropriate summary of theoretical research into film during the New Era. Through the analysis of *The Making of a Shadowplay Script* written by Hou Yao in 1926, Chen argues that China does have its own film aesthetics, and that it is the theory of staged film or shadowplay. What is more, this theory embodies the basic concept and history of Chinese film. Comparing this material with Western film theory, Chen points out that "old, grand and complete as it is, the system of Chinese film aesthetics is undergoing a profound crisis and is confronting the problem of making choices." What has emerged by the end of the New Era is the demand that Chinese film theory merge with that of the rest of the world.[2]

## NOTES

1. Li Tuo, Zhong Dafeng, Hao Dazheng, "Film: The Product of Science," *Film Art,* May 1988.

2. Chen Xihe, "Shadowplay: Chinese Film Aesthetics and Their Philosophical and Cultural Fundamentals," *Contemporary Film,* Spring 1986.

# 18 SHADOWPLAY: CHINESE FILM AESTHETICS AND THEIR PHILOSOPHICAL AND CULTURAL FUNDAMENTALS

Chen Xihe

Does China have its own theory of film? This question, which has caused considerable controversy in China for a long time, compels us to carry out a study from two points of view. The first is a comparative study between Chinese film aesthetics and those of the West. Is Chinese film aesthetics complete in terms of theoretical patterns as compared with Western film aesthetics? If not, in what sense is it incomplete? Can we pursue an alternative logic to understand the patterns of Chinese film aesthetics? Following this train of thought, we put the comparative study between Chinese and Western film aesthetics against the larger background of the basic differences between Chinese and Western philosophies and culture, and arrive at a new understanding. With this new understanding, we go back to do an "archaeological" study about the formation and development of Chinese film aesthetics. This study, with its horizontal comparison and vertical exploration, finally leads us to the recognition of the Chinese theory of film.

## SHADOWPLAY: THE CORE CONCEPT OF CHINESE FILM AESTHETICS

Just as the concepts of montage and the long take are the key concepts through which Western theorists understand film, this chapter takes the concept of the shadowplay, which appeared during the early period of

Chinese film, as the key concept through which the Chinese understand the medium.

In Chinese, shadowplay (*ying xi*) is a word group consisting of a modifier and the word it modifies. Its key word is play, which means a drama; shadow, which means the image on the screen, is only the modifier of play. The basic understanding of the relationship of shadowplay to film is that play is the origin of film, but shadow is its means of presentation.

Before shadowplay as an aesthetic concept can be deeply elucidated, it is necessary to explain it in historical terms. Shadowplay, first of all, refers to the concept of film and the pattern that occupied the dominant position in early Chinese filmmaking. As a concept of film, shadowplay reflected the basic understanding of filmmakers about the medium and influenced the features of filmmaking at that time. According to Chinese filmmakers before and during the 1920s, film was neither the direct recording of reality, nor a game of shooting and editing, but a drama. "When film initially came to China, it was called a shadowplay. People simply spoke of going to see a shadowplay. This tells us that film is derived from drama" (Bao Tianxiao 1973). "Shadowplay is a kind of drama. It possesses all the same values as drama" (Hou Yao 1926). "Although shadowplay is a new independent thing, as regards its properties of presentation (i.e., showing a story by actors or actresses), it is still drama. Although the forms of drama differ, its properties are fully the same" (Xu Zhudai 1926). Looking at film as drama was the central concept of film at that time. Under the guidance of this idea, early Chinese filmmakers established a set of shadowplay patterns that could be likened to stage dramas recorded by the camera. It is a specific phenomenon of the history of early Chinese film art.

However, as an aesthetic concept, shadowplay goes beyond the specific historical category of early Chinese film, and becomes a basic concept that summarizes the overall traditional understanding of Chinese film and covers its entire eight-year history. In recent times, the technical factors of film form have undergone a few changes, yet the basic concept by which Chinese understand film remains unchanged, and its influence extends directly to the dramatic film idea of the 1980s. However, a complete set of film aesthetics, which took this concept as its core, had been established in the 1920s, almost as early as the French avant-garde film theories and the montage films of the Soviet Union. On this subject, the historical contribution made by Hou Yao and his theoretical study, *The Making of a Shadowplay Script*, should be given special mention.

Hou Yao was a major filmmaker of the Great Wall Picture Company, which was built in May 1921. He was born in Kuangdong, and graduated in education from Southeast University in Nanjing, but he was fond of drama and joined the Literature Studies Society (a famous Chinese literary group in the 1920s). Most contributions of the Great Wall Picture Company in the first two years were scripted or directed by Hou Yao. The first film of Great Wall, *A Forsaken Woman,* was adapted by Hou Yao from his drama of the same title. His theoretical work, *The Making of a Shadowplay Script,* completed in 1925, was published in 1926 by the Taidong Press, Nanjing. In this book, he started from the unique philosophical and cultural ideology of China, and built a Chinese (or Oriental) system of film aesthetic theory.

## THE ONTOLOGY OF SHADOWPLAY AESTHETICS: FROM PLAY TO SHADOW

In the foreword of his book, Hou Yao claims bluntly: "I am a person who claims that the script is central. I believe that unless there is a good script, there cannot be a good drama. The shadowplay is a kind of drama; therefore, the filmscript is the soul of film." Deducing that the filmscript is the soul of film because the script is the center of drama, the author's premise is that "shadowplay is a kind of drama." Here then, the author considers play as the origin of film; that is, Hou Yao argues that film as a formal system should be understood from the level of play rather than the level of shadow. He takes play, which relates to the overall script and story, rather than shadow, which relates to the individual shot and image, as the essence of film and the starting point of film ontology.

Looking at the level of play as the essence of film is actually looking at film as a story system organized in accordance with dramatic principles. Thus script, which forms the basis of film story, naturally becomes the soul of film, and study of the script naturally becomes the major object of film theory. The study of the script is not just a study of productive techniques and strategies, but is also primarily a study of ontology in shadowplay aesthetics. It certainly is no accident that for several decades there have been numerous books and articles studying problems of the script and film literature in Chinese film theory, and that today in China there are many journals of film literature. Their numbers far exceed that of the study of pure film form (e.g., image, sound, shot, and editing). This is an inevitable outcome of the shadowplay concept.

What, then, is shadow? Shadow is simply the means of presenting a story. Hou Yao's understanding of image and shot is that they must be subordinate to script and story:

*Harmony.* A picture should pay attention to harmony in either aspects of quality or quantity. Those pictures that cannot harmonize with the characters and plots in play, no matter how beautiful they are, aren't harmonious in quality (Chapter 7, Section 2).

*Continuity.* The first shot, for example, shows us a man crying "Help!" on an isolated island surrounded by an ocean. The next shows us the man watching a play in a theatre. Because the two are continuous, the spectators wonder how the man on the island got to the theatre. If a shot that shows us someone rescuing the man by boat is inserted between the shots, the continuity isn't lacking (Chapter 7, Section 4).

Here Hou Yao takes pictures and editing as the only concrete skills through which to display plots and characters and assure continuity. He never treats shadow as an independent means of expression or discusses it in an ontological sense.

Hou Yao's thinking, as a matter of fact, has continued to the present. In the early 1980s Chinese film circles held a major debate over the issue of the nature of film. This debate was summarized appropriately by Guo Qing as follows: "The whole discussion makes one strong impression: People pay more attention to the dramatic and literary character (of film) than to the cinematic character itself. The main reason for this is that many look upon the dramatic and literary character as the essence" (*Film Art,* August 1983). The most representative opinion expressed was that of Zhang Junxiang, a leading filmmaker and critic of China, who said: "Film is simply literature, literature (or story) presented by means of film" (*Film Communication,* November 1980). In other words, the difference between film and literature is that film is a story shown by the image on the screen and literature is a story shown by the word on the paper. This view received a broad positive response.

Western film theories, however, are different from the Chinese. Their studies of the nature of film take the concrete image and shot as a starting point. For example, montage aesthetics pays attention to the relationship between shots; long-take aesthetics studies the relationship of subjects within a single shot that are various distances from the camera; structuralism/semiology analyzes the relationship between sensual (visual, aural) elements and linguistics, and so on. Nevertheless, among them there are many different opinions and views, which frequently enough contradict one another, though their taking the basic material and substance of film — image and shot — as a starting point to explain the nature of film is the same. Bazin emphasizes this point specifically: "We shall begin, necessarily, with the photographic image, the primitive element of the ultimate synthesis, and go from there" (*What Is Cinema?* vol. 1, trans. Hugh Grey, 2 vols., Berkeley, 1967).

To sum up, in terms of understanding cinematic form, the Chinese take the level of story as the key; Westerners take the level of image as the key. The Chinese take image as the means of presenting story; Westerners take story as one element of film. The Chinese pay attention to the dramatic and literary characteristics of story; Westerners pay attention to the characteristics of montage (editing) and the long take (shot). The Chinese study montage and the long take only in the sense of how to present story; Westerners study story only in a limited or technique sense. Fundamentally speaking, these differences reflect two different cultures and thinking methods. The Chinese understand any objective thing primarily through a synthetic method and view it as a whole without undertaking an analytical process. This method, called "primitive synthesis" by contemporary Chinese scholars, makes Chinese film theory focus primarily on the level of story. The Westerners approach a thing first through an analytical method, which makes them focus primarily on image and shot. The two different methods yield two different kinds of film aesthetics. From this, we can understand why Chinese film aesthetics cannot be classified into the categories of Western formalism or realism.

## THE ONTOLOGY OF SHADOWPLAY AESTHETICS: FORM FUNCTION TO STRUCTURE

The film theory of Hou Yao, as a complete system, put the problem of the social function of film first. At the beginning of the introductory chapter, he first states the four functions of drama: representing, criticizing, mediating, and beautifying life. Then he turns to film:

> Shadowplay is a kind of drama. It possesses all the values of drama. It possesses not only the four functions of representing, criticizing, mediating, and beautifying life, but also has larger influence than other kinds of drama. The reasons are as follows: the shadowplay is (a) more lifelike; (b) more economic; (c) more widespread and permanent; (d) an educational tool.

Among the four points, the last again emphasizes the function of shadowplay as an educational tool. Thus shadowplay aesthetics proceeds from functions of drama, combining them with social and historical conditions to become an aesthetics of film with the social function as its core.

Proceeding from the functions, Hou Yao approaches the basic structure of film. However, since at the onset he grasps film from the level of story, this approach to the film structure becomes a study of the basic elements and structural forms of story (Chapters 3 and 4) rather than that of image and shot. First of all, he makes the following stipulations for the essential factors to be included in the cinematic materials:

1. Crisis — the plots, in which characters confront such dangers as falling off a cliff, or a car turning over;
2. Conflict — a happening in a character's inner world, such as a conflict of ideas or behaviors;
3. Calamity — such as robbery, war, flood, fire, famine, disease, and so on (Chapter 3).

These stipulations about the essential factors of cinematic materials come entirely from dramatic principles. Furthermore, since the author takes social and educational functions as its core, moves toward film structure from the functions and determines film structure according to them, various aspects of social problems become the raw materials of film. The author generalizes the materials into sixteen categories: problems of health, sexual desire, women, marital, family, education, work, occupational, legal, political, military, religious, moral, contemporary thought, international, and life (Chapter 3).

Still beginning with social and educational functions, Hou prescribes the following to select film materials:

In order to make a shadowplay, one should select true, good, and beautiful materials. He should never take anything that is ugly, vulgar, inhuman, stale, or monotonous, or which goes against the spirit of the age. Otherwise, shadowplay would harm society more than bad novels (Chapter 3).

The author goes on to enumerate thirty-two kinds of materials that should not be put into shadowplay according to the stated principles. He claims strongly: "If we take the knowledge, customs, skills, ideas, and attitudes that life should have as the materials of the shadowplay, then shadowplay becomes an educational amusement and a true art." (Chapter 3). Finally, Hou Yao lists twenty-one kinds of materials that should be the materials of shadowplay. Through Hou's approach, the aesthetics of shadowplay actually become the ethics of shadowplay.

This manner of constructing film theory, which takes social functions as its core, remains the mainstream of Chinese film aesthetics. According to Maoism, arts are "a component part of the entire revolutionary apparatus" and "a weapon for uniting and educating people, and attacking and eliminating the enemy" (*Collected Writings of Mao Zedong,* vol. 8, p. 112). Mao goes on to say, "Arts should serve the political needs of the class and the party" (vol. 8, 134). These ideas establish a basis for the film aesthetics of the new China. Starting from its social and political functions, Chinese film aesthetics approaches the materials and forms of film, and classifies them into sociological and political categories: industrial problems, agricultural problems, military problems, reformation problems, and the like.

Western film aesthetics first approaches the structure of film, which includes the material of film and the methods of treating it and its forms, and then goes on to the function of film. Eisenstein claims that the raw material of film is the shot; however, pieces of unedited shots are no more than mechanical reproductions of reality. As such, they cannot in themselves be art. Only when these shots are arranged in montage patterns does film become art. Eisenstein states this doctrine repeatedly:

> The shot, considered as material for the purpose of composition, is more resistant than granite. This resistance is specific to it. The shot's tendency toward complete factual immutability is rooted in its nature. This resistance has largely determined the richness and variety of montage forms and styles — for montage becomes the mightiest means for a really important creative remolding of nature (*The Film Form,* trans. and ed. Jay Leyda. New York, 1949, p. 5).

Therefore, Eisenstein believes that reality speaks very obscurely, if at all. It is up to the filmmaker to rip reality apart and rebuild it into a system capable of generating the greatest possible emotional effect. The very sense of shock montage can convey confirms this. Eisenstein asserts an audience-oriented definition: "A work of art, understood dynamically, is just this process of arranging images in the feelings and mind of the spectator" (*The Film Sense,* trans. and ed. Jay Leyda. New York, 1942, p. 17).

For Bazin, brute reality is at the heart of cinema's appeal. Of course, the raw material of cinema is not reality itself, but the tracings left by reality on celluloid. Not only has the world made a tracing of itself in cinema, it has nearly duplicated its visual reality for us. Cinema then stands beside the world, looking just like the world. While it is incorrect to speak of reality appearing on the screen, Bazin provides a more exact term borrowed from geometry. Cinema, he says, is an asymptote of reality, moving even closer to it, forever dependent on it. Therefore, Bazin intensely opposes the overuse of montage, stipulates limitation for its use, and energetically encourages the technique of depth of field to preserve the ambiguity of reality itself. Bazin argues that cinema is as an "open sesame" to universes unknown, that cinema as a new sense, reliable like our natural senses, gives us knowledge of empirical reality otherwise unavailable. Cinema unveils a world. Thus cinema can provide a common nonideological understanding of the earth from which people can begin to forge new and lasting social reforms.

Metz, as a representative of structuralism-semiology, argues that every art form, indeed every communicational system, has a specific material of expression that sets it off from other systems. The raw material of cinema is by no means reality itself or a particular means of signification like montage, but the channels of information to which we pay attention when we watch a film. These include images that are photographic, moving, and multiple; graphic traces that include all written material we read off the screen; recorded speech; recorded music; and recorded noise or sound effects. At the heart of the field of film is cinematographic fact and at the core of cinematographic fact is the process of signification — the human process of asserting messages by means of sign systems, which are made of the above channels of information. The radical semioticians claim that the human process of cinematic signification is corrupted by the dominant ideology, and used to insist on the reality of the world we live in and the way we live in it through the surface reality of cinematography. It destroys every possibility of meaning except for the neurotic repetition of the dominant ideology. These critics plead that we must create a new culture, a new reality, one that will stop repressing all but bourgeois desires and all but certain social classes. We need a whole new cinema, which will expose the human process of how we transform matter into significance at every level, and establish a whole new vision of the world.

Although the film aesthetics of the West make different statements about film, all of them progress from the basic structure of film, and the natural potentials of the medium, to the function of film in order to explore its nature and determine its position in the world. If the differences of both kinds of film aesthetics can be generalized in a single sentence, then, the Chinese is a kind of function-aesthetics, taking the ethical and political spirit as its core, whereas Western film aesthetics is a kind of substance-aesthetics, taking the scientific spirit as its core. Of course, structural-semiological theory also emphasizes function, but it takes the rigorous scientific studies of basic structure as a prerequisite. Thus both types of film aesthetics yield a series of differences in the questions of film structure and function. Among them, the largest is in the understanding of the material of film. The Chinese understand film material as the various problems of life and aspects of social activities; the Westerners understand it in terms of its basic substance and possibilities. Chinese consider the film substance subordinate and study it little, concentrating their attention on society and life; the West studies it intensely to find its potentials to react on society and life. Tracing these differences to their source, it is in the difference between the two cultural spirits. The cultural spirit of the West, using science as its model, treats film aesthetics with an epistemological consideration; the cultural spirit of the Chinese, using ethics as its model, treats it with an axiological consideration. It leads the Chinese, in their approach to film, to place particular stress on the social and instrumental values of film, and the West to emphasize the natural and noninstrumental values.

One other point: as *The Making of a Shadowplay Script* has clearly demonstrated, shadowplay aesthetics as an ontology closely integrates with the theory of technique. Except for the introductory chapter, which is given solely to ontology, the book deals with theoretical aspects of both ontology and techniques, or solely with the theory of technique. This treatment is also a basic characteristic of contemporary Chinese film theories.

## SHADOWPLAY AESTHETICS ITSELF AS THEORY

China is a nation that emphasizes practice and underestimates speculative theory. Starting with Confucius, many Chinese philosophers have looked upon speculative theory as harmful and useless, which characterizes the model of Chinese thought as a pragmatic-rational spirit. "It does not explore, discuss, and argue difficult philosophic problems and believes that it is unnecessary to deal with this kind of pure abstract speculation, but that it is important to deal appropriately with real life" (Li Zehou 1985, p. 46). This traditional spirit also affects the field of film theory.

Even though China has an eighty-year history of filmmaking, theoretical reflection about this practice primarily maintains a practical and empirical level, and does not ascend to the higher and more abstract levels of speculative theory. China often only formulates theoretical hypotheses, which are implied in its criticism or summaries of its filmmaking without detailed elucidation. The best writers on the subject, such as Hou Yao and Zhang Junxiang, consciously fuse their cognition of film into film criticism and summaries of filmmaking, which often leads people to believe that China has no film theories or aesthetics. This, however, is not the case. Although Chinese film aesthetics has never been developed into purely theoretical patterns, as has Western film aesthetics, it is nonetheless a Chinese way of thought and expression.

In contrast with Chinese film theories, many Western film theories follow more pure theoretical pattern. One of the most typical examples is Seigfried Kracauer's *Theory of Film: The Redemption of Physical Reality*. Others, such as Rudolf Arnheim's *Film As Art,* Jean Mitry's *Aesthetics and Psychology of Cinema,* and Christian Metz's *Language and Cinema,* all have a strong speculative and theoretical color. Even Bazin's thoughts on the nature of film, which closely connect with his practice of film criticism, are full of the spirit of a philosophical speculation, which is related to the development of speculative logic and analytical philosophy in the West.

## THE THEORETICAL MODEL OF SHADOWPLAY AESTHETICS

According to the foregoing description and analysis, we can build a theoretical model for shadowplay aesthetics. In terms of form, shadowplay aesthetics divides film into two levels: drama and image. Drama refers to the level of narrative structure, and is often called *interior form* by Chinese film artists. Its stylistic principle is dramatization. Image refers to the level of cinematic language, and is often called *exterior form.* Its stylistic principle is narrative continuity in story and plot. In both formal levels, interior form is primary and determinant in that it determines the nature of film — film is a kind of drama. Exterior form is secondary and subordinate. In terms of content, shadowplay aesthetics concentrates highly on the social function of film and demands that film communicate specific, ready-made ideologies of ethics or politics. In terms of the relationship between form and content, it absolutely emphasizes content over form, and insists that form obey content. Consequently, the fundamental nature of film as a whole is that of an educational tool.

The theoretical construction and principles of shadowplay aesthetics and their relationship with traditional philosophies and culture can be presented as shown in Figure 1.

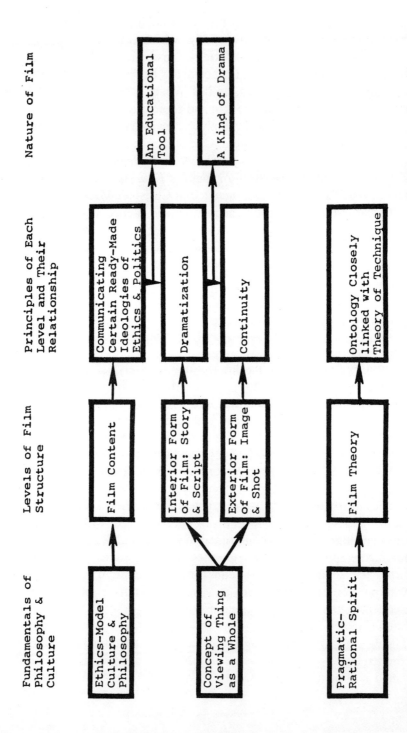

Fundamentals of Philosophy & Culture

Levels of Film Structure

Principles of Each Level and Their Relationship

Nature of Film

Ethics—Model Culture & Philosophy

Film Content

Communicating Certain Ready-Made Ideologies of Ethics & Politics

An Educational Tool

Concept of Viewing Thing as a Whole

Interior Form of Film: Story & Script

Dramatization

A Kind of Drama

Exterior Form of Film: Image & Shot

Continuity

Pragmatic-Rational Spirit

Film Theory

Ontology Closely linked with Theory of Technique

FIGURE 1 — The Theoretical Construction and Principles of Shadowplay Aesthetics and Their Relationship with Traditional Chinese Philosophies and Culture

## CONCLUSION

Now we can see that shadowplay aesthetics, as an ideology, is an expression of the Chinese soul and spirit, and closely related to the traditional Chinese culture-spirit. For a long time, it led the concept of film and filmmaking of China. It took shadowplay as its key concept, and developed a set of theoretical ideas about filmmaking, criticism, and appreciation, which influenced most artists, critics, and audiences, and became a powerful system and network covering all aspects of film theory and aesthetics in China. In comparison with montage, long take, and other Western film theories, it affected the theory and filmmaking of China more broadly and deeply, and for a far longer time. From *Story of an Orphan Saving His Grandfather* and *A Forsaken Woman* of the 1920s to *Xi'an Incident, At Middle Age,* and *The Herdsman* of the 1980s, many outstanding films all relate to this film aesthetic, which has created a unique cinematic tradition in China.

However, this huge, old, complete system of film aesthetics is experiencing a deep crisis at a time when traditional Chinese culture has had large-scale exchanges and major collisions with Western culture. In 1979 a leading art critic, Bai Jingchen, wrote his pioneering article, "Throwing Away the Walking Stick of Drama," and shortly thereafter, famous critics Zhang Nuanxin, Li Tuo, and Zhong Dianfei issued their articles calling for "The Modernization of Film Language" and "The Divorce Between Film and Drama," thus initiating a challenge to the traditional concept of shadowplay. As if in response to this theoretical call, a number of films emerged during and after 1979, taking up the challenge — *One and Eight, Yellow Earth, In the Wild Mountains, Black Cannon Incident, Old Well,* and *Red Sorghum* among them. In seeking a more active and modern film style, these films initiated an attack on the traditional shadowplay from the perspective of creative practice. Chinese film aesthetics is facing a new transformation.

What direction should be taken is a question the times bring to us. This is not, however, an isolated question. It is relevant to the future of the entire traditional Chinese culture. As we urgently transcend this tradition, perhaps we first should soberly reflect upon that tradition. Just as film art is stimulated by ploughing back the work of the past, so film theory may be stimulated by ploughing back the thought of the past. The limitations and weaknesses of older theories reveal paths to be avoided just as their achievements reveal, cumulatively, the problems and doctrines that a new theory must take into account.

We are now at the point of taking the first step.

## REFERENCES

Andrew, J. Dudley. *The Major Film Theories*. New York: Oxford University Press, 1976.

Bai Jingsheng. "Throwing Away the Walking Stick of Drama." *Film Art Reference*, January 1979.

Bao Tianxiao. *A Reminiscence of Chuanyinglou*. Rev. ed. Hong Kong: Dahua Press, 1973.

Chen Jihua. *History of the Development of Chinese Film*. Beijing: Chinese Film Press, 1963.

Gao Qing and Wang Zhongqian. "A Summary of the Discussion about the Dramatic Character of Film, the Literary Character of Film, and the Cinematic Character of Film." *Film Art*, no. 8, 1983.

Henderson, Brian. "Two Types of Film Theory." *Movies and Methods*. Berkeley: University of California Press, 1976.

Hou Yao. *The Making of a Shadowplay Script*. Nanjing: Taidong Press, 1926.

Li Zehou. *On the Thought History of the Chinese Ancient*. Beijing: People Press, 1985.

Mao Zedong. *Collected Writings of Mao Zedong*, vol. 8. Tokyo: Chang-change Press, 1983.

Nichols, Bill. *Movies and Methods*. Berkeley: University of California Press, 1976.

Perkins, V. F. "A Critical History of Early Film Theory." *Movies and Methods*. Berkeley: University of California Press, 1976.

Semsel, George S., ed. *Chinese Film: The State of the Art in the People's Republic*. New York: Praeger, 1987.

Xu Zhudai. "Shadowplay Is a Drama." *Mingxing Special Issue*, no. 4, December 1926.

Zhang Junxiang. "Film Is Just Literature." *Film Communication*, no. 11, 1980.

Zhang Nuanxin and Li Tuo. "The Modernization of Film Language." *Film Art*, no. 3, 1979.

Zhong Dianfei. "The Divorce Between Film and Drama." *Film Communication*, no. 10, 1980.

# BIBLIOGRAPHY

Ai Mingzi, Li Tianji, and Meng Senhui. "A Subject Never to Forget." *New Film Scripts,* February 1982.

Bai Jingsheng. "Throwing Away the Walking Stick of Drama." *Film Art Reference,* January 1979.

Bao Tianxiao. *A Reminiscence about Chuanyinglou.* Rev. ed. Hong Kong: Dahua Press, 1973.

Chen Huangmei. "Don't Forget Literature." *Film Scenario,* January 1982.

Chen Lide. "Exploration and Innovation Must Originate from Life." *Film Art,* January 1980.

Chen Xihe. "Shadowplay: Chinese Film Aesthetics and Their Philosophical and Cultural Fundamentals." *Contemporary Film,* Spring 1986.

Cheng Jihua. *History of the Development of Chinese Film.* Beijing: Chinese Film Press, 1963.

Dai Jinhua. "A Discussion with Shao Mujun." *Film Art,* December 1986.

Ding Yinnan. "The Change of Film Concept and the Demand of the Audience." *The Explorations of Film Directing,* vol. 2, Beijing: China Film Publishing House, 1982.

Gao Qing and Wang Zhongqian. "A Summary of the Discussion about the Dramatic, Literary, and Cinematic Characteristics of Film." *Film Art*, no. 8, 1983.

Han Xiaolei. "An Experiment of Truthfully Presenting Contemporary Youth." *Film Culture*, August 1983.

___. "Is Film Nationalization Scientific?" *Journal of Literature and Art*, July 1980.

Hou Yao. *The Making of a Shadowplay Script*. Nanjing: Taidong Press, 1926.

Huang Shixian. "Film Should Seek the Beauty of Its Form." *Film Art Reference*, no. 21, 1980.

Li Jie. "Xie Jin's Era Should End." *Wenhui Daily*, August 1, 1986.

Li Jisheng. "Theory, Reality, and Styles of Study." *Film Art*, August 1988.

Li Shaobai. "My Understanding of Film Innovation." *Film Art*, December 1986.

___. "Trivial Ideas on Film Nationalization." *Film Culture*, January 1981.

Li Shaobai, Rong Weijing, and Li Shun. "Issues on Film Theory and Criticism." *Film Art*, February 1988.

Li Tuo, Zhong Dafeng, Zhou Chuanji, and Hao Dazheng. "What Is Cinema? A New Look at the Question." *Film Art*, May 1988.

Lu Zhuguo. "Strive to Strengthen the Literary Quality of Film." *Screen and Audience*, August 1982.

Luo Yijun. "The Argument over Film Nationalization." *Film Art*, April 1985.

___. "The National Style in the Films of the 1930s." *Film Aesthetics*. Zhong Dianfei, ed. Beijing: Culture Association Publishers, 1983.

___. "Preliminary Research on the National Style of Film." *Film Art*, October and December 1981.

___. "The Style on the Screen in Beijing — The Ancient City." *Film Art*, October 1984.

___. "Three Problems of Film Nationalization." *Guangming Daily*, November 2, 1983.

Ma Zhonggai. "The Saying 'Film Nationalization' Is Also Imported." *Film Culture*, January 1981.

Mao Zedong. *Collected Writings of Mao Zedong,* vol. 8. Tokyo: Chang-change press, 1983.

Semsel, George S., ed. *Chinese Film: The State of the Art in the People's Republic.* New York: Praeger, 1987.

Shao Mujun. "About *Love-forsaken Corner.*" *Film Art,* April 1982.

___. "The Argument over Similarity and Difference." *Film Art,* November 1985.

___. "Modernization and the Modernists." *Film Art,* May 1979.

___. "Notes on Film Aesthetics." *Film Art,* November 1984.

___. "Pure and Impure — An Analysis of the Direction of Contemporary Film Theory." *Film Art,* March 1988.

___. "The Road of Innovation in Chinese Cinema." *Film Art,* September 1986.

___. "Summary of Casual Thinking on Film Aesthetics." *Film Art,* November 1984.

Shen Yiaoting, Wu Yigong, and Song Cong. "Film Art is Directors' Art." *Wenhui Daily,* November 2, 1980.

Song Cong. "The Exploration of Contemporary Film Concept." *Film Art Reference,* August 1983.

Song Jianbo. "Thoughts on the Literary Value of Film." *Film Literature,* December 1982.

Tian Shen. "Film Should Belong to Literature." *Film Literature,* September 1982.

Wang Lian. "I'm All for 'Don't Forget Literature'." *New Film Scripts,* February 1982.

Wang Yuanjian. "Film: A Visual Form of Literature." *Film Literature,* September 1980.

Rong Weijing. "On the Presentation of Nationalism through Film." *Film Art,* October 1986.

Wu Yigong. "To Be a Loyal Artist to the People." *Film Art,* June 1987.

Xia Hong. "The Debate on *Horse Thief.*" *Film Art,* July 1987.

Xia Yan. "About Chinese Film." *Research on Literature,* June 1980.

Xie Fei. "My View of the Concept of Film." *Film Art,* December 1984.

Xie Jin. "Speech at the Board Meeting of the China Film Association." *Film Art,* October 1986.

Xu Zhudai. "Shadowplay Is Drama." *Mingxing Special Issue,* no. 4, December 1926.

Yang Ni. "Film Is Film: A Response to Tan Peisheng." *Film Art,* October 1983.

Yang Yianjin. "No Nationalization in the Forms of Presentational Techniques." *Journal of Literature and Art,* July 1980.

Yie Dan. "Film Can't Separate from Literature." *New Film Scripts,* February 1982.

Yu Min. "Diversification, Not Prescriptions." *New Film Scripts,* February 1983.

Yuan Wenshu. "About Film Study." *Reference of World Cinema,* June 1980.

___. "Film Tradition and Innovation." *Film Art,* June 1987.

Zhang Junxiang. "Essay Done in Film Terms." *Film Culture,* February 1980.

___. "Film Is about Literature." *Film Communication,* no. 11, 1980.

___. "A Letter to Comrade Xia Yan." *People's Daily,* November 3, 1986.

Zhang Nuanxin. "Exploration of the New Concept of Film." *The Explorations of Film Directing,* vol. 2. Beijing: China Publishing House, 1982.

Zhang Nuanxin and Li Tuo. "The Modernization of Film Language." *Film Art,* March 1979.

Zhang Wei. "Query on the Literary Quality of Film." *Film Literature,* February 1982.

Zheng Dongtian. "The Aesthetics of *Neighbors.*" *Film Art,* July 1983.

___. "Only Seven Years: An Exploration of Middle-Aged and Young Directors — (1979–1986)." *Contemporary Cinema,* January 1987.

Zheng Xuelai. "On Film Literature and Film Characteristics." *New Film Scripts,* May 1982.

Zhong Dafeng. "Also on the Tradition and Innovation of Film." *Film Art,* December 1986.

Zhong Dianfei. "The Divorce between Film and Drama." *Film Communication,* no. 10, 1980.

___. "Film Form and Film's National Form." *Film Culture,* January 1981.

___. "Film Literature Should Make a Fresh Start." *New Film Scripts*, January 1983.

___. "Issues on Cinematic Aesthetics." *Research on Literature*, June 1980.

___. "A Letter to Ding Qiao." *Film News Report*, October 1980.

___. "Notes on Film Awards." *Popular Film*, June 1986.

Zhu Dake. "The Drawback of Xie Jin's Model." *Wenhui Daily*, July 18, 1986.

Zhou Chaunji and Li Tuo. "An Important School of Cinematic Aesthetics — About the Theory of the Long Take." *Film Culture*, no. 1, 1980.

# INDEX

The Pinyin phonetics for Chinese film titles are included in parentheses alongside the English translation.

*My Memories of Old Beijing* (Chen Nan Jiu Shi), 64, 65, 68, 83, 88, 94, 163, 170, 183, 184, 185
*My Name Is Ivan* [USSR], 61
*My Sixty Years* (Wo Zhe Yi Bei Zi), 169
*Myriad of Lights* (Wan Jia Deng Huo), 155, 169
*Mysterious Buddha* (Shen Mi De Da Fuo), 82

*Narrow Lane* (Xiao Jie), 45, 56, 88, 94
*Neighbors* (Lin Ju), 56, 88, 94, 170
"New Star" (Xin Xing) [TV], 148
*New Women* (Xin Nu Xing), 155
*New Year's Sacrifice* (Zhu Fu), 157
*Nie Er* (Nie Er), 169
*Nine Days of One Year* [USSR], 60
nondramatic film, 59, 60, 62, 63, 64, 67, 68, 69, 71, 72, 73, 77, 166

*Old Well* (Lao Jing), 191, 203
*Olive Twist,* 106
*On the Hunting Ground* (Lie Chang Zha Sa), 90, 96, 134, 141, 174
*One and Eight* (Yi Ge He Ba Ge), 84, 90, 95, 119, 141, 174, 203
open-door policy, xvii, xxii, 3, 84, 103, 141, 177
*Opium War, The* (Jia Wu Feng Yun), 157
Ostrosky, Alexander, 42
*Othello,* 65
*Our Discharged Soldiers,* 170
*Our Fields* (Wo Men De Tian Ye), 88
*Our Kitten* (Wo Men De Xiao Hua Mao), 184
*Our Niu Baishui* (Zan Men De Niu Baishui), 81

*Paisa* [Italy], 61
Pang Pu, 172
*Patton,* 160
Peng dehuai, 176
Peng Zhen, 176
*Personal Life, A* [USSR], 77
*Pioneer* (Chuang Ye), 106
*Place of Rehabilitation* (Zhai Sheng Zhi Di), 78

*Plunder of Plums and Peaches* (Tao Li Jie), 155
*Poetics,* 121
*Prairie Fire, The* (Liao Yuan), 34
*Pride's Deadly Fury* (Wu Lin Zhi), 44
psychology, xv, 29, 36, 63, 80, 89, 96, 115, 116, 129, 146, 148, 152, 162, 166
Pudovkin, V. I., xiii, 13

*Red Detachment of Women, The* (Hong Se Niang, Zi Jun), 108, 169
*Red Flag of Cuigang* (Cui Gang Hong Qi), 169
*Red Flower on Tianshan* (Tian Shan De Hong Hua), 169
*Red Sorghum* (Hong Gao Liang), xix, 191, 203
Resnais, Alain, 72, 165, 176
*Reverberations of Life* (Sheng Huo De Chan Yin), 86, 91, 161
*Rickshaw Boy* (Luo Tuo Xiang Zi), 163, 170
*River Without Buoys* (Mei You Hang Biao De He Liu), 88
*Rome, Eleven O'Clock* [Italy], 61
*Rome, Open City* [Italy], 61
Romm, Mikhail, 60, 61
Rong Ge, 137
Rong Weijing, 99
Rosselini, Roberto, 72
Rotha, Paul, 111
Ru Principle, 145

*Sacrifice* (Zhu Fu), 169
*Sacrificed Youth* (Qing Chun Ji), 90, 94, 96, 134, 174
*Scar,* 170
Schaffner, Frank, 160
*Scholartree Village* (Huai Shu Zhuang), 169
*Scripture for Women* (Nu Er Jing), 182
*Secret Decree* (Die Xue Hei Gu), 90
semiology (semiotics), xi, xvii, 195, 199
*Serfs* (Nong Nu), 169
Semsel, George, xiii, xviii, xxi, 37, 170
Shakespeare, William, 26, 51, 67
Shanghai clique, 181, 187

# ABOUT THE EDITORS
# AND CONTRIBUTORS

**Bai Jingsheng,** film critic, is associate professor, Department of Literature, Beijing Film Institute. He is a graduate of the Department of Literature, China University. His major essays are "Throwing Away the Walking Stick of Drama," "On the Characteristics of Film Art," and "The Development of Montage." He has also written short stories, some of which are "Thrill in Heaven," "Sunset," and "Stage."

**Chen Xihe,** critic, holds a B.A. in literature, and an M.A. from the Graduate College of the China Film Art Research Center, 1985. A research fellow of the China Film Art Research Center, he has a Ph.D. in progress from Ohio State University. He is a columnist for *Beiying Huabao* and a special contributor to *Film Art*. His major works include *Film Literature and Theatre*.

**Hou Jianping** has translated a number of English-language literary and philosophical works into Chinese, including short stories by Isaac Bashevis Singer and a book on the concept of the absurd. As a translator at the Beijing headquarters of the China Film Import and Export Corporation, she subtitled numerous Chinese films into English. Her most recent writing deals extensively with women directors in China.

**Li Jie,** critic, is a lecturer at Huadong Normal University. He is a graduate of the Graduate College, Huandong Normal University. His major works include "Literature Is Another Perspective of Humanity"; *Individuality, Personality, and Creativity* (a collection of essays); and short stories and novellas.

**Li Tuo,** writer and critic, is deputy editor-in-chief of *Beijing Literature.* His works include short stories and literary and art criticism.

**Luo Yijun,** film critic, is secretary of the Secretariat, China Film Association, and research fellow of the China Film Association. He is the director of the China Film Critics Society. A 1948 graduate of Beijing University, his major works include *The Storming Screen* (a collection of essays).

**George S. Semsel,** associate professor in the Ohio University School of Film, is the author/editor of *Chinese Film: The State of the Art in the People's Republic.* Dr. Semsel, recently named a Fulbright Scholar to China, is currently in residence at Sukhothai Thammathirat Open University in Thailand, where he was reassigned after the People's Republic of China cancelled its program.

**Shao Mujun** is a film critic and translator. He is secretary of the Secretariat of the China Film Association and a research fellow of the China Film Association. He is a 1949 graduate from the English Department, St. John's University, Shanghai, and a graduate of the Foreign Languages Department, Graduate College, Qinghua University. His major works include *Survey of Western Film History* and *In the Sea of the Silver Screen* (a collection of essays).

**Rong Weijing,** film critic, is deputy managing editor of *Film Art,* China Film Association. A graduate of the Chinese department, Shandong University, his major works include "Defense and Reevaluation — The Confusion of Film Theory," "We Need No Regrets," "The Responsibility of Criticism and Responsible Criticism," and "Six Features of American Culture."

**Wu Yigong,** director, is chief of the Shanghai Film Bureau and general director of the Shanghai Film Corporation. He is a graduate of the Directing Department, Beijing Film Institute. His films include *Evening*

*Rain, My Memories of Old Beijing, Sister, College in Exile,* and *The Misfortune of the Young Master.*

**Xia Hong,** a graduate of Fudan University, is managing editor of *Film Art* (*Dianying Yishu*), a scholarly journal published by the China Film Association. Xia's film articles have appeared in a number of publications in China. He is the guest editor of *Wide Angle*'s issue on Chinese cinema.

**Xie Fei** is a film director and critic. He is a board member of the China Film Association, the China Film Critics Society, and CILECT. He is director and associate professor, Beijing Film Institute. He is a 1965 graduate of the Directing Department, Beijing Film Institute. His films include *Hua Wa* (1978), *Our Fields* (1983), and *Girl from Hunan* (1986).

**Yang Ni,** film critic, is editor of *Film Art,* China Film Association. She is a member of the Chinese World Cinema Society and the China Film Critics Society. She is a 1969 graduate of the Chinese Department of Beijing Normal University.

**Yu Min,** screenwriter and critic, is a consultant to the China Film Association. He has written the script for *Bridge*; a novel, *The First Contract*; essays including "Exploration"; and a translation, *On Acting Performance.*

**Yuan Wenshu,** screenwriter and critic, is a consultant to the China Film Association. He is former vice-chairman and general secretary of the Secretariat, China Film Association. His major works include *A Collection of Frontier Dramas, The Common Enemy of the Nation, The Systems of Russian Drama* (translation), and the essays "Characters, Personalities, and Plots in Film," and "The Exploration of Film."

**Zhang Junxiang** is a director of theater and film as well as a scriptwriter and film theoretician. He is former chief of the Shanghai Film Bureau, deputy chief of the Film Bureau of the Ministry of Culture, vice-chairman of the China Film Association, and honorary president of the China Film Critics Society. He graduated from the Drama College of Yale University, 1939. His films include *Homecoming, Doctor Bethune, Red Flag of Cuigang,* and *Sparkling Fire.* He is the author of "Basic

Directing Techniques" (dramatic theory) and "The Special Representational Means of Film" (film theory).

**Zhang Nuanxin** is director and chief of the Fine Art Department at the Youth Film Studio of the Beijing Film Institute. A 1963 graduate of the Directing Department of the Beijing Film Institute, her films include *Sha' ou, Sacrificed Youth,* and *Tears of Hua Jiao.*

**Zheng Dongtian,** film director and critic, is chairman and associate professor of directing, Beijing Film Institute. His major works include the films *Neighbors* and *The Building of Love* and the essays "Thoughts on *Yellow Earth,*" "Notes on *In the Wild Mountains,*" and "After the Combination."

**Zheng Xuelai,** critic, is research professor and director, Institute of Foreign Arts, Central Arts Academy of China. He is editor-in-chief of *Journal of World Arts and Aesthetics, Journal of Contemporary Foreign Arts,* and *World Film History* (12 volumes). He is vice-chairman of the Chinese World Cinema Society and serves on the board of directors of the China Film Association. His major works are *Problems of Film Aesthetics* (1982), *On the Stanislavsky Method* (1984), and *Collected Papers on Filmology* (1986).

**Zhong Dianfei** is an art and literary critic and film theoretician. He is a research fellow at the China Film Art Research Center. He serves on the Chairman's Committee of the China Film Association and is president of the China Film Critics Society. His major works include *A Collection of Deep Thinking, Announcement of the Struggle,* "The Drum of Film," and "Strategies of Film." He served as editor-in-chief of *Film Aesthetics, 1982*; *Film Aesthetics, 1984*; and *Film Aesthetics.*

**Zhu Dake,** critic, is a member of the Shanghai Branch of the China Film Association. He is assistant professor of the Literary Research Institute, Shanghai Normal University. He is a graduate of the Chinese department, Huadong Normal University. His major works include "On the Procedure of Film," "Xie Jin's Model — A Signal of the Decline of Contemporary Film," "Ethics — The Cultural Essence of Xie Jin's Films," and "Shallow Literature."